CRAZY PLATES

CRAZY PLATES

Low-Fat Food So Good, You'll Swear It's Bad for You!

Janet & Greta Podleski

Cartoons by Ted Martin

A PERIGEE BOOK

A Perigee Book
Published by The Berkley Publishing Group
A division of Penguin Putnam Inc.
375 Hudson Street
New York, New York 10014

Crazy Plates is a trademark of Granet Publishing Inc.
Cartoons by Ted Martin. Edited by Fina Scroppo and Cheryl Embrett. Design consultants: Chuck Temple and Kevin Strang. Front cover photography by Susan Ashukian. Front cover food styling by Julie Zambonelli. Back cover food photography by Robert Wigington. Back cover food styling by Ruth Gangbar.

Granet Publishing Inc. edition published 1999
First Perigee edition: February 2000

The Penguin Putnam Inc. World Wide Web site address is http://www.penguinputnam.com

Library of Congress Cataloging-in-Publication Data

Podleski, Janet, 1965–
    Crazy Plates : low-fat food so good, you'll swear it's bad for you! / Janet & Greta Podleski ; cartoons by Ted Martin.
        p.   cm.
    ISBN 0-399-52584-X (tp)
    1. Cookery   2. Low-fat diets—Recipes.   3. Food—Humor.
    I. Podleski, Greta, 1966– II. Title.
TW714.P635   2000   99-40792
641.5'638—dc21   CIP

The following product and company names appearing in the book are trademarks or trade names of their respective companies: 7-Up, Batman, Betty Crocker, Bran Flakes, Burger King, Chiquita, Coca-Cola, Crisco, Crock-Pot, Dole, Dramamine, Eatmore, Esso, FedEx, Fig Newton, Flintstones, Fudgsicle, Heinz, James Bond, Jeopardy, Kahlúa, KFC, La-Z-boy, McDonald's, Mighty Mouse, Miracle Whip, Nike, Nintendo, Oatmeal Crisp Raisin Cereal, Oreo, Pepperidge Farm, Pizza Hut, Pringles, Quarter Pounder, Rototiller, Scrabble, Sesame Street, SnackWell's, Snickers, Spam, Tae Bo, Tim Hortons, Tupperware, Twinkie, Twix, Velcro, Wendy's

Recipe analysis calculated using Nutribase Professional Nutrition Manager software (Cybersoft, Inc.). When a choice of ingredients is listed, analysis is calculated using the first ingredient. Optional ingredients are not included in the analysis.

In view of the complex, individual, and specific nature of health and fitness problems, this book is not intended to replace professional medical advice. The authors and publisher expressly disclaim any responsibility for any liability, loss, or risk, personal or otherwise, which is incurred as a consequence, directly or indirectly, of the use and application of any of the contents of this book.

To our wonderful and very supportive sisters,
Helen, Margie, Theresa, and Donna.
We blame them for our warped personalities.
Six girls. One bathroom. You do the math!

Contents

Introduction

When the Podleski sisters first decided about a year ago to create a second cookbook, frankly, I was somewhat skeptical. I felt any effort, even an outstanding one, was almost sure to disappoint. Nothing, I argued, could live up to *Looneyspoons: Low-fat food made fun!*, Janet and Greta's 1997 smash hit.

I was wrong. Very wrong.

Crazy Plates is phenomenal. In fact, I'm not sure that I have ever come across another book so thoughtfully and painstakingly put together.

What you have here is truly a labor of love. Showing extraordinary passion and great attention to detail, Janet and Greta have spent 12 months living, breathing, and sleeping this book. These two never cease to amaze me. So much of their excellence is due to their high expectations. They didn't set out to create a second book just as good as *Looneyspoons*; they set out to create an even better one.

Greta sequestered herself in her kitchen for months on end. She slipped out only to buy groceries for testing recipes, to take care of urgent personal matters (like showering), and, of course, to sleep (we argued a cot by the oven would have sufficed!).

Along with my parents, many of their friends, neighbors, and our office staff, I was lucky enough to be one of the taste testers. We all loved each of Greta's creations but, of course, that wasn't good enough for her. Until we were presented with dishes that would literally have us begging for more, pleading for seconds, demanding just one more bite, Greta would keep diligently tinkering and modifying.

The result? The food in this book is the tastiest I've ever eaten—the fact that it's low-fat is a bonus! My father, a man not normally prone to hyperbole, announced, just before eating his fifth piece of *Must Bake Carrot Cake* (p. 155), that Greta is the Michelangelo of low-fat food. Janet and I think that a *Rainman* comparison is more appropriate—Greta may be more of an *idiot savant*. Name any high-fat meal and she can tell you immediately how to enhance its taste, yet decrease its fat, through creative substitutions. The fact that she watches *Jeopardy* every night is probably not a coincidence.

As Greta developed her recipes, Janet began her thorough search for interesting information that would not only educate readers, but also entertain and motivate them. Drawing on readers' feedback from *Looneyspoons*, Janet knew what areas people wanted and needed to know more about. So, she compiled a treasure chest of relevant health tips by reading dozens of books, hundreds of magazines, and by visiting key health sites on the Internet.

By wrapping that information in humor, Janet has, once again, taken the intimidation out of a normally very dry subject. As you read through *Crazy Plates* you'll find yourself laughing out loud, yet learning valuable tips, too. Janet has a great turn of phrase and, as you'll soon become painfully aware, a unique ability to *pun-ish* her readers with corny plays on words.

Working together, the two sisters have spent countless late nights laying out and perfecting each page of this book. As dramatic as it sounds, I am in awe of their pride in craftsmanship. From Janet's meticulous (some would argue, obsessive) placement of Ted Martin's wonderful cartoons to Greta's rigorous approach to editing, they simply will not settle for anything less than their best. Their very best.

The feedback from our editor, John Duff, has confirmed my excitement. He was constantly sending back *Crazy Plates* pages with comments such as, "What a cute cartoon," "Fantastic information," "This recipe looks unbelievable—I can hardly wait to try it!", and, "Wow, this is great stuff!"

In fact, I'm not sure I can say it any better—this *is* great stuff. I'm very proud to work with Janet and Greta and I'm thrilled to be a small part of this project.

Again, the three of us wish you good reading and healthy eating!

Dave Chilton, Bestselling author and
star of the PBS series *The Weathy Barber*
February 2000

Just the Snacks, Ma'am

Scrumptious snacks and appetizers

Strip T's

Sesame seed and coconut-crusted
turkey strips with warm dipping sauce

If you add these crispy, baked turkey
strips to your cooking repertoire, you'll take it
off—you'll take it *all* off! Your excess weight,
that is. That's because we've stripped away
most of the fat—and we're not teasing, either.

1/2 cup shredded, sweetened coconut
2 tbsp sesame seeds
1/2 cup unseasoned, dry
   bread crumbs
1-1/2 pounds turkey breast,
   cut into 1/2-inch-wide strips
2 egg whites
2 tsp sesame oil
Non-stick cooking spray

Dipping Sauce
1/2 cup plum sauce
1/3 cup unsweetened pineapple juice
1-1/2 tsp each mustard and cornstarch

- Place coconut and sesame seeds in a dry skillet over medium heat. Cook until golden brown, stirring frequently. Transfer toasted coconut and sesame seeds to a pie plate. Add bread crumbs and mix well.

- Place turkey strips in a large bowl. In a small bowl, lightly beat egg whites and sesame oil. Pour over turkey and mix until all pieces are coated. Working one at a time, roll turkey strips in coconut mixture. Place on a large baking sheet that has been sprayed with non-stick spray. Repeat with remaining strips and coconut mixture. Spray tops of strips with a light coating of non-stick spray. Bake at 425° for 10 minutes. Remove from oven and turn pieces over. Spray other side with a light coating of non-stick spray. Return to oven and bake for 5 more minutes.

- While strips are cooking, prepare sauce. Combine plum sauce, pineapple juice, mustard, and cornstarch in a small saucepan. Cook over medium heat until sauce is bubbly and has thickened.

- Transfer turkey strips to a platter and place dipping sauce in center. Serve immediately.

Makes 6 servings

What's
in it
for me?

Per serving: 280 calories, 6.8 g fat,
3.1 g saturated fat, 33.3 g protein,
20.4 g carbohydrate, 1 g fiber,
83 mg cholesterol, 186.4 mg sodium
% calories from fat: 22

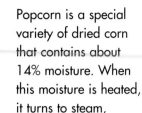

Who'da
Thunk?

Why does popcorn pop?

Popcorn is a special
variety of dried corn
that contains about
14% moisture. When
this moisture is heated,
it turns to steam,
creating a pressure inside the kernel of
about 135 pounds per square inch. When
the pressure becomes too great, "pop"
goes the corn. The hull bursts open and
the kernel's starchy content explodes and
expands up to 35 times its original size
while turning the kernel inside out.
Incidentally, if you're getting lots of "old
maids" (unpopped kernels), it's usually
because the corn has dried out. Without
moisture, a kernel can't pop!

Not a Fungi to be Around

Although they're found in the vegetable
section of the grocery store, mushrooms
aren't truly vegetables. They're fungi, and
some are deadly. Now, don't get all
excited—they're perfectly safe when you
buy them at the supermarket. But, if you
pick and eat mushrooms out in a field
without knowing what you're doing, it
may be the last thing you ever do. Since
there's no feature that distinguishes toxic
mushrooms from the edible kind, never
gather or eat wild mushrooms unless a
mushroom expert has identified them as
safe. Be warned: There are no specific
antidotes to some of their lethal poisons!
The *morel* of the story: Err on the side of
caution and buy your mushrooms at the
store.

I'm on a new tranquilizer diet.
I haven't lost an ounce, but
I don't care.

THE E FILES

So, you think you're the epitome of physical fitness, huh? Squash on Monday, volleyball on Wednesday, a trip to the gym Thursday, a pack of cigarettes *every* day. *Thunder crack! Dramatic doom music!* There are no ifs, ands, or *butts* about it—nicotine is bad news for muscles and for athletes. In fact, it decreases blood flow to muscles, making them tire faster. What's more, less blood flow means lactic acid stays in the muscles longer, so it takes them more time to recover between workouts. And don't forget about your lungs—if you smoke, you have less lung power for aerobic exercise, the kind that burns fat. Ironically, "lighting up" might make you heavier!

SAY IT AIN'T SO!

Do friends call you "a big ham"? Either you're the life of the party or you've been eating too many ham and cheese sandwiches. Did you know that ham and cheese on a croissant (three ounces of ham, two ounces of Swiss cheese, one tablespoon of mayonnaise) weighs in at a whopping 730 calories and 51 grams of fat? And some people eat two. Better not be you, big ham—unless you *want* the porky nickname.

Dippity-do-da Fruit Dip

Creamy fruit dip with a hint of strawberry and orange flavor

My, oh my, what a wonderful day! With plenty of fruit dip headin' your way...you'll sing, "Dippity-do-da, yippee, hooray!"

1 cup marshmallow cream
4 oz light cream cheese, softened
1/2 cup low-fat, strawberry-flavored yogurt
  (see hint below)
1 tbsp frozen orange juice concentrate, thawed

- In a small bowl, beat together marshmallow cream and cream cheese on medium speed of electric mixer. Beat until smooth. Add yogurt and orange juice concentrate. Beat on low speed until well blended.

- Cover and refrigerate dip for 1 hour before serving.

Makes about 1-1/2 cups

Hint: Use fruit-bottom yogurt in this recipe for a thicker dip. Stirred yogurts tend to produce a dip that's runny.

Per serving (2 tbsp): 87 calories, 1.7 g fat,
1 g saturated fat, 1.5 g protein,
16.8 g carbohydrate, 0 g fiber,
3.3 mg cholesterol, 66.8 mg sodium
% calories from fat: 18

What's in it for me?

I've got to stop eating so many cornflakes.
I'm going soggy in the bathtub.

JUST THE SNACKS, MA'AM

Our Caps Runneth Over

Crab-stuffed mushroom caps

Our mushroom caps are so stuffed with savory stuff, there's really not *mushroom* for improvement. They're delicious with a CAPital "D."

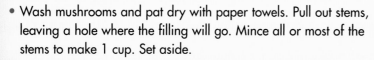

16 large white mushrooms with stems
1 tsp olive oil
2 tbsp minced onions
1 can (4-1/4 oz) crabmeat, drained
2 tbsp each unseasoned, dry bread crumbs, low-fat mayonnaise, and chopped, fresh parsley
1 tbsp grated Parmesan cheese
1 egg
1/4 tsp salt
1/8 tsp black pepper
2 or 3 drops hot pepper sauce

- Wash mushrooms and pat dry with paper towels. Pull out stems, leaving a hole where the filling will go. Mince all or most of the stems to make 1 cup. Set aside.

- Heat olive oil in a medium, non-stick skillet over medium heat. Add minced stems and onions. Cook and stir until vegetables are tender, about 3 to 4 minutes. Be careful not to burn them.

- In a medium bowl, combine mushroom-onion mixture with all remaining ingredients. Using a teaspoon, stuff mushrooms with filling, mounding on top.

- Arrange stuffed mushrooms in a single layer in a shallow baking pan. Bake at 400° for 15 minutes. Serve hot or at room temperature.

Makes 16 stuffed mushrooms

What's in it for me?

Per mushroom: 26 calories, 0.9 g fat, 0.2 g saturated fat, 2.7 g protein, 2.3 g carbohydrate, 0.3 g fiber, 19 mg cholesterol, 97.5 mg sodium
% calories from fat: 29

When it comes to wearing slacks, often the end doesn't justify the jeans.

Fresh food isn't always more nutritious than processed food.

FAT OR FICTION?

Most people think that fresh food is more nutritious than processed food. But some of the time, they're wrong. The truth is, sensible food processing, such as canning, drying, and freezing, makes food safer, extends its shelf life, and may increase its nutritional value. Take milk, for example. Straight from the cow, it contains all kinds of nasty organisms that are destroyed by processing. Adding vitamin D makes it more nutritious, and skimming the fat reduces the cholesterol, saturated fat, and calories. And if you think that all preservatives are hazardous to your health, think again. Antioxidant preservatives like vitamin C prevent food from going rancid, while others protect against food poisoning. So, it seems that when preservatives and processing methods are used judiciously, they can extend *your* shelf life!

YOU DO THE MATH

Oh, for pizza sake! It's just a piddly piece of pepperoni pie! Unfortunately, the average slice of pepperoni pizza contains a mammoth 16 grams of fat—and who eats just one slice? On your next trip to the pizza parlor, why not trade two slices of sausage-topped pizza for two of the vegetarian variety? Based on one trip a week, you'll save 11,752 calories and 936 grams of fat in a year! That's almost 14 days' worth of fat! So, if you're the type that likes to live on the *wedge*, just make sure it's the healthier kind.

Totally Useless Pizza Trivia

Cliff Clavins of the world unite! Here's a list of completely irrelevant pizza facts that's guaranteed not to impress your friends!

- Although we consider the beloved pizza to be Italian, it actually originated in Greece. The Greeks came up with the idea of the edible plate, which is really what a pizza is—a big, delicious plate with many types of food served on it.

- Americans eat approximately 100 acres of pizza a day, or 350 slices a second.

- Each year, Pizza Hut uses 80 million pounds of tomatoes and 350 million pounds of flour (the yield of 300,000 acres of wheat).

- Pizza delivery people have made the following observations:
  - Women tip better than men;
  - the longer the driveway, the smaller the tip;
  - a new car in the driveway usually means a smaller tip;
  - during TV newscasts, most pizza is ordered while the weather report is on;
  - most people answer the door shoeless;
  - during heat waves, people with fans cooling their homes tipped drivers 23% less than those with air conditioning.

- Super Bowl Sunday is the number-one day for pizza delivery. Other top-selling pizza days of the year include New Year's Eve, New Year's Day, Thanksgiving Eve, Halloween, and days of inclement weather.

- Americans' favorite pizza toppings, in order, are pepperoni, beef, Italian sausage, mushrooms, and green peppers.

Pocket Science

Pizza pockets stuffed with Canadian bacon, mushrooms, and cheese

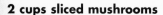

It was a laboratory of love that led to this invention, but you don't have to be a *pocket* scientist to experiment with these delightfully tasty pizza sandwiches.

2 cups sliced mushrooms
4 oz Canadian bacon, chopped
1 tbsp chopped, fresh oregano, or 1 tsp dried
1 pkg (1 pound) frozen pizza dough, thawed
1 cup pizza sauce
1/2 cup shredded, part-skim mozzarella cheese (2 oz)
1 egg white, lightly beaten

- Preheat oven to 400°.

- Spray a medium, non-stick skillet with non-stick spray. Add mushrooms and cook over medium heat until tender, about 4 minutes. Add bacon and cook for 2 more minutes. Stir in oregano and remove from heat.

- Divide pizza dough into 2 pieces. On a lightly floured surface, roll out each piece to an 8 x 8-inch square (or as close as you can get to a square!). Using a sharp knife, cut each large square into 4 smaller squares.

- Working one at a time, transfer squares to a baking sheet that has been sprayed with non-stick spray. Spoon 1 tablespoon sauce in center of square. Top with 1 tablespoon mushroom-bacon mixture and 1 tablespoon cheese. Fold dough over filling to create a triangle, stretching it a bit if you need to. Pinch edges closed or press down on edges with the tines of a fork to seal. Repeat with remaining crusts and filling.

- Brush tops of pizza pockets lightly with egg white. Bake for 13 to 15 minutes, until golden brown and puffed up. To serve, cut pizza pockets in half and arrange them on a serving platter. Warm up the extra pizza sauce and serve it as a dip.

Makes 8 servings

Per serving: 207 calories, 4.5 g fat, 1 g saturated fat, 11.9 g protein, 29.9 g carbohydrate, 1.4 g fiber, 10.6 mg cholesterol, 730.8 mg sodium % calories from fat: 19

What's in it for us?

Jerry Springrolls

Vegetable-filled spring rolls with a
spicy, Thai dipping sauce

Today's topic: Snacks from both sides of the tracks.

You'll be the host with the most when you serve your friends these
light-tasting spring rolls. We've lowered the fat rating by censoring
all the heavyweight, controversial ingredients.

Dipping Sauce

3/4 cup water

2 tsp cornstarch

1/3 cup seasoned rice vinegar

1/4 cup brown sugar

1-1/2 tbsp reduced-sodium soy sauce

1 tbsp grated gingerroot

1 clove garlic, minced

1/4 tsp crushed red pepper flakes

2 oz rice vermicelli noodles,
    uncooked (see Cooking 101)

1 cup each grated carrots and
    chopped bean sprouts

1/2 cup peeled, seeded, and
    finely chopped cucumber

1/2 cup chopped green onions and
    chopped, fresh mint leaves

2 tsp sesame oil

14 6-inch rice papers (see Cooking 101)

- Whisk together all sauce ingredients in a small
  saucepan. Heat over medium-high heat until mixture
  comes to a boil and thickens slightly. Remove from
  heat and let cool to room temperature.

- Boil vermicelli in a large pot of water for 4 minutes,
  until tender. Drain, rinse with cold water, and drain
  again. Blot dry using paper towels.

- Coarsely chop noodles and place them in a medium
  bowl along with carrots, bean sprouts, cucumber, green
  onions, and mint leaves. Mix well. Add sesame oil and
  mix again.

- Fill a mixing bowl with 3 inches of hot water. Keep
  some boiling water handy to add to the bowl as the
  water cools. Working one at a time, soak rice papers in
  hot water for about 30 seconds, or until soft and pliable
  (time will vary with brand of rice paper). Transfer to a
  clean kitchen towel, lay wrapper flat, and blot dry.

- Place 1/4 cup filling in center of wrapper. Using your
  fingers, shape filling into a 3-inch-long cylinder. Fold
  bottom edge over filling and roll once to enclose. Fold
  in sides and continue to roll up tightly. (Pressing down
  on filling as you roll helps to tighten it.) Place seam-side
  down on a plate and cover with a damp towel. Repeat
  process with remaining wrappers and filling. Keep at
  room temperature until ready to serve.

- Serve spring rolls with dipping sauce within 3 hours of
  making them, otherwise they'll dry out.

Makes 14 spring rolls

What's in it for me?

Per roll: 62 calories, 0.8 g fat,
0.1 g saturated fat, 1.2 g protein,
12.4 g carbohydrate, 0.7 g fiber,
0 mg cholesterol, 71.8 mg sodium
% calories from fat: 12

COOKING
101

Rice papers, made from rice flour and water, look like translucent tortillas. They
must be softened by soaking in water before using. Packaged dry and in plastic
wrap, look for rice papers at well-stocked grocery stores or Asian markets. Be
careful not to confuse rice papers with spring roll wrappers, which are made
from wheat flour and are meant to be deep-fried. Rice vermicelli (or rice-flour
noodles) are extremely thin, almost thread-like noodles. You'll find them in the
Oriental-food aisle of most supermarkets.

JUST THE SNACKS, MA'AM

Are the skins of potatoes really that good for you?

If your mother was like many, she was convinced that the most nutritious part of the potato was the skin. (She probably said the same thing about bread crusts, too.) Raw potato skins have about the same nutrient content as the raw flesh, with slightly higher levels of calcium and zinc. Baking the potatoes, however, causes more vitamins to accumulate in the skins. They're also a good source of fiber, so mom was kinda right to insist that you eat your skins. But, one thing mom probably didn't know is that potato peels contain a naturally occurring poison called solanine. It's the vegetable's defense against soil pests, which is why it's concentrated in the skin. After harvest, solanine levels can become toxic if the potato is exposed to too much light. No need to panic, though. Just avoid potatoes with green-tinged skins—they're the dud spuds.

TRIVIAL TIDBIT

In ancient times, salt was highly valued—so much so that spilling salt became an unlucky omen among the Romans. At one time, Roman soldiers were paid in salt or given a sum of money to buy it. This money was known as *salarium*, the origin of our word "salary."

The Skins Game

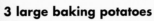

Crispy potato skins topped with cheddar cheese and bacon bits

When you *putt* these tasty skins in front of the gallery, you'll have their *undivotted* attention, *fore* sure!

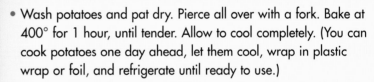

Keep your eyes on the ball.

3 large baking potatoes
1 tsp olive oil
1 tsp seasoned salt
3/4 cup shredded, reduced-fat sharp cheddar cheese (3 oz)
3 slices bacon, cooked crisp and crumbled
1 tbsp chopped, fresh cilantro or parsley
1/2 cup each salsa and low-fat sour cream

- Wash potatoes and pat dry. Pierce all over with a fork. Bake at 400° for 1 hour, until tender. Allow to cool completely. (You can cook potatoes one day ahead, let them cool, wrap in plastic wrap or foil, and refrigerate until ready to use.)

- Cut potatoes in half lengthwise. Using a teaspoon, scoop out the flesh, leaving a 1/4-inch-thick shell. Slice each half into three wedges. Lightly brush both sides of skins with olive oil.

- Arrange skins in a single layer on a cookie sheet that has been sprayed with non-stick spray. Sprinkle with seasoned salt. Broil skins for 5 minutes. Remove from oven and sprinkle with cheese, bacon, and cilantro. Return to oven and broil for 2 to 3 more minutes, until cheese is bubbly. Serve hot skins with salsa and sour cream.

Makes 18 skins

Per skin: 70 calories, 1.7 g fat, 0.7 g saturated fat, 3.2 g protein, 10.9 g carbohydrate, 0.9 g fiber, 4.7 mg cholesterol, 171 mg sodium % calories from fat: 22

What's in it for me?

I sent my wife out to get something for my liver. She came back with a pound of onions.

Spread Yourself Thin

Creamy seafood spread for crackers

It's incredible—and spreadable! Did we mention that it's edible? The only thing regrettable is that it won't last long. *Sea* for yourself!

4 oz light cream cheese, softened

1/4 cup seafood cocktail sauce

1 tsp lemon juice

1/4 tsp each ground cumin and chili powder

8 oz chopped, cooked shrimp

8 oz chopped, lump crabmeat

1/3 cup minced green onions

- In a large bowl, beat together cream cheese and cocktail sauce on high speed of electric mixer. Beat until smooth.
- Add lemon juice, cumin, and chili powder and beat until well blended.
- Stir in shrimp, crabmeat, and onions. Mix well. Cover and refrigerate for at least 2 hours before serving.
- Serve seafood spread with low-fat crackers.

Makes about 2-1/2 cups

What's in it for me? ➜ Per serving (1/4 cup): 78 calories, 2.6 g fat, 1.3 g saturated fat, 8.9 g protein, 5.2 g carbohydrate, 0.1 g fiber, 52.7 mg cholesterol, 383.4 mg sodium % calories from fat: 29

If you wish to grow thinner, diminish your dinner.

H.S. Leigh

A Far-Fetched Theory?

They say you can't teach an old dog new tricks. Maybe so. But we've certainly learned a few smart eating tricks by paying attention to the way our dog, Crisco, eats. Despite his high-fat name, it appears that our Jack Russell terrier is one healthy, low-fat hound. It's not likely that our pooch will ever have a paunch. That's because he eats only when he's hungry, and only enough to satisfy himself. Unlike his masters, who've been conditioned to clean their plates right down to the china pattern, he often leaves his bowl unfinished. He doesn't eat simply because he's feeling lonely, bored, tired, or down in the dumps. He never bites off more than he can chew, and most importantly, he drinks plenty of water. We've never observed him staring blankly into the vast expanse of the refrigerator, waiting for something inside to call out his name. And if Crisco could reach for his own snack, we'd bet dollars to dog biscuits that he'd *chews* something nutritionally complete and balanced—*collie-flour*, perhaps?

If you're watching your cholesterol levels, shrimp is a definite no-no.

One of the popular misconceptions about shrimp is that eating it sends your cholesterol levels skyrocketing. Though shrimp has roughly twice as much cholesterol as meat, it contains far less fat than meat—plus, the fat in shrimp is largely unsaturated. That's important because foods high in saturated fats are more responsible for upping cholesterol levels than foods high in dietary cholesterol. Shrimp is also a great source of heart-healthy omega-3 fatty acids. And it's a healthy, low-fat food, unless it's breaded and fried or served in a butter sauce. So, when it comes to shrimp, there's really no need to skimp—just don't be *shellfish*!

When marinating foods, always use a glass or ceramic container. Most marinades contain an acidic ingredient such as lemon juice, vinegar, or wine, which can react with metal and cause off-flavors in the food. To save on cleanup, try marinating your fish or meat in a large plastic bag with a zip closure. Set the bag on a plate or in a shallow bowl and refrigerate, turning the bag occasionally to distribute the marinade. If using leftover marinade as a sauce for your finished dish, be sure to boil it first to destroy any bacteria that may have been transferred from the raw food.

Booze-infused drinks, such as specialty coffees, fancy fruity cocktails, and dreamy, ice-creamy liquid concoctions, may be all the rage these days, but top those trendy beverages with whipped cream and your libation is liable to linger longer than you'd like. Whipped cream can add 16 to 18 grams of fat to your drink—and to your rump! If you want to hang with the *thin* crowd, just remember: It's hip to skip the whip.

Shrimply Irresistible

Marinated, grilled shrimp skewers with fiery fruit salsa

Super-lean and super-scrumptious, these shrimp skewers are *shrimple* to prepare, even for a *shrimpleton*.

3 tbsp reduced-sodium soy sauce
2 tbsp each lime juice and brown sugar
1 tbsp each olive oil and ketchup
2 cloves garlic, minced
1 tsp ground coriander
1/2 tsp ground cumin
24 fresh or frozen uncooked jumbo shrimp (thaw first if using frozen)

Fruit Salsa
3/4 cup orange segments
3/4 cup peeled, cored, and diced Granny Smith apples
2 tbsp lime juice
2 green onions, white part only, minced
1 tbsp chopped, fresh mint or cilantro
1 tsp sugar
1/2 tsp crushed red pepper flakes

6 wooden or metal skewers

- In a small bowl, combine soy sauce, lime juice, brown sugar, olive oil, ketchup, garlic, coriander, and cumin. Remove shells from shrimp, leaving tails intact. Pour marinade over shrimp in a shallow, glass baking dish or in a heavy-duty, resealable plastic bag. Make sure each piece of shrimp is coated with marinade. Refrigerate for 1 hour. If using wooden skewers, soak them in water until ready to use.

- Meanwhile, prepare salsa. Put all salsa ingredients in a blender or food processor and pulse on and off until mixture is pureed. Pour into a small, glass serving bowl and refrigerate until ready to serve.

- Remove shrimp from marinade and thread 4 pieces onto each skewer. Grill over medium-hot coals for 3 to 4 minutes per side, basting with extra marinade. Serve immediately with fruit salsa.

Makes 6 servings

Per serving: 164 calories, 4.1 g fat, 0.3 g saturated fat, 18.3 g protein, 13.6 g carbohydrate, 1.2 g fiber, 129.2 mg cholesterol, 457.5 mg sodium % calories from fat: 23

What's in it for me?

Fairest Wheels

Tortilla pinwheels with chicken, cream cheese, and hot red-pepper jelly

This appetizing chicken pinwheel recipe won first prize in the State Fair's "Fairest of the Fare" recipe contest. And you can say "farewell" when you serve them to your family.

1 cup finely chopped, cooked chicken
1/2 cup chopped lettuce
1/2 cup shredded, reduced-fat sharp cheddar cheese (2 oz)
1/3 cup each chopped green onions and minced red bell pepper
4 oz light cream cheese, softened
2 tbsp low-fat sour cream
1 tbsp hot red-pepper jelly (see tip in margin)
3 9-inch flour tortillas

- In a medium bowl, combine chicken, lettuce, cheddar cheese, green onions, and red pepper. Set aside.

- In a small bowl, beat together cream cheese, sour cream, and red-pepper jelly on low speed of electric mixer. Spread 1/3 cream cheese mixture over one side of tortilla. Sprinkle with 1/3 chicken mixture, leaving a 1/2-inch border at the top just covered with cream cheese mixture (so you can seal it closed). Roll up tightly, jelly-roll style. Wrap tortilla roll in plastic wrap. Repeat with remaining tortillas and filling.

- Refrigerate for 2 hours. Trim off the ends and cut each roll into 8 slices. Serve cold.

Makes 24 pinwheels

What's in it for me?

Per pinwheel: 44 calories, 1.6 g fat, 0.9 g saturated fat, 2.9 g protein, 5.5 g carbohydrate, 1.1 g fiber, 6.1 mg cholesterol, 120.2 mg sodium
% calories from fat: 30

What the heck is hot red-pepper jelly and where can I buy it?

Hot red-pepper jelly is a condiment made from red chili peppers, sugar, vinegar, and spices. It enhances the flavor of meats, poultry, and sauces with a touch of heat. You can mix hot red-pepper jelly with plain cream cheese to create a tasty spread for crackers. You'll find it in a jar near the ketchup at your grocery store.

THE **E** FILES

Each day you fail to flex your muscles, they get weaker. "So, what? Big deal! Muscle shmuscle!" Well, it is a big deal if you're battling the bulge. That's because fading muscle tone leads to increased body fat and loss of *flex* appeal. For each pound of muscle you add to your body, you'll burn an extra 75 calories a day to maintain it. In contrast, if you add a pound of fat, you'll be calling on a puny two calories a day. So, the less muscle you have, the fewer calories you can consume, even if you're just trying to maintain your weight. And who wants to eat like a gerbil just to keep their weight steady? Grab some barbells and start lifting your way to a leaner body—it's worth the *weight*.

I just swallowed a frog... I'm liable to croak any minute!

The Dunk Tank

Three kinds of dips for dunking

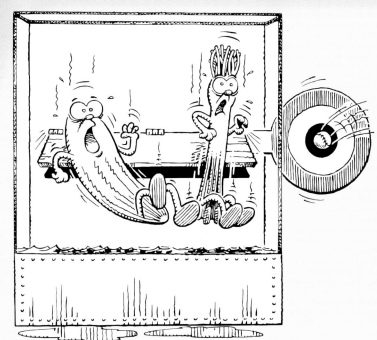

These low-fat dips will delight your lips! You'll give *tanks* when all is said and *dunked*.

Black Bean Dip
For pita chips or baked tortilla chips

1 can (15 oz) black beans, drained and rinsed
1/4 cup minced onions
2 tbsp chopped, fresh cilantro
1 tbsp lime juice
2 cloves garlic, minced
1/2 tsp ground coriander
1/4 tsp each ground cumin and black pepper
1/3 cup low-fat sour cream

- Combine all ingredients except sour cream in a blender or food processor and whirl until smooth. Transfer mixture to a small bowl and stir in sour cream. Cover and refrigerate until serving time.

Makes about 1-3/4 cups

Tzatziki
For warm, fresh pita triangles

1 cup low-fat, plain yogurt
1 cup peeled, seeded, and diced English cucumber
1/4 cup chopped green onions
3 tbsp chopped, fresh mint leaves
1 clove garlic, minced
1/4 tsp salt
1/8 tsp black pepper

- Combine all ingredients in a small bowl. Refrigerate for 1 hour before serving.

Makes about 2 cups

Tangy Plum Dip
For chicken nuggets or chicken skewers

1 cup yellow plum or apricot jam
1/4 cup orange juice
2 tbsp white vinegar
1 tsp dry mustard powder
1 tsp reduced-sodium soy sauce
1/2 tsp grated orange zest

- Combine all ingredients in a small saucepan. Cook over medium heat until jam is melted and dip is bubbly. Serve warm.

Makes about 1-1/4 cups

TZATZIKI Per serving (1/4 cup):
15 calories, 0.2 g fat,
0 g saturated fat, 1.5 g protein,
2.4 g carbohydrate, 0.2 g fiber,
0.6 mg cholesterol, 90.1 mg sodium
% calories from fat: 11

TANGY PLUM Per serving (2 tbsp):
58 calories, 0.1 g fat,
0 g saturated fat, 0.2 g protein,
15.4 g carbohydrate, 0.3 g fiber,
0 mg cholesterol, 35.8 mg sodium
% calories from fat: 1

BLACK BEAN Per serving (1/4 cup):
51 calories, 0.8 g fat,
0.1 g saturated fat, 4.7 g protein,
11.3 g carbohydrate, 3.5 g fiber,
0.8 mg cholesterol, 28.3 mg sodium
% calories from fat: 10

What's in it for me?

TRIVIAL TIDBIT

Almost $7 out of every $100 spent on eating outside the home is gobbled up by McDonald's.

Satayday Night Fever

Chicken satay with peanut dipping sauce

A low-fat chicken satay that includes a creamy peanut dipping sauce? What *Gibbs*? And simple to make, too? *Discos* here, and *discos* there—how easy can it *Bee*? *Gees*!

4 large boneless, skinless chicken breast halves, cut into 1-inch cubes
2 tbsp reduced-sodium soy sauce
1 tbsp each honey and lemon juice
2 tsp grated gingerroot
1 clove garlic, minced

Peanut Dipping Sauce
1/2 cup low-fat chicken broth
3 tbsp each light peanut butter and grape jelly
1 tbsp reduced-sodium soy sauce
1 tsp each grated lemon zest and sesame oil
1/2 tsp ground coriander
1/4 tsp crushed red pepper flakes

8 wooden or metal skewers

- Place chicken pieces in a large, heavy-duty, resealable plastic bag. In a small bowl, combine soy sauce, honey, lemon juice, gingerroot, and garlic. Pour marinade over chicken pieces in bag. Seal and refrigerate for at least 2 hours, or overnight if possible.

- If using wooden skewers, soak them in water for at least 20 minutes before using to prevent burning. Prepare grill. Thread chicken cubes onto skewers. Discard marinade. Grill for about 10 minutes, turning often to cook all sides. (If you prefer, cook chicken under broiler, 4 inches from heat, for about 8 minutes total.)

- While chicken is cooking, prepare dipping sauce. Combine all sauce ingredients in a blender and whirl for 30 seconds. Transfer to a small saucepan. Heat over medium heat until mixture is bubbly and has thickened. Transfer to a serving dish. Serve hot chicken skewers with dipping sauce.

Makes 8 skewers

What's in it for me?

Per skewer (with sauce): 146 calories, 3.6 g fat, 0.7 g saturated fat, 18.1 g protein, 10 g carbohydrate, 0.1 g fiber, 41.1 mg cholesterol, 331.6 mg sodium
% calories from fat: 22

COOKING 101

Satay (pronounced sah-TAY) is a favorite Southeast Asian appetizer consisting of small, marinated cubes of meat, fish, or poultry threaded onto skewers and grilled or broiled. In Malaysia and Indonesia, it's common to see roadside vendors selling satay made from their own closely guarded secret recipes. To create a beautiful, glossy finish, seasoned satay pros often brush the marinated meat with a mixture of one tablespoon of sugar dissolved in one-quarter cup of water just before cooking.

YOU DO THE MATH

Do you have a fear of frying? We do. That's because the fat content of fried snacks can be really scary! Just one ounce of tortilla chips—a wee handful—contains eight grams of fat. But, let's say you swap a more realistic two handfuls, or two ounces, of low-fat, baked tortilla chips for the fried version just once a week. You'll save 3,120 calories and 728 grams of fat a year—more than 10 days' worth of fat! So, when it comes to eating fried chips, it's better to be a scaredy-cat than a fat cat.

Order! Order in the court!

I'll have a cheeseburger, fries, and a Coke.

Romaine Empire

A kingdom of salads that's sure to empress

The Rice Squad

Brown rice salad with
bacon and almonds

It's the crime of the century! Someone
robbed the flavor bank and dumped
their stash in our salad! Now everyone thinks it's
our fault that rice tastes so good. We suppose
there's a grain of truth to that, but until we
consult our attorney, yum's the word.

Dressing

1 cup low-fat sour cream
1 tbsp each red wine vinegar
  and lime juice
2 tsp honey
1/2 tsp ground cumin
1/4 tsp each chili powder and salt
1/8 tsp black pepper

4 cups cooked brown rice
1 cup each diced red bell pepper and chopped green onions
1/2 cup frozen green peas, thawed
1/4 cup toasted, sliced almonds (see tip on p. 30)
2 slices bacon, cooked and crumbled
2 tbsp chopped, fresh cilantro or parsley

- To make dressing, combine first 8 ingredients in a small bowl.
  Refrigerate until ready to use.

- Combine all remaining ingredients in a large bowl. Add dressing
  and mix well. Chill until cold.

Makes 8 servings

What's
in it
for me?

Per serving: 185 calories, 4.2 g fat,
1 g saturated fat, 6.7 g protein,
31 g carbohydrate, 3.4 g fiber,
3.9 mg cholesterol, 195.3 mg sodium
% calories from fat: 20

Anybody seen this
grainy character?

WANTED
RAW
OR
COOKED

FRONT SIDE

Couch potatoes, stand to attention...if
you're able! Seasoned sofa spuds are
paying a dear price for their leisurely
lifestyle. Inactive people have a higher
risk of developing heart disease,
diabetes, colon cancer, obesity, and
osteoporosis. The solution is simply to
put activity back into everyday life.
A good start would be peeling
yourself off the couch, Potato. And that's
not a half-baked idea, either. Becoming
active doesn't just protect you against
life-threatening illnesses: It'll help you
sleep better, ward off colds, improve your
outlook on life, make you feel 10 years
younger, and decrease your odds of
being in a nursing home when you get
older. So, if you like to lie around, you've
got a real *lie-ability*.

TRIVIAL
TIDBIT

According to the National
Cancer Institute, high-fat
salad dressing is the
number-one source of
fat in the diets of North
American women ages
19 to 50. Looks like we're all dressed up
with nowhere to grow—except around
our midriffs!

He's in such bad shape, if he tried to run a bath,
he'd come in second.

Breakfast at Tiffany's (or anyone else's place)

Remember when mom said we should eat breakfast like a king, lunch like a prince, and dinner like a pauper? Well, mom was one smart cookie, and she even has medical experts backing her up. Too bad we aren't listening: 58% of North Americans don't eat breakfast! Yet it's been proven that dieters who eat breakfast end up losing more weight than those who don't. And doctors say that people who don't "break the fast" by regularly denying themselves food for 14 hours or so, are more likely to develop gallstones. Oh, the gall of it! To make matters worse, when you skip breakfast, your blood-sugar levels take a steep nosedive, and that can hinder late-morning problem-solving abilities. So, if you don't eat breakfast, you may end up like yesterday's coffee—a little weak in the bean!

Did you know it takes eight pounds of milk to make one pound of cheese? While this super-concentrated food may be a great source of calcium, it's also high in fat and cholesterol. An ounce of cheddar cheese contains nine grams of fat. And an ounce is pretty puny, too— about one and a half slices of processed cheese, one-quarter cup of shredded cheese, or a cube the size of a domino. Still, the average North American eats two pounds of cheese a month! That's enough to feed Mighty Mouse and his entire mousehold for a year! Remember: Everything in moderation.

Laugh at your mistakes.
Everyone else does.

Greek is the Word

Greek-style salad with penne pasta, tomatoes, feta cheese, and fresh oregano

If you find yourself saying, "It's all Greek to me," then you must be talking about this incredible-tasting pasta and vegetable medley. *Feta* up with ordinary salads? Ours is food for the gods!

1 pound penne pasta, uncooked (about 5 cups dry)
1-1/2 cups peeled, seeded, and diced English cucumber
3 medium tomatoes, seeded and chopped
1 cup crumbled feta cheese (4 oz)
1/2 cup chopped red onions
1/4 cup each chopped green onions and pitted, sliced black olives
1/4 cup chopped, fresh oregano, or 1 tbsp dried

Dressing
1/2 cup low-sodium, low-fat chicken broth
1/4 cup red wine vinegar
1 tbsp each olive oil and lemon juice
1 tsp each Dijon mustard and sugar
1 clove garlic, minced
1/4 tsp black pepper

- Cook pasta according to package directions. Drain. Rinse with cold water and drain again.

- In a large bowl, toss together pasta, cucumber, tomatoes, feta cheese, onions, olives, and oregano. Set aside.

- In a small bowl, whisk together all dressing ingredients. Pour over salad and mix well. Season with more black pepper, if desired. Cover and refrigerate for at least 1 hour before serving.

Makes 8 servings

Per serving: 312 calories, 7.8 g fat, 2.8 g saturated fat, 10.7 g protein, 47.5 g carbohydrate, 1 g fiber, 16.7 mg cholesterol, 295.5 mg sodium % calories from fat: 23

What's in it for me?

Eata Fajita Salad

Warm chicken fajita salad with chili-lime dressing

Eata fajita and savor the flavor! Traditional fajita fillings—spicy chicken, peppers, and onions—make a *filling* salad when they're served on crunchy greens and topped with grated cheese. Giddy-up!

1/2 cup low-fat sour cream
2-1/2 tbsp lime juice
1 tsp sugar
1/4 tsp each chili powder and ground cumin
4 boneless, skinless chicken breast halves, cut into thin strips
1 cup each sliced green and red bell peppers
1 small red onion, thinly sliced into rings
1/2 cup salsa
2 tbsp chopped, fresh cilantro
8 cups shredded romaine lettuce
1/2 cup shredded, reduced-fat sharp cheddar cheese (2 oz)

• In a small bowl, combine sour cream, 1-1/2 tablespoons of the lime juice, sugar, chili powder, and cumin. Refrigerate dressing until ready to use.

• Spray a large, non-stick wok or skillet with non-stick spray. Add chicken. Cook and stir over medium-high heat until chicken is no longer pink. Continue to cook until chicken is lightly browned. Add peppers and onions. Cook for 3 more minutes. Add salsa and cook for 2 more minutes.

• Stir in remaining 1 tablespoon lime juice and cilantro. Mix well. Remove from heat.

• To assemble salad, divide lettuce among 4 serving plates. Top with warm chicken mixture. Spoon dressing over salad. Sprinkle with cheese. Serve immediately.

Makes 4 servings

What's in it for us?

Per serving: 250 calories, 4.8 g fat, 2.2 g saturated fat, 35.4 g protein, 16.9 g carbohydrate, 3.9 g fiber, 77.8 mg cholesterol, 387.2 mg sodium
% calories from fat: 17

The words "fat-free" on a package are your license to fill.

FAT OR FICTION?

Someone notify James Bond! We're talking about a conspiracy of epicurean proportions—specifically, foods labeled "fat-free." Nutritionists call it the "SnackWell's Syndrome," after the line of non-fat food products that people gobble up like there's no tomorrow. It's a common misconception that fat-free foods give you free rein to overindulge. Take fat-free brownies, for instance. Until recently, people who were concerned about their figures would never snack on brownies. Now they polish off two or three at a time. Despite the low-fat or fat-free hype on the label, those chocolate-dipped, caramel-laced, cream-filled mini-cakes can still make you fat. That's because they still have plenty of calories, and if you consume more calories than you burn, well, expect your pants to pop in 007 minutes! Any excess calories, whether they're from fat, carbohydrates, or protein, are stored as fat. Clearly, waistlines of the world are expanding, and the fate of our figures depends largely on our license to kill fat-free misconceptions!

You Do The Math

If you load up on mayo, it's your hips that will pay-o! Next time you make yourself a sandwich, try swapping two teaspoons of mustard for the same amount of mayonnaise. Based on two sandwiches a week, you'll save 6,240 calories and 718 grams of fat in a year. That's more than 10 days' worth of fat! So, go ahead and spread yourself thin—just don't bite off more than you can chew.

Ultra Light Miracle Whip works well in this recipe and in others calling for a low-fat, mayonnaise-type dressing. Broccoli slaw mix is made of grated broccoli stems and often includes grated carrots, too. Look for it where you find pre-packaged salads at the grocery store. If you can't find it, you can always substitute regular coleslaw mix.

What fruit juice's residues are worth a fortune?

The residue from making orange juice is a hot commodity. Elements from the discarded pulp, seeds, and peel are used to make food products, such as cake mixes, candies, and soft drinks. The residues also find their way into paints and perfumes. More than 100 million pounds of orange-peel oil are sold annually for cooking purposes (it's unsaturated, by the way), and it's also the base for a synthetic spearmint oil that Coca-Cola buys in quantity for use as a flavoring. We propose a new company slogan: Coke, it's the peel thing.

Broccoli Mountain High

Broccoli coleslaw with turkey bacon and a creamy dressing

Shout it from the top: This broccoli coleslaw is full of crunch and full of flavor! Just be careful not to cause an avalanche. Sure to *peak* your interest, it's worth climbing the highest mountain for.

**1/3 cup low-fat mayonnaise
  (see Cooking 101)
2 tbsp white
  vinegar
1 tbsp sugar
1/2 tsp celery seed
6 cups broccoli
  slaw mix
  (see Cooking 101)
1 large red apple,
  unpeeled, cored,
  and diced
1 cup grated carrots
4 slices turkey bacon, cooked
  and chopped into small pieces**

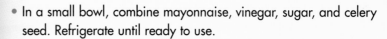

- In a small bowl, combine mayonnaise, vinegar, sugar, and celery seed. Refrigerate until ready to use.

- In a large bowl, toss together broccoli slaw mix, apple, carrots, and cooked bacon. Add dressing and mix well. Refrigerate for 1 hour before serving.

Makes 6 servings

Per serving: 72 calories, 2.2 g fat, 0.6 g saturated fat, 4.3 g protein, 11.4 g carbohydrate, 3.2 g fiber, 8.3 mg cholesterol, 263.6 mg sodium % calories from fat: 24

What's in it for me?

She says she eats like a bird, and since a bird consumes four times its weight in food every day, she'll be a round robin in no time.

Crabsolutely Fabulous Pasta Salad

Shell pasta with crabmeat and vegetables in a creamy, mustard-dill dressing

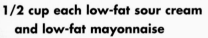

We've got the gift of crab! Our creamy pasta salad with crabmeat and dill will really give you something to talk about. Plus, it's crabnormally easy to make, even for the crabsent-minded.

1/2 cup each low-fat sour cream and low-fat mayonnaise
1 tbsp each lemon juice, honey mustard, and minced, fresh dill
1/2 tsp salt
1/4 tsp black pepper
12 oz medium shell pasta, uncooked (about 5 cups dry)
1 pound lump crabmeat (real or imitation), chopped
1/2 cup each diced red and green bell peppers
1/2 cup chopped green onions

- In a small bowl, combine sour cream, mayonnaise, lemon juice, honey mustard, dill, salt, and pepper. Refrigerate dressing until ready to use.

- Cook shells according to package directions. Drain well. Rinse with cold water and drain again. Transfer pasta to a large bowl. Add crabmeat, bell peppers, onions, and dressing. Mix well. Cover and refrigerate until ready to serve.

Makes 8 servings

What's in it for me? ➡ Per serving: 230 calories, 1.8 g fat, 0.1 g saturated fat, 15.2 g protein, 38.5 g carbohydrate, 0.4 g fiber, 1 mg cholesterol, 531.2 mg sodium
% calories from fat: 7

Cats became the longest-running Broadway musical in history. And as a special treat, the cast was given tuna instead of dry food.

David Letterman

In Defense of Decaf

Have you been lying awake at night wondering how they take the caffeine out of coffee? Thought so. Did you know it was the beans they take it from? Maybe you thought it was a straight liquid transaction that took place in a huge vat somewhere. Heck no, Joe! Several decaffeination methods are currently in use. In the water-process method, coffee beans are simply soaked in water to remove the caffeine. Unfortunately, much of the flavor comes out in the wash. Then there's the direct-contact method where the beans are treated with methylene chloride. This was the best way to preserve flavor, until the chemical was banned for use in hair sprays when studies showed that it caused cancer in animals. No need to lose sleep though—now coffee makers use carbon dioxide. Whew! Our DEcaf has been DEchemmed and DEtermined safe. DElightful!

THE E FILES

Rise and shine your walking shoes! Studies show that exercisers who work out in the morning are 50% more likely to stick with it. If you're struggling to fit exercise into an already hectic schedule, the wee hours of the morning may be the least distracting. Later in the day, excuses can mount up, or you may be too wiped out to work out. Another incentive to hop, skip, and jump out of the sack is that exercising in the a.m. helps set the tone for the p.m. Activity not only jump-starts your metabolism and gets your blood pumping, but it also gives your brain a jolt, actually improving communication between brain cells. When you spring out of bed, you'll wake up on the bright side!

What the heck is mango chutney and where can I buy it?

Mango chutney is a spicy condiment made from mangoes, onions, vinegar, and spices. The sweetness of the fruit provides a nice contrast to the spicy and sour flavorings. It's most commonly used on grilled meats, or to add zing to sauces and salad dressings. You'll find it in a jar near the ketchup at your grocery store.

Who'da Thunk?

Who invented Melba toast?

Melba toast, a mainstay in the dieter's arsenal for years, originated when several pieces of burnt toast were served to Australian opera star Nellie Melba at The Savoy Hotel in London. The prima donna had been on a diet, ordered toast, and was mistakenly served overtoasted, crisp, crunchy slices. Instead of cringing over the chef's *crumby* miscue, she loved it. So much so, that the maître d' named them in her honor and put Melba's toast on the menu.

My husband is losing five pounds a week on a new diet. In a year and a half, I should be rid of him completely!

Chicken and Mango Tango

Tangy, warm chicken and mango salad

Got a hunger pang-o? Then taste the Tango! Chicken and sweet peppers dance with chunks of fresh mango in a spicy dressing.

Dressing
1/3 cup low-fat, vanilla-flavored yogurt
1-1/2 tbsp each lime juice and mango chutney
   (see tip in margin)
1 tbsp seasoned rice vinegar
1 tsp honey
1/4 tsp each ground cumin, ground coriander, and paprika

1 tsp olive oil
4 boneless, skinless chicken breast halves, cut into strips
   or cubes
2 tsp grated gingerroot
1 clove garlic, minced
1-1/2 cups peeled, sliced mangoes
1 cup sliced red bell pepper
1/3 cup chopped green onions
8 cups torn romaine or mixed lettuces

- Combine all dressing ingredients in a small bowl. Set aside until ready to use.

- Heat the olive oil in a large skillet or wok. Add chicken, gingerroot, and garlic. Cook and stir over medium-high heat until chicken is no longer pink. Add mangoes, bell peppers, and green onions. Cook for 3 more minutes, until peppers begin to soften and mangoes are heated through. Stir in dressing. Remove from heat.

- Divide lettuce among 4 serving plates. Spoon warm chicken and mango mixture over lettuce. Serve immediately.

Makes 4 servings

Per serving: 239 calories, 3.4 g fat, 0.5 g saturated fat, 30.2 g protein, 23.1 g carbohydrate, 3.7 g fiber, 68.2 mg cholesterol, 185.3 mg sodium % calories from fat: 12

What's in it for me?

Where's Waldorf?

Chopped apples and toasted walnuts
tossed with rotini pasta in a light, creamy dressing

If you've been searching high and low for a Waldorf salad that isn't packed with fat, our slimmed-down version is what you're after.

Dressing

**3/4 cup low-fat, vanilla-
   flavored yogurt**
2 tsp honey mustard
1 tsp grated lemon zest
1/2 tsp salt
1/8 tsp black pepper

**4 cups cooked rotini pasta
   (about 2 cups dry)**
**3 cups chopped, unpeeled Red
   Delicious apples**
1 cup diced celery
1/3 cup toasted, chopped walnuts (see Cooking 101)
1/4 cup minced red onions
2 tbsp chopped, fresh parsley

- Combine yogurt, honey mustard, lemon zest, salt, and black pepper in a small bowl. Refrigerate until ready to use.
- Toss remaining ingredients in a large bowl. Add dressing and mix well. Chill for 1 hour before serving.

Makes 4 to 6 servings

What's in it for me?

Per serving (based on 6 servings): 174 calories,
4.5 g fat, 0.3 g saturated fat, 5.6 g protein,
29.3 g carbohydrate, 2.3 g fiber,
0.6 mg cholesterol, 253.8 mg sodium
% calories from fat: 23

Toasting nuts before using them in recipes intensifies their flavor. To toast nuts, place them in a dry skillet over medium heat. Shake the pan often, and roast walnuts for four to five minutes, until fragrant. Cool before using. Because nuts have a high fat content, they go rancid quickly. The best way to store shelled nuts is in an airtight container in the refrigerator, where they'll keep for about four months.

Good to the Core

You know what they say: "Two apples a day gets the doctor's OK!" Well, that's not exactly what they say, but eating two apples a day is probably a smart idea. Apples are chock-full of nutritional goodies, from pectin, a soluble fiber that helps lower cholesterol, to flavonoids, natural chemicals that appear to protect your heart. And every time you crunch an apple, you may be doing your eyes a favor, too. One of the flavonoids in apples actually protects against cataracts. So really, what they're saying is that regular daily consumption of apples keeps the cardiologist and the ophthalmologist at bay. Or, in plain English, an apple a day keeps all the doctors away.

Waldorf salad, originally a mixture of apples, celery, and mayonnaise, was invented by Oscar Tschirky in 1893. Oscar was a maître d' at the Waldorf-Astoria Hotel in New York City.

TRIVIAL TIDBIT

Take your pick.

Pick! If they're anything like the last batch, I'll need a hammer and chisel!

The Dressing Room

Flavorful, low-fat salad dressings

It's time to change the way you dress—your salads, that is! Why cloak them with fat-laden dressings when you can dress them up with our tasty, low-fat renditions?

Creamy Italian

1 cup low-fat sour cream
2 tbsp red wine vinegar
1 tbsp each grated Parmesan cheese, lemon juice, and honey
1 clove garlic, minced
2 green onions, white parts only, minced
1/2 tsp dried oregano
1/4 tsp each salt and black pepper

- Combine all ingredients in a small bowl. Refrigerate for 1 hour before using. Store in an airtight container or jar with lid in the refrigerator. Shake well before using. Will keep for 3 to 4 days.

Makes about 1-1/4 cups

Oriental Dressing
(tangy; good for Asian coleslaw)

1/2 cup frozen pineapple juice concentrate, thawed
1/3 cup seasoned rice vinegar
1 tbsp each reduced-sodium soy sauce and sesame oil
2 tsp grated gingerroot
1 tsp cornstarch
1 clove garlic, minced

- Whisk together all ingredients in a medium saucepan. Bring mixture to a boil over medium-high heat. Cook for 1 minute, until slightly thickened. Cool to room temperature. Refrigerate for up to 3 days.

Makes about 1 cup

Tropical Dressing
(for fruit salad)

3/4 cup diced kiwifruit
1/2 cup mashed ripe banana
1/2 cup low-fat, vanilla-flavored yogurt
2 tbsp frozen pineapple juice concentrate, thawed
1/2 tsp coconut extract

- For thick dressing, mash kiwi with a fork and stir together all ingredients in a medium bowl. For thinner dressing, whirl all ingredients together in a blender. Best if used within 24 hours.

Makes about 1-1/2 cups

CREAMY ITALIAN Per serving (2 tbsp):
28 calories, 0.5 g fat, 0.3 g saturated fat,
1.7 g protein, 4.5 g carbohydrate, 0 g fiber,
2 mg cholesterol, 108.1 mg sodium
% calories from fat: 15

ORIENTAL DRESSING Per serving (2 tbsp):
51 calories, 1.8 g fat, 0.3 g saturated fat,
0.4 g protein, 8.1 g carbohydrate, 0 g fiber,
0 mg cholesterol, 76.9 mg sodium
% calories from fat: 33*
*higher than our other recipes, but still very low in fat for salad dressing

TROPICAL DRESSING Per serving (1/4 cup):
49 calories, 0.2 g fat, 0 g saturated fat,
1.2 g protein, 11.4 g carbohydrate,
1.2 g fiber, 0.4 mg cholesterol,
12.7 mg sodium
% calories from fat: 3

What's in it for me?

Hearty laughter is a good way to jog internally without having to go outdoors.

Norman Cousins
Anatomy of an Illness

Nat's King Coleslaw

Asian coleslaw with a sesame-ginger dressing

It's unforgettable, in every way. But how can coleslaw so unforgettable be so incredible, too? We've added sesame oil and gingerroot to make our coleslaw fit for a king.

You've got a good head on your shoulders.

Dressing

1/2 cup seasoned rice vinegar
1/4 cup pure maple syrup (see hint below)
2 tbsp reduced-sodium soy sauce
1 tbsp sesame oil
1 tsp grated gingerroot

1 large pkg (1 pound) coleslaw mix (see hint below)
2 cups bean sprouts
1/3 cup chopped green onions
1 large Red Delicious apple, unpeeled, cored, and shredded

- To make dressing, whisk together vinegar, maple syrup, soy sauce, sesame oil, and gingerroot in a small bowl.

- In a large bowl, combine coleslaw mix, bean sprouts, green onions, and apple. Pour dressing over salad and mix well. Refrigerate for 1 hour before serving.

Makes 6 to 8 servings

Hint: If you don't have any maple syrup, use honey instead. You can substitute 6 cups shredded green cabbage, 1 cup shredded red cabbage, and 1 cup shredded carrots for the coleslaw mix.

What's in it for me?

Per serving (based on 8 servings): 79 calories, 2 g fat, 0.3 g saturated fat, 1.5 g protein, 14.8 g carbohydrate, 2.5 g fiber, 0 mg cholesterol, 171.3 mg sodium
% calories from fat: 22

His idea of a balanced diet is having a bacon double cheeseburger in each hand.

SAY IT AIN'T SO!

Have you seen the magic show that's playing down at the deli? They take perfectly healthy foods and, abracadabra, they make them unhealthy. Like when they turn cabbage into oil-soaked coleslaw. Three-quarters of a cup has 36 grams of fat and more than 400 calories! Then they turn potatoes into potato salad. Might as well eat a bag of chips, because a paltry three-quarters of a cup has 18 grams of fat and almost 300 calories. Chicken breast vanishes and reappears as chicken salad. Drown it in mayonnaise and this "salad" has more fat than a cheeseburger. And how about when they turn fruit into fruit salad? Oh yeah, fruit salad is healthy! Never mind. Your best bet is to find a deli that goes easy on the oil and butter, and uses low-fat versions of mayonnaise and sour cream.

YOU DO THE MATH

Keep your eyes on the size of your fries! If your cravings take over and you just can't resist an order of French fries, then at least opt for the small size. By replacing a large serving of fries with a small serving just once a week, you'll save 9,360 calories and 520 grams of fat in a year. That's more than seven days' worth of fat! So, if you don't want French fries to form a merger with your waistline, downsizing is the way to go.

If you want to lose weight, don't eat snacks.

FAT OR FICTION?

Au contraire. Not only are "grazers" less likely to overeat than those who restrict their food intake, but regular eaters are also teaching their bodies to expect a steady source of fuel. That's important. If your body figures you'll be eating again soon, it won't have to become an expert at storing fat. Every time you eat, you initiate the thermic effect of food, a temporary increase in your metabolism to help you digest and absorb nutrients. The most effective heat-generating foods are carbohydrates and lean protein. As far as your metabolism is concerned, eating a high-carbohydrate snack is like tossing a load of dry, crackling leaves on a campfire. The flames leap up and consume the fuel quickly and efficiently. If you have a snack that's high in fat, it's like using kindling that's damp. The fire has to struggle to burn it, and you end up with more smoke than heat. To keep that fire burning, you've gotta slip in a snack, Jack. When you skip the *amazing graze*, you haven't got a prayer.

TRIVIAL TIDBIT

It's easy to fall into the habit of matching your dining companion bite for bite, but if your companion is male, and you're a female, it's a sure route to Adipose Alley. The average North American woman needs one-third fewer calories than her male counterpart. So, if you're dining with your beau, aim to eat about two-thirds as much as he does, otherwise you'll *expand by your man*.

Gobbledegood Turkey Salad

Chunks of turkey breast, pineapple, and orange segments in a sweet, mango dressing

If you're watching your weight, there's no need to give up creamy salads cold turkey. You can gobble up this tropical delight guilt-free.

Dressing
**1/3 cup low-fat
  sour cream
2 tbsp mango chutney
  (see p. 29)
1 tbsp each lemon juice
  and honey
1/4 tsp curry powder**

**4 cups chopped, cooked turkey breast
1 cup each diced red bell pepper and diced celery
1 cup each diced pineapple and halved orange segments
  (see hint below)
1/2 cup chopped green onions**

- To make dressing, combine sour cream, mango chutney, lemon juice, honey, and curry powder in a small bowl. Refrigerate until ready to use.

- In a large bowl, combine turkey, red pepper, celery, pineapple, orange segments, and green onions. Add dressing and mix well. Refrigerate for 1 hour before serving.

Makes 6 servings

Hint: If using canned mandarin oranges, drain well and keep them whole.

Per serving: 181 calories, 1.2 g fat, 0.3 g saturated fat, 24.5 g protein, 18.5 g carbohydrate, 2.1 g fiber, 63.6 mg cholesterol, 198.9 mg sodium
% calories from fat: 6

What's in it for me?

Put Up Your Cukes

Cool cucumber salad with creamy, dill dressing

There's a lot of punch packed into this simple cucumber salad, so expect to duke it out with your friends for the leftovers.

1 cup low-fat sour cream or plain yogurt
1/4 cup chopped green onions
1 tbsp each lemon juice and sugar
1 tbsp minced, fresh dill
1/4 tsp salt
6 cups peeled, seeded, and diced English cucumbers (see hint below)

• To make dressing, combine all ingredients except cucumbers in a small bowl. Cover and refrigerate for 30 minutes.

• Add dressing to diced cucumbers in a medium bowl. Mix well. Refrigerate until ready to serve. Best if eaten within 24 hours.

Makes 6 servings

Hint: When a recipe calls for seeded cucumbers, split the cucumber lengthwise and scrape out the seeds and watery membrane with a spoon. Salads made from seeded cucumbers stay fresh longer.

What's in it for me?

Per serving: 55 calories, 0.8 g fat, 0.3 g saturated fat, 3.2 g protein, 9.6 g carbohydrate, 0.9 g fiber, 2.7 mg cholesterol, 166.9 mg sodium
% calories from fat: 13

Why do pregnant women crave pickles?

It's no old wives' tale—pregnant women really do sometimes crave unusual foods like pickles. These seemingly irrational cravings are actually the body's way of asking for certain lacking nutrients. In the case of pickles, it's salt that the body is yearning for. Though women have been warned for years to reduce their salt intake, a pregnant woman needs more salt than she would normally require. That's because she needs to make about 40% more blood than normal to feed the placenta, and the key ingredient to maintaining this higher level of blood is salt. The fetus needs lots of salt, too, since it's constantly bathed in a saline solution. So, when she peppers you with requests for anchovies and pretzels, just take it with a grain of salt.

TRIVIAL TIDBIT

Your heart, an organ that's just a bit larger than your fist, pumps 2,000 gallons of blood every day. That's enough to fill up 100 refrigerators with gallon jugs.

Football player's wife: I hate it when my husband calls leftovers "replays."
TV executive's wife: My husband calls them "reruns."
Mortician's wife: Be grateful. My husband refers to them as "remains."

When they reach middle age, most people start to wonder: Will I have enough money for retirement? What they really should be taking stock of is the following: Will I have enough muscle to play with my grandchildren, to pick up grocery bags, to tend the garden, or to swing a golf club? Will I have the strength to have any fun at all? Even if you've never invested in exercise, it's not too late to get in on the action and reap the returns. Like a miracle anti-aging potion, exercise can offset, delay, prevent, and even reverse many of the common conditions associated with growing older. One consequence of being active is that you could live longer and stronger than your neighbors. Imagine! You could be climbing Mount Everest when your friends can barely climb the stairs!

Today, my friends, we shed a tear for another helpless victim of vegetable corruption. We cry for the onion, an innocent, inherently healthy food that has been dragged into the dark underworld of fat-wielding, adipose outlaws. Yes, we mourn for all onions who have been ruthlessly transformed into...onion rings! Four measly rings contain 160 calories, and 60% of those calories come from fat. It's a crying shame! And a frying shame, too! Word out on the street is that the Vegetable Bureau of Investigations is looking into the matter.

Name That Tuna Salad

Tuna tossed with cannellini beans, tomatoes, and fresh basil

Go ahead. Call our tuna salad whatever you want. Just don't call it bland or boring. Loaded with fiber and easy to make, it's the perfect lunch to take to the office.

I can name that tuna in three bites!

Alba Core Gill Finley

1 can (15 oz) cannellini beans (white kidney beans), drained and rinsed

1 can (6 oz) water-packed tuna, drained

2 cups diced tomatoes

1/2 cup minced red onions

2 tbsp chopped, fresh basil or mint leaves

1 tbsp olive oil

2 tsp each red wine vinegar and lemon juice

1 tsp sugar

1 clove garlic, minced

1/2 tsp Dijon mustard

1/4 tsp each salt and black pepper

- In a large bowl, combine beans, tuna, tomatoes, red onions, and basil. Stir gently to avoid smashing the beans.

- In a small bowl, whisk together olive oil, vinegar, lemon juice, sugar, garlic, mustard, salt, and pepper. Pour dressing over salad and mix well. May be served immediately or chilled before serving.

Makes 4 servings

Per serving: 204 calories, 4.7 g fat, 0.1 g saturated fat, 16.4 g protein, 23.8 g carbohydrate, 6.2 g fiber, 12.4 mg cholesterol, 566.7 mg sodium % calories from fat: 21

What's in it for me?

If you haven't any charity in your heart, you have the worst kind of heart trouble.

Bob Hope

ROMAINE EMPIRE

My Fair Ladle

Savory soups that require you to Doolittle

Looking for Mr. Goodbarley

Long, slow simmering makes the beef really tender in this barley soup

The search is over! Hearty, hungry-man soup so satisfying, we can *barley* contain our excitement!

1-1/2 pounds stewing beef, trimmed of fat and cut into bite-sized pieces
1 cup each chopped celery, chopped carrots, and chopped onions
1 clove garlic, minced
7 cups water
4 tsp beef bouillon powder
1 cup tomato sauce
2/3 cup pearl barley
1-1/2 tsp dried marjoram
3/4 tsp dried thyme
1/2 tsp black pepper
Salt to taste
1/3 cup chopped, fresh parsley

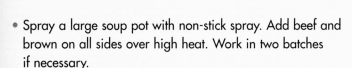

She's quite a dish!

- Spray a large soup pot with non-stick spray. Add beef and brown on all sides over high heat. Work in two batches if necessary.
- Reduce heat to medium. Add celery, carrots, onions, and garlic. Cook and stir for 5 more minutes. Add all remaining ingredients to pot, except parsley. Bring to a boil. Reduce heat to medium-low. Cover and simmer for 1-1/2 hours, until beef is very tender. Stir in parsley and serve hot.

Makes 8 servings

What's in it for us?

Per serving: 203 calories, 4.9 g fat, 1.4 g saturated fat, 21.7 g protein, 18.8 g carbohydrate, 2.9 g fiber, 50.2 mg cholesterol, 702.3 mg sodium
% calories from fat: 21

I used to have an hourglass figure—
then the sands of time shifted.

FAT OR **FICTION?**

Celery has "negative calories," so it's a miracle weight-loss food.

Don't put a lot of *stalk* in that claim. Celery isn't a miracle diet food. It may be low in calories, but chewing it doesn't burn more calories than it contains. An eight-inch stalk has just six calories, but chewing celery, or anything for that matter, burns about the same amount of calories as...well...just sitting! Celery, iceberg lettuce, and cucumbers are nearly calorie-free, not because of the energy it takes to chew them, but because of their high water content. Another dieting myth gone down the drain! But it's no myth that celery is good for you. In fact, it contains a chemical that helps reduce high blood pressure. So, there's still a lot of punch in celery's crunch!

YOU DO THE MATH

Snacking on olives can leave you in a high-fat pickle. But if you trade two ounces of olives for two ounces of baby dills once a week, you'll save 3,016 calories and 312 grams of fat in a year. That's more than four days' worth of fat! In this case, it's better to *dillydally*, just don't eat *olive* them.

Where did the expression "spill the beans" come from?

Legend has it that members of Greek societies used to vote on the admission of new members by dropping beans into jars or helmets. White beans signified a "yes" vote and black beans a "no." As tensions mounted and the anticipation became unbearable, anxious voters would accidentally knock over the jar or helmet, revealing the secret vote. In other words, they would spill the beans.

Okay, here's the situation: You're working late, you're famished, ready to faint, and the only relief available is the packaged food from...*Vendo-Death!* Beware of certain vending-machine snacks that masquerade as low-fat, healthy foods. Take trail mix, for example. A measly half cup has as much fat as a chocolate-glazed donut. Then there's the yogurt-covered nuts and raisins. The coating is a mixture of oil, sugar, and yogurt powder—more like NOgurt than yogurt! And how about those pretzel-combo thingys. When you stuff cheese in them, they're not pretzels anymore. Polish off just three-and-a-half ounces and you've choked down 17 grams of fat. If you make regular trips to the vending machine, you're really *dying* for a snack!

Is it true that cannibals don't eat clowns because they taste funny?

Bean Me Up, Scotty

Spicy black-bean soup with a sour cream swirl

Captain's log: It's the most enterprising combination of ingredients on the planet. Soup that boldly goes where no soup has gone before.

2 tsp olive oil
1 cup each chopped onions, chopped red bell pepper, and chopped carrots
1 clove garlic, minced
1 jalapeño pepper, seeded and minced
3 cups low-fat beef broth
1 cup tomato sauce
4 cups canned black beans, drained and rinsed
2 tbsp chopped, fresh cilantro
1 tbsp each lemon juice and brown sugar
2 tsp dried oregano
1 tsp each chili powder, ground cumin, and Worcestershire sauce
1/2 tsp dried thyme
1/4 tsp black pepper
6 tbsp low-fat sour cream
Chopped, fresh cilantro for garnish (optional)

- Heat olive oil in a large soup pot over medium heat. Add onions, red pepper, carrots, garlic, and jalapeño. Cook and stir for 5 minutes, until vegetables begin to soften. Add all remaining ingredients, except sour cream. Bring to a boil. Reduce heat to medium-low and simmer, covered, for 10 minutes.

- Working in batches, transfer soup to a blender or food processor and puree until smooth. Return to pot. Top each bowl of soup with a tablespoon of sour cream. Garnish with chopped cilantro, if desired.

Makes 6 servings

Per serving: 161 calories, 3.5 g fat, 0.1 g saturated fat, 11.3 g protein, 33.9 g carbohydrate, 9 g fiber, 1 mg cholesterol, 458.7 mg sodium % calories from fat: 15

What's in it for me?

MY FAIR LADLE

Obi Wonton Kenobi

Simple Chinese soup with chicken-filled wontons

What makes our wonton soup outta this world? Why, it's the *light-sabery* broth, of course. May the *forks* be with you! (Or, in this case, a spoon might be better.)

Filling

8 oz skinless ground chicken or turkey
1/4 cup minced green onions
2 tsp reduced-sodium soy sauce
1 tsp each grated gingerroot, sesame oil, and cornstarch
1 egg white
1/4 tsp salt

30 wonton wrappers (see Cooking 101)

Broth

6 cups low-sodium, low-fat chicken broth
1/4 cup chopped green onions
1/4 cup fresh basil leaves, cut into thin strips
1 tbsp reduced-sodium soy sauce
2 tsp sesame oil
1 tsp grated gingerroot

• Combine all filling ingredients in a medium bowl. Mix well. Working one at a time, place 1 teaspoon of filling in center of wonton wrapper. Fold one side over to enclose filling, making a triangle. Moisten edges and press down to seal. Bring the two points of the base of the triangle around filling, overlap them, moisten, and press together. Place filled wonton on a tray and cover with a damp kitchen towel. Repeat with remaining wontons.

• To cook wontons, bring a large pot of water to a boil over high heat. Add wontons. Stir once or twice to prevent wontons from sticking together. Boil for 5 minutes. Remove wontons using a slotted spoon. Drain well.

• To make soup, bring broth to a boil in a medium pot. Add onions, basil, soy sauce, sesame oil, and gingerroot. Simmer, uncovered, for 2 minutes.

• To serve soup, place 5 wontons in the bottom of each soup bowl. Ladle hot broth over wontons and serve immediately.

Makes 6 servings

What's in it for me?

Per serving: 210 calories, 4.4 g fat, 0.6 g saturated fat, 16.3 g protein, 26 g carbohydrate, 0.8 g fiber, 21.9 mg cholesterol, 592.1 mg sodium
% calories from fat: 19

COOKING 101

Wontons are a Chinese specialty similar to Italian ravioli. The paper-thin dough used to surround the filling comes prepackaged as wonton wrappers or wonton skins. Look for them in plastic wrap in the produce department of your grocery store. They dry out very quickly, so keep them covered with a damp towel while using.

Any Way You Slice It

Some say "tomato," some say "tomahto." No matter how you say it, they're good for you. Tomatoes are rich in antioxidants, which protect against cancer-causing cell damage. One of these natural cancer-fighting agents is lycopene, a close relative of beta carotene. Attention all men! Research shows that males who consume tomatoes or tomato-based foods at least four times a week—pizza included (hold the high-fat toppings)—have 20% less risk of prostate cancer than those who don't eat tomatoes. And the cooked kind appear to be best. It seems that cooking releases the fat-soluble lycopenes, and that a small amount of oil intensifies the effect. It's easy to add more tomatoes to your diet: in addition to pizza, there's pasta sauce, soup, sandwiches, juice, salsa, chili, and bruschetta. Sliced, diced, or chopped—no matter how you prepare them, tomatoes can't be topped!

THE E FILES

Put more spring in your offspring! Even if you don't want to be more active for your own sake, at least do it for your children. When both parents are active, children are nearly six times more likely to follow in their footsteps. And that would be a good thing, considering that obesity in children is reaching near-epidemic levels in North America. So, turn off the TV, hide the Nintendo joystick, and unplug the computer. Make exercise a priority, make it fun, and make it a family affair. By teaching Buffy and Jody proper *sweatiquette*, you'll stop them from becoming couch potatoes while they're still small fries.

Bow-link for Dollars

Spicy turkey sausage and bow-tie pasta soup

If the thought of turkey kielbasa teamed with pasta and veggies *strikes* your fancy, this soup's right up your *alley*. So good, there'll be nothing to *spare*.

8 oz turkey kielbasa, casing removed, cut into bite-sized pieces
1-1/2 cups chopped onions
1 clove garlic, minced
5 cups low-sodium, low-fat beef broth
1 can (14-1/2 oz) Italian-style stewed tomatoes, undrained
2 cups chopped zucchini
4 oz bow-tie pasta, uncooked (about 2 cups dry)
1/4 cup each chopped, fresh basil leaves and parsley
1 tbsp balsamic or red wine vinegar
1 tsp honey
3/4 tsp dried Italian seasoning
1/2 tsp salt
1/4 teaspoon black pepper

- Spray a large soup pot with non-stick spray. Add sausage, onions, and garlic. Cook and stir over medium heat for 5 minutes, until onions begin to soften.

- Add all remaining ingredients. Bring to a boil. Reduce heat to medium-low. Cover and simmer for 15 minutes, until pasta is tender. Serve hot.

Makes 6 servings

Per serving: 173 calories, 3.2 g fat, 0.1 g saturated fat, 12 g protein, 25.1 g carbohydrate, 2.3 g fiber, 26.7 mg cholesterol, 660.1 mg sodium
% calories from fat: 16

What's in it for me?

He must be eating army food—everything goes to the front.

Skinny Minestrone

This colorful minestrone is sure to become a family favorite

Our hearty minestrone is bursting with vegetable goodness! It's skinny on fat, not on flavor!

2 tsp olive oil
3/4 cup chopped Spanish onions
1/2 cup diced celery
2 cloves garlic, minced
1 can (28 oz) diced tomatoes, undrained
3 cups low-sodium, low-fat chicken or vegetable broth
3 cups vegetable cocktail (V-8 juice)
1 cup each chopped carrots, chopped zucchini, and chopped green cabbage
1 cup canned chickpeas, drained and rinsed
2 oz baby shells or tubetti pasta, uncooked (1/2 cup dry)
3 tbsp chopped, fresh parsley
1 bay leaf
2 tsp dried basil
1 tsp dried oregano
1/2 tsp each dried thyme and black pepper

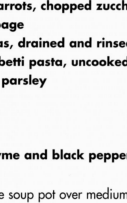

- Heat olive oil in a large soup pot over medium heat. Add onions, celery, and garlic. Cook and stir for 3 minutes, until vegetables begin to soften.

- Add all remaining ingredients. Bring to a boil. Reduce heat to medium-low. Simmer, partially covered, for 30 minutes. Serve hot.

Makes 8 servings

What's in it for me?

Per serving: 128 calories, 2.1 g fat, 0 g saturated fat, 5.7 g protein, 23.3 g carbohydrate, 2 g fiber, 0 mg cholesterol, 402.4 mg sodium
% calories from fat: 14

A high-fiber diet can help you control your weight.

FAT OR FICTION?

Our grandmothers called fiber "roughage," and all *well-regulated* households know that roughage is good for you. But why all the fuss over fiber? Because undigestible fiber acts like a personal scouring pad for internal use only. Besides increasing and softening stools, fiber speeds waste material through your intestines, making it less likely that suspicious, disease-promoting substances will spend time loitering in your system. But what grandma may not have told you is that fiber helps you manage your weight, too. Eating high-fiber foods keeps you feeling fuller longer, reducing your temptation to nibble. Fiber also slows the entry of sugar into the bloodstream, minimizing the highs and lows that make you crave sweet snacks. And high-fiber foods can transport dietary fats through your system before they're fully absorbed, reducing the amount of fat that gets into your bloodstream. When grandma made you eat your broccoli, beans, bran, and blueberries, she wasn't just being an old fart!

Yuk! your breath smells like garbage!

What do you expect? I'm eating junk food.

Split peas are a variety of yellow or green pea grown specifically for drying. Unlike whole dried peas, they don't require soaking before cooking. You'd be doing your body a favor by incorporating these tiny health nuggets into your diet. Just one cup of cooked split peas has a whopping 16 grams of fiber and less than one gram of fat!

Gimme Five!

Health experts implore us to eat at least five servings of fruits and vegetables every day, but the food industry sure isn't helping the cause. Nope, instead of promoting fruits and vegetables, it spends millions of dollars on fancy packaging and slick ads that push fat-free snacks and sweets. This commercialization of the low-fat diet means huge profits for manufacturers. If only fruits and vegetables were afforded the same promotional opportunities. Imagine what it might say on their labels: High in fiber! No cholesterol! Low in fat and calories! With phytochemicals and other health-giving nutrients! Why buy into this five-a-day quota that health experts are selling? To help prevent heart disease, stroke, degenerative diseases, premature aging, and cancers of the lung, colon, stomach, esophagus, mouth, throat, and possibly bladder and cervix. How many reasons do you need?

If at first you don't succeed...pretend that's not what you were trying to do in the first place.

Give Peas a Chance

Velvety smooth, minted pea soup that's very high in fiber

When two peas in a *pot* are united with a handful of other luscious goodies, the result is a silky smooth soup that lives in perfect harmony with your taste buds.

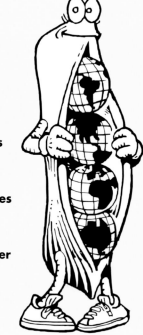

1 tsp olive oil
1 cup chopped onions
2 cloves garlic, minced
5 cups low-fat chicken or
** vegetable broth**
1-1/2 cups chopped carrots
1-1/2 cups dried, green split peas
** (see Cooking 101)**
1 cup peeled, cubed potatoes
1/2 cup chopped, fresh mint leaves
1 tbsp grated gingerroot
1/2 tsp dried sage
1/4 tsp each salt and black pepper
2 cups shredded romaine lettuce
1 cup frozen green peas
1/2 cup evaporated 2% milk

- Heat olive oil in a large soup pot over medium heat. Add onions and garlic. Cook and stir for 3 minutes. Add broth, carrots, split peas, potatoes, mint, gingerroot, sage, salt, and pepper. Bring to a boil. Reduce heat to medium-low. Cover and simmer for 30 minutes.

- Add lettuce and frozen peas. Simmer for 5 more minutes, until lettuce is wilted and peas are heated through.

- Working in batches, transfer mixture to a blender or food processor. Puree until smooth. Return soup to pot. Stir in evaporated milk and serve immediately.

Makes 6 generous servings

Per serving: 267 calories, 2 g fat, 0.4 g saturated fat, 18.8 g protein, 46.2 g carbohydrate, 16.1 g fiber, 1.7 mg cholesterol, 568.4 mg sodium % calories from fat: 7

What's in it for me?

We're Yammin'

Roasted sweet-potato soup
with orange and ginger

Yammed if you do and yammed if you don't. If you
do make this ever-so-yammy recipe, it'll be a
huge hit with the entire *yamily*. And if you
don't, you'll be missing out, yammit!

**6 cups peeled, cubed yams or sweet
  potatoes (about 3 large)**
1-1/2 cups coarsely chopped onions
1 tbsp olive oil
1 clove garlic, minced
5 cups low-fat chicken broth
**1 tbsp each grated orange zest
  and gingerroot**
1 whole clove
**1/2 tsp each ground cumin
  and salt**
1/4 tsp black pepper
6 tbsp low-fat sour cream
Chopped, fresh cilantro for garnish (optional)

- Spray a shallow roasting pan with non-stick spray. Add yams,
  onions, olive oil, and garlic. Stir well. Roast, uncovered, at 425°
  for 25 minutes. Stir once, halfway through cooking time.

- Transfer mixture to a soup pot. Add broth, orange zest,
  gingerroot, clove, cumin, salt, and pepper. Bring to a boil.
  Reduce heat to medium-low and simmer, covered, for 10 minutes.

- Working in batches, transfer soup to a blender or food processor
  and puree until smooth. Serve hot with a swirl of sour cream in
  the center. Garnish with fresh cilantro, if desired.

Makes 6 servings

What's in it for me?

Per serving: 209 calories, 3.7 g fat,
0.2 g saturated fat, 5.6 g protein,
39.2 g carbohydrate, 4.9 g fiber,
1 mg cholesterol, 292 mg sodium
% calories from fat: 16

*If exercise could be packaged into a pill,
it would be the single-most prescribed and
beneficial medicine in the nation.*

Dr. Robert Butler
Mount Sinai Medical Center, New York City

Who'da Thunk?

Who invented the potato chip?

George Crum, a cook at
the Moon Lake Lodge
Resort in Saratoga
Springs, NY, is credited
with the invention of
potato chips in 1853.
One day, a particularly fussy guest who
had just returned from Paris sent back an
order of fried potatoes because they were
not "properly thin." Crum prepared a
thinner batch, which was also sent back.
He took exception to this criticism and
promptly whittled a potato into thin,
near-transparent slices, soaked them in
ice water, and fried them in a kettle of
boiling oil, then salted them. As the story
goes, he sent the ridiculously thin slices
back to the persnickety customer. Much to
his surprise, he received accolades
instead of insults! And the love of potato
chips has continued. Per capita, North
Americans eat about 6.1 pounds of
potato chips a year! At 10 grams of fat
per handful, that's a Crummy snack to eat
on a regular basis.

SAY IT AIN'T SO!

Canned "miracle meat" made its debut on
dinner plates during the Second World
War. Innocent-looking enough, the pink
pork product in the rectangular can
contains 24 grams of fat in a puny
three-ounce serving—what you'd find in
your average fast-food hamburger!
Convenient as it may be, processed
luncheon meat in a can isn't something to
oink out on regularly, unless you want
your midriff to *spam* three continents!

What the heck is lemongrass and where can I buy it?

Lemongrass is an herb that grows in slender green stalks that look a bit like woody leeks. It's what gives a lemony flavor and aroma to Southeast Asian dishes. Only the bottom four to six inches of the stalk are used in cooking. Many supermarkets carry lemongrass in the produce section, or look for it at Asian markets. In a pinch, substitute one teaspoon of grated lemon zest for one stalk of lemongrass.

YOU DO THE MATH

Does the fat in peanuts drive you nutty? It should. Just one cup of peanuts has a mind-boggling 720 calories and 63 grams of fat. If you swap your peanuts for two cups of pretzels just once a week, you'll save an astounding 20,280 calories and 3,120 grams of fat in a year. That's more than 46 days' worth of fat! C'mon baby, let's do the twist!

Help! I've accidentally swallowed a spoon!

Well, just lie down and don't stir.

EMERGENCY

ABSOLUTELY NO RESERVATIONS

Chicken Soup for the Bowl

Asian chicken soup with coconut and coriander

Fill up your bowl and warm your soul with a chicken soup that's even better than mom's. Far East ingredients give it a far-out flavor.

2 pounds skinless, bone-in chicken thighs and drumsticks (about 8 pieces)
6 cups low-fat chicken broth
3 stalks lemongrass, cut into 1-inch pieces (see tip in margin)
1 tbsp grated gingerroot
10 black peppercorns
1/2 tsp each ground coriander and crushed red pepper flakes
2 cups sliced mushrooms
1 cup light coconut milk
1/4 cup chopped green onions
1 tsp sugar
1/2 tsp coconut extract
2 tbsp chopped, fresh cilantro
1 tbsp lime juice
2 cups cooked white rice

- In a large soup pot, combine chicken pieces, broth, lemongrass, gingerroot, peppercorns, coriander, and crushed red pepper flakes. Bring to a boil. Reduce heat and simmer, partially covered, for 30 minutes. Skim off any foam.

- Remove chicken pieces. Strip the chicken off the bones and set aside. Discard bones.

- Using a wire strainer, strain the broth and discard the solids. Return broth to soup pot and stir in cooked chicken, mushrooms, coconut milk, green onions, sugar, and coconut extract. Cook over medium heat until mushrooms are tender, about 10 minutes. Stir in cilantro, lime juice, and cooked rice. Serve hot.

Makes 6 servings

Per serving: 231 calories, 6.7 g fat, 2.2 g saturated fat, 22.2 g protein, 20 g carbohydrate, 0.6 g fiber, 70 mg cholesterol, 156.8 mg sodium % calories from fat: 26

What's in it for me?

MY FAIR LADLE

45

Fundalentil Soup

Make this big batch of tomato and lentil soup one day ahead for the best flavor

It's fun to make, it's fun to eat, and *fundalentilly*, it's good for you! What more could you ask for? A second helping, of course.

1 tsp olive oil
1-1/2 cups chopped onions
1 cup chopped celery
2 cloves garlic, minced
7 cups low-fat chicken broth
1 can (28 oz) diced tomatoes, undrained
1 can (10-3/4 oz) reduced-fat tomato soup, undiluted
2 cups dried brown or green lentils
2 cups chopped carrots
2 cups peeled, diced yams or sweet potatoes
2 tsp dried oregano
1-1/2 tsp ground cumin
1 tsp each ground coriander and salt
1/2 tsp black pepper
1/8 tsp ground nutmeg
2 cups packed, chopped, fresh spinach

• Heat olive oil in a large soup pot over medium heat. Add onions, celery, and garlic. Cook and stir for 3 to 4 minutes, until vegetables begin to soften.

• Add all remaining ingredients, except spinach. Bring to a boil. Reduce heat to medium-low, cover, and simmer for 30 minutes, stirring occasionally. Add spinach and simmer for 15 more minutes. Serve hot.

Makes 12 servings

What's in it for me?

Per serving: 199 calories, 2 g fat, 0.1 g saturated fat, 12.3 g protein, 34.9 g carbohydrate, 12.2 g fiber, 0 mg cholesterol, 361.6 mg sodium % calories from fat: 9

THE E FILES

Snowblowers, riding lawn mowers, remote controls, automatic garage-door openers—energy- and time-saving devices are everywhere. Why walk when you can ride in a golf cart? Why weed by hand when there's the Wonderful Whirling Weed Wacker? Here's why: A researcher in the United Kingdom estimated that over the last 25 years, the average person's energy expenditure has dropped by 800 calories a day. That's almost 300,000 calories a year! A 170-pound man would have to jog for 555 hours in order to burn off that amount. Holy shin-splints, Batman! That weed wacker doesn't sound so wonderful anymore. If modern conveniences are meant to save time, why not use that time for physical activity? Dishwashers, washing machines, microwave ovens, and VCRs all give you more flexibility, freeing up time to walk, ride a bike, or play tennis. By putting your muscles to work, you're not giving technology a chance to zap your health.

What common household spice is also a hallucinogen?

Who'da Thunk?

Call the Spice Squad! You're busted! Though most commonly used to flavor eggnog, pies, cakes, or soups, nutmeg can also be a hallucinogenic drug. It's true! Nutmeg contains the chemical myristin, which has properties similar to the drug mescaline, and if taken in large quantities, nutmeg can actually produce hallucinations and a feeling of euphoria. No need to trash your stash, though. You'd have to down an absurd amount to reach Fantasy Island—and you'd probably get sick to your stomach before you got there. In culinary proportions, you can rest assured that nutmeg is a safe spice, not a Scary Spice.

Penny Wise, Pound Foolish

Each year, billions of dollars are spent on organized weight-loss programs. Some are run by qualified medical and nutrition experts and can really help people. Others are run by unqualified staff and often make unrealistic claims. If it sounds too good to be true, then it probably is. Beware of fraudulent weight-loss schemes that promise "immediate, don't-lift-a-finger results," or ones that use words like "magic," "miracle," "secret," "revolutionary," or "effortless" in their advertising. There's no miracle weight-loss solution. There's no magic pill that'll melt away flab and incinerate cellulite. If losing weight was such a cinch, no one would be heavy, right? A healthy, varied, low-fat diet along with some regular exercise is the only *weigh* to shed pounds. And if you need assistance, talk to a registered dietitian who can help you make small, gradual, and permanent changes to your eating and lifestyle habits.

TRIVIAL TIDBIT When you go food shopping, leave the kids at home. Studies show that if you bring a child along, you'll spend 29% more on groceries if you're female, and 66% more if you're male. Also, Dad's a lot more likely to buy food with kid appeal (meaning high in sugar), like Marshmallow Krispie Crunch Cereal.

Happy-Go-Leeky

Creamy leek and potato soup with fresh dill

It's your *leeky* day! This soup is not only *dillectable*, but it's also *potatotally* scrumptious.

- **1 tbsp butter**
- **2 cups sliced leeks (white parts, plus 1 inch of green parts)**
- **1 cup chopped celery**
- **4 cups low-fat chicken or vegetable broth**
- **3 cups peeled, diced potatoes**
- **1 cup chopped carrots**
- **3/4 tsp dried thyme**
- **1/2 tsp salt**
- **1/4 tsp black pepper**
- **1 cup buttermilk**
- **1 tbsp minced, fresh dill**

- Melt butter in a large soup pot over medium heat. Add leeks and celery. Cook and stir for 5 minutes, until vegetables begin to soften.

- Add broth, potatoes, carrots, thyme, salt, and pepper. Bring to a boil. Reduce heat to medium-low, cover, and simmer for 20 minutes.

- Working in batches, transfer soup to a blender or food processor and puree until smooth. Return to pot. Stir in buttermilk and dill. Serve hot.

Makes 6 servings

Per serving: 134 calories, 2.6 g fat, 1.5 g saturated fat, 5.7 g protein, 23.4 g carbohydrate, 2.8 g fiber, 6.6 mg cholesterol, 586.2 mg sodium
% calories from fat: 16

What's in it for me?

She's served so many TV dinners, she thinks she's in show business.

The Souper Bowl

Hearty, creamy, turkey and vegetable chowder

We interrupt this cookbook to bring you coverage of Chowderbowl XXIV, live from Bowlivia. The crowd favorites—turkey and vegetables—are sure to score extra points with a hungry clan.

8 oz boneless, skinless turkey breast, cut into 1-inch cubes
3 oz Canadian bacon, diced
1/2 cup chopped onions
3 cups low-fat chicken broth
2 cups diced carrots
1 cup peeled, cubed potatoes
1 tsp dried thyme
1/2 tsp dried rosemary
1/4 tsp black pepper
2 cups broccoli florets
1 can (15 oz) cream-style corn
1 cup frozen or canned corn kernels
1/2 cup low-fat sour cream mixed with 1 tsp cornstarch

- Spray a large soup pot with non-stick spray. Add turkey and cook over medium-high heat until no longer pink. Add bacon and onions and cook for 2 more minutes. Add broth, carrots, potatoes, thyme, rosemary, and pepper. Bring to a boil. Reduce heat to medium-low, cover, and simmer for 8 minutes.

- Stir in broccoli and simmer for 3 more minutes. Add creamed corn and corn kernels. Cook for 2 more minutes, until corn is heated through. Stir in sour cream mixture and serve immediately.

Makes 4 servings

What's in it for us?

Per serving: 325 calories, 4.1 g fat, 0.7 g saturated fat, 27.3 g protein, 51.4 g carbohydrate, 4.2 g fiber, 47.5 mg cholesterol, 900.6 mg sodium
% calories from fat: 10

Where's the best place to eat along the highway? Wherever there's a fork in the road.

Weight! Touch that Dial!

Turn off the tube and adjust the volume on your eating! Watching television promotes mindless snacking, an automatic eating motion that makes it easy to forget about the quality and quantity of your food. It's not easy to distinguish between feelings of hunger and satiety when you're in *The Twilight Zone*, or lost in *Another World*. Television also has a measurable effect on metabolism. Researchers at Memphis State University monitored young girls watching *The Wonder Years* and found that their metabolic rate dropped as much as 16% below resting levels. In other words, they burned fewer calories watching TV than they would have sitting still with the TV off!

Let's face it, everyone wants to look and feel younger than their years. If there's a potion, pill, cream, or scheme that guarantees the glow of youth, people are willing to pay top dollar for it. But is that $3,000 face-lift really necessary? What most people need is a simple forklift—to pry them off the couch, that is! Many supposedly age-related changes in the body are simply a matter of being out of shape. Inactivity carries a hefty price tag: loss of muscle tone and strength, stiff joints, lack of zip, slower metabolism, increased body fat, and a less efficient heart. Cancel the plastic surgery! Toss the ACME Age-Defying Cream! Exercise is the magical youth serum we've all been searching for and it doesn't cost a cent. Activity now! Don't delay! Call 1-800-GET-YUNG.

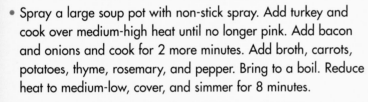

What the heck is savoy cabbage and where can I buy it?

Savoy cabbage is a light green, mellow-flavored cabbage with crinkled leaves that is considered by many to be the finest cabbage for cooking. You'll find it in the produce department of most well-stocked grocery stores. If you can't find it, use the standard, smooth, light green cabbage in its place. By the way, the word cabbage comes from the French word *caboche,* which is a colloquial term for "swollen head."

Got the blues? If you thought blue corn chips were nutritionally superior to regular corn chips, prepare for despair. Blue corn turns pale gray, brown, or lavender when processed. But the special corn doesn't make a healthier chip. No, the high fat content of tortilla chips comes from the vegetable oil they're fried in, not the small amount of fat found naturally in corn. A measly handful typically contains six to nine grams of fat, which supply 50% or more of its 130 to 150 calories! Blue hue? Boo hoo!

Cabbage Patch Soup

A meal in a pot

This savory cabbage creation is definitely at the head of its class.

1 pound extra-lean ground beef
1 cup each chopped celery and chopped onions
1/2 cup chopped green bell pepper
1 clove garlic, minced
1 can (28 oz) diced tomatoes, undrained
1 can (6 oz) tomato paste
5 cups low-sodium, low-fat beef broth
2 cups peeled, cubed potatoes
1 cup chopped carrots
1/4 cup chopped, fresh parsley
2 tbsp red wine vinegar
1 tbsp sugar
1 bay leaf
1-1/2 tsp dried basil
1 tsp paprika
1/2 tsp each salt and black pepper
3 cups thinly sliced savoy cabbage (see tip in margin)

- In a large soup pot, cook beef, celery, onions, green pepper, and garlic over medium-high heat until beef is browned. Add all remaining ingredients, except cabbage. Bring to a boil. Reduce heat to medium-low. Cover and simmer for 30 minutes.

- Stir in cabbage and simmer for 30 more minutes. Remove bay leaf before serving.

Makes 8 servings

Per serving: 198 calories, 6.4 g fat, 2.4 g saturated fat, 14.9 g protein, 21.8 g carbohydrate, 3.5 g fiber, 34.3 mg cholesterol, 531.3 mg sodium % calories from fat: 28

What's in it for me?

Mulligatawnski

Southern Indian soup with curried chicken, apples, and rice

Get *curried* away with Greta's scrumptious version of mulligatawny soup.

- **1 tbsp butter or margarine**
- **1 cup each chopped celery, chopped onions, and chopped carrots**
- **1 clove garlic, minced**
- **4 boneless, skinless chicken breast halves, cut into 1-inch cubes**
- **2 tsp curry powder**
- **1 tsp chili powder**
- **1/2 tsp ground cumin**
- **3 whole cloves**
- **6 cups low-fat chicken broth**
- **1 can (14-1/2 oz) plum tomatoes, drained, cut up**
- **1/2 cup uncooked, long-grain white rice**
- **1 tsp salt**
- **1/2 tsp black pepper**
- **2 cups peeled, cored, and diced Granny Smith apples**
- **1/4 cup chopped, fresh parsley**
- **3/4 cup low-fat sour cream or yogurt**
- **1 tbsp lemon juice**

- Melt butter in a large soup pot over medium heat. Add celery, onions, carrots, and garlic. Cook and stir for 3 to 4 minutes, until vegetables begin to soften.

- Add chicken. Cook until chicken is no longer pink. Add curry powder, chili powder, cumin, and cloves. Cook and stir for 2 more minutes. Add broth, tomatoes, rice, salt, and pepper. Bring to a boil. Reduce heat to medium-low. Cover and simmer for 15 minutes.

- Add apples and parsley. Simmer for 10 more minutes. Remove from heat. Stir in sour cream and lemon juice. Serve hot.

Makes 8 servings

What's in it for me? → Per serving: 202 calories, 3.5 g fat, 1.1 g saturated fat, 19.4 g protein, 22.3 g carbohydrate, 2.4 g fiber, 42.9 mg cholesterol, 605.5 mg sodium
% calories from fat: 16

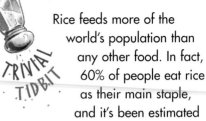

Rice feeds more of the world's population than any other food. In fact, 60% of people eat rice as their main staple, and it's been estimated that some one billion people worldwide are involved in growing it. The Chinese, who have been eating rice for 4,000 years, consume about a pound a day per person. And instead of saying "Hello" as a greeting, it's common for them to ask, "Have you had your rice yet?"

YOU DO THE MATH

Go ahead. *Bake* my day! Just be aware that if you trade your high-fat, butter-flavored croissant for a plain bagel once a week, you'll save 3,120 calories and 884 grams of fat in a year. That's more than 13 days' worth of fat! So, on your next trip to the pastry shop, be sure to choose baked goods that aren't *bads*.

Bring Home the Bakin'

Muffins, loaves, and other baked goodies

IT'S NICE TO BE KNEADED

Isn't She Loafly?

Chocolaty, chocolate-chip zucchini loaf

Isn't she wonderful? Isn't she special? She's a delectable, chocolate-chip zucchini loaf that's moist and delicious without a ton of fat. A real beauty!

2-1/2 cups all-purpose flour
1/2 cup unsweetened cocoa powder
1-1/2 tsp baking powder
1 tsp each baking soda and cinnamon
3/4 tsp salt
1-1/2 cups sugar
3/4 cup fat-free egg substitute, or
   3 whole eggs (see Cooking 101)
1/2 cup unsweetened applesauce
1/3 cup vegetable oil
2 tsp vanilla
2 cups packed, grated zucchini
1/2 cup mini chocolate chips

- Preheat oven to 350°. Spray two 8 x 4-inch loaf pans with non-stick spray. Set aside.

- In a large bowl, combine flour, cocoa, baking powder, baking soda, cinnamon, and salt. Set aside.

- In a medium bowl, whisk together sugar, egg substitute, applesauce, vegetable oil, and vanilla. Stir in zucchini. Add wet ingredients to dry ingredients. Stir just until dry ingredients are moistened. Fold in chocolate chips.

- Spread batter evenly in prepared pans. Bake for 50 minutes, or until a toothpick inserted in center of loaf comes out clean. Cool for 5 minutes in pans. Remove from pans and let cool on a wire rack before serving.

Makes 2 loaves, 10 slices each

What's in it for me?

Per slice: 184 calories, 5.3 g fat, 1.5 g saturated fat, 3.2 g protein, 32.1 g carbohydrate, 1.4 g fiber, 0 mg cholesterol, 185.4 mg sodium
% calories from fat: 25

A positive attitude may not solve all your problems, but it will annoy enough people to make it worth the effort.

Herm Albright

COOKING 101

Fat-free egg substitute is a liquid egg product sold frozen in cartons. Its main ingredient is egg white (about 80%), and other ingredients can include non-fat milk, tofu, added vitamins and minerals, and artificial colors. Egg substitute is cholesterol-free, and can be used in cooking and baking in many of the same ways as regular eggs. One-quarter cup egg substitute is the equivalent of one whole egg.

Who invented bagels?

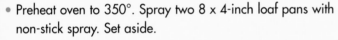

Who'da Thunk?

Legend has it that many years ago, a greedy king in a small European country decided it was time once again to raise taxes. Since he had already taxed almost everything in the kingdom, he elected to target ovens that were used by Jewish bakers. With already thin profit margins, the bakers couldn't afford to pay the new tax and many had to close shop. Eventually, one of the distraught bakers observed his wife making noodles by rolling her dough into small circles and putting them into boiling water. He thought, "What if I rolled some of my dough into rings and boiled it, too?" When he tried it, his little circles of dough bounced merrily in the boiling water, plumped up into firm donut shapes, and became chewy and delicious. Bagels were born! The new treat's name came from a variation of the Yiddish word *beygl*. But that's not the *hole* story. Word spread about the boiled bread rings, and the king was so impressed, he cancelled the tax. Good thing the baker used his noodle!

Washing windows, scrubbing floors, and sweeping driveways are more than just spring-cleaning activities. In fact, we should cherish these chores for two reasons: They fight dirt and grime—*and* they fight fat! According to the new fitness rules, anything that gets your body moving counts as exercise, including moderate, everyday activities like vacuuming and mowing the lawn. Who'da thunk? Twenty years with your head in a dirty oven, scraping, scrubbing...firming, toning! Indeed, housework can be a great fat burner and muscle toner, especially when you put some effort into it. So, put on your Calvin Kleans, crank up the tunes, and spring into action!

YOU DO THE MATH

The condition of your physique can often be measured by your *chip-to-waist* ratio. So, if potato chips are your snack of choice, you might want to munch on this: By substituting two cups of low-fat microwave popcorn for two cups of potato chips once a week, you'll save 13,156 calories and 936 grams of fat in a year. That's almost 14 days' worth of fat! When the chips are downed, the flab's way up.

Takin' Care of Biscuits

Melt-in-your-mouth whole wheat and cheddar biscuits

Let's call this eating to order and get down to biscuits! First on the agenda: The planned merger between whole wheat dough and tangy, tasty cheddar cheese. Everyone in *flavor* say, "Aye'm hungry!"

1-1/4 cups all-purpose flour
3/4 cup whole wheat flour
2 tsp baking powder
1 tsp baking soda
1/4 tsp salt
1/8 tsp cayenne pepper
1/2 cup shredded, reduced-fat sharp cheddar cheese (2 oz)
3 tbsp butter or margarine
1 cup buttermilk
1 tsp honey

- Preheat oven to 425°.
- In a medium bowl, combine both flours, baking powder, baking soda, salt, and cayenne pepper. Stir in cheese. Using a pastry blender, cut in butter until mixture resembles coarse crumbs.
- Combine buttermilk and honey. Add to dry ingredients. Using a fork, stir to form a soft dough. Turn dough out onto a lightly floured surface. Form a ball. Roll out dough to 3/4-inch thickness. Cut into 2-1/2-inch rounds using a biscuit or cookie cutter. Place biscuits on a cookie sheet that has been sprayed with non-stick spray. Bake for 12 minutes, until biscuits have puffed up and are light golden brown. Serve warm.

Makes 14 biscuits

Per biscuit: 105 calories, 3.6 g fat, 2.1 g saturated fat, 3.9 g protein, 14.8 g carbohydrate, 1.1 g fiber, 10.1 mg cholesterol, 230 mg sodium
% calories from fat: 30

What's in it for me?

His doctor put him on a seven-day diet,
but he ate the whole thing in one meal.

Corn in the U.S.A.

Comforting corn muffins for dunking in chili or stew

If Utaht corn muffins were O-high-o in fat, think again! In our revamped version, oil's no longer the Maine ingredient, so you Kentucky an extra one in your lunch bag and still fit into that New Jersey.

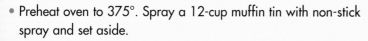

1 cup all-purpose flour
1 cup yellow cornmeal
2 tbsp sugar
1-1/2 tsp baking powder
1/2 tsp baking soda
1/4 tsp salt
1 can (15 oz) cream-style corn
1/2 cup buttermilk
1 egg
2 tbsp butter or margarine, melted
1 can (4 oz) diced green chilies

- Preheat oven to 375°. Spray a 12-cup muffin tin with non-stick spray and set aside.

- In a large bowl, combine flour, cornmeal, sugar, baking powder, baking soda, and salt. Set aside.

- In a medium bowl, whisk together corn, buttermilk, egg, melted butter, and diced green chilies. Add wet ingredients to dry ingredients. Stir just until dry ingredients are moistened.

- Divide batter among 12 muffin cups. Bake for 20 minutes, or until a toothpick inserted in center of muffin comes out clean. Be careful not to overbake. Remove muffins from tin and cool slightly on a wire rack. Best served warm.

Makes 12 muffins

What's in it for me?

Per muffin: 149 calories, 3 g fat,
1.4 g saturated fat, 3.6 g protein,
28 g carbohydrate, 1.3 g fiber,
23.5 mg cholesterol, 345.7 mg sodium
% calories from fat: 18

Margarine has less fat and calories than butter.

FAT OR FICTION?

Which is butter—better or margarine? Oops! Having a little trouble with our vowel movements again. That's which is *better*? Most people don't realize that butter and margarine have the same amount of fat and calories per tablespoon—about 11 grams of fat and 100 calories. So, how are they different? Well, butter contains cholesterol and margarine doesn't. Butter also has more saturated fat. But here's where things get slippery: Margarine is made from vegetable oil, and in order to make the oil spreadable and increase its shelf life, manufacturers put it through a process called hydrogenation. This turns the healthy, unsaturated fats into unhealthy ones called trans fatty acids. These may increase the risk of heart disease even more than saturated fats do. A solution? Look for margarines labeled "non-hydrogenated." And remember, man does not live on spread alone. If your diet is otherwise low in fat, the occasional pat of butter or tablespoon of margarine won't kill you.

Did you hear about the new overnight coffee delivery service? It's called Federal Espresso.

Truth or Health Consequences

We have no trouble believing that if we swallow arsenic, we'll surely die. But, despite all the scientific evidence, we still have trouble convincing ourselves that a healthy diet improves our quality of life. Let's clear this up right here and now! Even if your weight is normal, low-fat eating can reduce your risk for five of the 10 leading causes of death: heart disease, stroke, atherosclerosis, diabetes, and certain cancers. Eating smart means choosing foods that will make you feel and look your best, give you energy, keep you at a healthy weight, and improve the quality of your every waking hour. You only have one body, so you'd better feed it with respect. Become a believer! When it comes to the benefits of a healthy diet, the proof is in the low-fat pudding.

SAY IT AIN'T SO!

Cappuccino. Mochaccino. Frappaccino. Sure are a whole *latte* choices at the gourmet coffee shop—and a whole *latte* fat if they're made with whole milk! A 12-ounce whole milk cappuccino can have about seven more grams of fat than its non-fat counterpart. Same goes for the iced varieties. If you're longing for latte, be sure to ask for the skinny variety (or "skimmy," to be more precise). Non-fat milk froths as nicely as the full-fat stuff, so your taste buds won't even know the difference.

You know, I really don't think I need buns of steel. I'd be happy with buns of cinnamon.

Ellen DeGeneres

Mercedes Buns

No one will believe these warm cinnamon buns are low in fat and calories

A luxurious breakfast treat for the pastry lover in you, these cinnamon buns drizzled with creamy glaze are a *wheel* hit with everyone.

1 loaf (1 pound) frozen bread dough, thawed
1 tbsp butter, melted
1/2 cup packed brown sugar
2 tsp cinnamon
1/2 cup icing sugar
1 oz light cream cheese
1 tbsp 2% milk

- Spray a 9 x 13-inch baking pan with non-stick spray and set aside.

- Roll out dough on a lightly floured surface to a 9 x 12-inch rectangle. Use your hands to stretch dough if necessary. Brush top of dough with 1/2 melted butter. Mix brown sugar and cinnamon in a small bowl. Sprinkle 3/4 sugar mixture over dough. Spread evenly to edges. Roll up dough jelly-roll style. (You should end up with a 12-inch long loaf.) Pinch edges to seal. Using a very sharp, serrated knife, slice loaf into 12 equal pieces. Arrange pieces close together in baking pan. Cover with a kitchen towel and let rise in a warm place until double in size, about 1 hour.

- Just before dough has finished rising, preheat oven to 350°. Brush buns with remaining melted butter and sprinkle with remaining cinnamon-sugar mixture. Bake for 25 to 30 minutes, or until puffed up and light golden brown.

- While buns are baking, prepare glaze. In a small bowl, beat together icing sugar, cream cheese, and milk on high speed of electric mixer until smooth. Remove buns from oven and drizzle with glaze. Serve warm. Cover leftovers with foil or plastic wrap and store at room temperature.

Makes 12 buns

Hint: These buns taste best when you heat them individually in the microwave for 15 to 20 seconds. The microwave softens the dough and makes them even more scrumptious!

Per bun: 167 calories, 2.9 g fat,
0.9 g saturated fat, 4.1 g protein,
31.7 g carbohydrate, 0.8 g fiber,
3.5 mg cholesterol, 229.6 mg sodium
% calories from fat: 16

What's in it for me?

BRING HOME THE BAKIN'

No Business Like Dough Business

Basic pizza dough for two 12-inch, thin-crust pizzas

Since everyone loves pizza, we thought the *yeast* we could do was create a simple crust that doesn't *knead* a lot of ingredients. The result: Our pizza dough is a *rising* star!

1 pkg active dry yeast
1 cup warm water (105° to 115°)
1 tbsp honey
2 cups all-purpose flour
1/2 cup whole wheat flour
1-1/2 tbsp olive oil
1 tsp salt
Olive oil cooking spray
2 tbsp cornmeal (optional)

- Pour yeast into a large bowl. Combine warm water and honey. Pour over yeast. Let sit for 5 to 10 minutes, until mixture is foamy. Meanwhile, combine all-purpose and whole wheat flours. Set aside.

- Add olive oil and salt to yeast mixture. Mix well. Add 1 cup flour mixture. Using a wooden spoon, stir until smooth. Add a second cup of flour mixture and continue to stir until dough forms a soft and sticky mass and comes away from the sides of the bowl.

- Flour the work surface and your hands with some of the remaining flour mixture. Turn dough out of bowl onto floured surface and knead in more flour until dough is smooth and elastic. Don't worry if you don't use up all of the flour. Shape dough into a ball. Spray a large bowl with olive oil spray and place dough inside. Cover with plastic wrap and let rise in a warm place for 45 to 60 minutes, until double in size (see Cooking 101).

- Spray two 12-inch pizza pans with olive oil spray and sprinkle lightly with cornmeal, if using. Punch down dough and return to work surface. Divide dough into 2 balls. Using a rolling pin, roll out each ball to a 12-inch circle. Place dough on pizza pan. Spray dough lightly with cooking spray. Add your favorite toppings and bake at 450° for 13 to 14 minutes.

Makes two 12-inch pizza crusts

What's in it for me?

Per crust: 695 calories, 13.1 g fat, 0.5 g saturated fat, 18.5 g protein, 127.4 g carbohydrate, 7 g fiber, 0 mg cholesterol, 1171.7 mg sodium
% calories from fat: 17

COOKING 101

Wherever you choose to let your dough rise, make sure it's free of drafts. They're enemies of yeast and cause the dough to rise slowly and unevenly. One of the best places for dough to rise is in your oven. Turn the oven to 200° for two minutes, then turn it off and place the covered bowl of dough inside.

Where did the term "baker's dozen" come from?

Who'da Thunk?

In ancient times, bakers were subject to severe penalties for short-weighting their customers. In Egypt, for example, bakers were sometimes nailed by the ear to their shop doors when caught selling light loaves. Bakers were *deafly* afraid therefore, when the English parliament passed a law in 1266 that strictly regulated bread weight. Since it was difficult at that time to make loaves a uniform weight, bakers began adding a thirteenth loaf to each shipment of 12 they sent to a shopkeeper or retailer. This freebie assured there would be no shortchanging, and more importantly, no ear-nailing.

You can't lose weight by talking about it. You have to keep your mouth shut.

The Old Farmer's Almanac

THE E FILES

If you want to burn fat and increase your overall fitness level, go to the dogs! The more you take your dog for a walk, the less fat you'll have to lose. That's because brisk walking burns between 200 and 300 calories an hour. Even slow walking uses 120 to 150 calories. What's more, sustained physical activity, such as walking for half an hour or more, burns proportionally more fat than carbohydrates. Release the hounds! If you don't have a hound, borrow one! Walk a friend's or neighbor's dog—you can be sure they, and their pooches, will be delighted. And you don't have to go for a long walk, either. Even three 10-minute walks spread out over a day can do wonders for your health. Now, no one likes to be hounded, and we really shouldn't bark orders, but we can't resist: Walk your dog and get a new *leash* on life!

TRIVIAL TIDBIT

If you boil an egg while singing all five verses and choruses of the hymn *Onward Christian Soldiers*, it'll be a perfectly soft-cooked egg when you come to amen.

Berried Treasure

Moist and luscious blueberry-bran muffins

Yo ho ho and a lot of yum! You'll gladly walk the plank for these mouthwatering muffins that hide blueberry nuggets inside a treasure chest of bran and peaches. They're as good as gold!

1-1/4 cups all-purpose flour
1-1/2 tsp baking soda
1 tsp cinnamon
1/2 tsp salt
1 can (15 oz) peaches in light syrup, undrained
2/3 cup packed brown sugar
1/2 cup fat-free egg substitute, or 2 whole eggs
3 tbsp vegetable oil
4 cups Bran Flakes cereal
1/2 cup blueberries (fresh or frozen)

I'll be hooked on these!

- Preheat oven to 375°. Spray a 12-cup muffin tin with non-stick spray and set aside.

- In a medium bowl, combine flour, baking soda, cinnamon, and salt. Set aside.

- Drain peaches and reserve 1/3 cup syrup. Pour peaches and reserved syrup into a blender and puree until smooth. In a large bowl, whisk together pureed peaches, brown sugar, egg substitute, and vegetable oil. Add Bran Flakes and mix well. Add flour mixture and stir just until dry ingredients are moistened. Do not overmix. Gently fold in blueberries.

- Divide batter among 12 muffin cups. Bake for 20 minutes, or until a toothpick inserted in center of muffin comes out clean. Serve warm.

Makes 12 muffins

Per muffin: 188 calories, 4 g fat, 0.6 g saturated fat, 3.7 g protein, 37.1 g carbohydrate, 2.9 g fiber, 0 mg cholesterol, 337 mg sodium
% calories from fat: 18

What's in it for me?

Why don't seagulls hang out at the bay?
'Cause then they'd be bagels.

Berry Maniloaf

This easy lemon loaf with raspberries makes a great afternoon snack

Our raspberry loaf will come along, just like a song, and brighten your day. You'll be singing its praises when you discover how simple it is to make.

1-3/4 cups all-purpose flour
1/2 cup sugar
2 tsp baking powder
1 tsp baking soda
1/2 tsp salt
1 cup low-fat, lemon-flavored yogurt
1/4 cup vegetable oil
1 egg
2 egg whites
1 tsp grated lemon zest
1 cup fresh or frozen raspberries (see Cooking 101)

- Preheat oven to 350°. Spray a 9 x 5-inch loaf pan with non-stick spray and set aside.

- In a large bowl, combine flour, sugar, baking powder, baking soda, and salt. Set aside.

- In a medium bowl, whisk together yogurt, oil, egg, egg whites, and lemon zest. Add wet ingredients to flour mixture and stir just until moistened. Gently fold in raspberries.

- Pour batter into prepared pan and bake for 50 minutes, or until a toothpick inserted in center of loaf comes out clean. Cool loaf in pan for 10 minutes. Remove from pan and let cool completely before slicing.

Makes 1 loaf, 12 slices

What's in it for me? →

Per slice: 161 calories, 5.3 g fat, 0.8 g saturated fat, 3.8 g protein, 25.1 g carbohydrate, 1.2 g fiber, 18.3 mg cholesterol, 285 mg sodium
% calories from fat: 29

Can't...smile... without...you... ♫

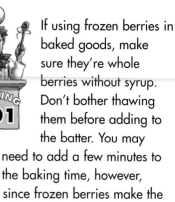

If using frozen berries in baked goods, make sure they're whole berries without syrup. Don't bother thawing them before adding to the batter. You may need to add a few minutes to the baking time, however, since frozen berries make the batter cold.

The Benefit of the Dough

We've got an APB on a fiber impostor! We repeat. A fiber impostor! Be on the lookout for enriched white bread pretending to be as nutritious as whole wheat bread. Don't be fooled. White bread is made from white flour that's had the bran and wheat germ removed in the milling process. No bran. No wheat germ. You know what that spells: No fiber! And we all know how good fiber's been to us regular folks who want to stay...well... regular. The suspect may be disguised as brown bread. Keep on your toes! Sometimes caramelized sugar is added to bring color to bread that's borderline nutritious. The only way to play it safe is to read the label first, ask questions later. Remember, words like "unbleached," "stone-ground," "enriched," or "wheat" may sound good, but if the first ingredient listed isn't "whole wheat," then the bread's mostly refined flour.

Who keeps track of the cookies you eat? The kitchen counter.

He's way over budget

COOKIES

SAY IT AIN'T SO!

If you're a frequent visitor to the pastry shop, better listen up. Most pastry shop items are loaded with fat—and more than you think! A cheese danish can contain more calories and two times as much fat as a fast-food hamburger. An old-fashioned cake donut has seven times the fat of one fruit-filled, low-fat cereal bar. And what about those big, beloved cinnamon buns? At 34 grams of fat each, YOU could end up with big buns if you don't practice moderation! Now, we're not saying you should boycott the pastry shop altogether, just make sure it has more soft rolls than you do.

YOU DO THE MATH

We'd like to propose a toast—preferably without butter! By spreading two teaspoons of fruit jam on your breakfast toast twice a week instead of the same amount of butter, you'll save 3,536 calories and 790 grams of fat in a year. That's almost 12 days' worth of fat! So, if you want to *preserve* your figure, don't let fat-filled butter dwell on your derrière from *smear* to eternity.

I'm tired of all this nonsense about beauty being only skin deep. That's deep enough. What do you want—an adorable pancreas?

Jean Kerr
The Snake Has All the Lines

The Grateful Bread

Super-moist and cake-like, this sweet apple and oat bread can be served for dessert

Grated apples, grated carrots, grated coconut—grate Scott! This bread has grate flavor!

1-1/2 cups all-purpose flour
1 cup quick-cooking rolled oats (not instant)
1 cup sugar
2 tsp each baking powder and cinnamon
1/2 tsp salt
1/4 tsp ground nutmeg
1/3 cup each shredded, sweetened coconut and chopped walnuts
1/2 cup evaporated 2% milk
1/2 cup fat-free egg substitute, or 2 whole eggs
1/3 cup unsweetened applesauce
2 tbsp canola oil
2 tsp vanilla
2 cups peeled, grated apples
1/2 cup grated carrots

You'll thank me for this!

- Preheat oven to 350°. Spray a 9 x 5-inch loaf pan with non-stick spray and set aside.

- In a large bowl, combine flour, oats, sugar, baking powder, cinnamon, salt, and nutmeg. Add coconut and walnuts. Mix well.

- In a medium bowl, whisk together evaporated milk, egg substitute, applesauce, oil, and vanilla. Stir in apples and carrots.

- Add wet ingredients to dry ingredients. Mix just until dry ingredients are moistened. Pour batter into pan. Spread evenly. Bake for 55 to 60 minutes, or until a toothpick inserted in center of loaf comes out clean. Cool for 10 minutes in pan. Remove bread from pan and let cool completely on a wire rack. Cover with plastic wrap and store in the refrigerator.

Makes 1 large loaf, 12 slices

Per slice: 240 calories, 6.2 g fat, 1.4 g saturated fat, 5.3 g protein, 42.5 g carbohydrate, 2.3 g fiber, 0.8 mg cholesterol, 212.6 mg sodium % calories from fat: 23

What's in it for us?

Stop and Smell the Rosemary Focaccia

Italian focaccia (foh-KAH-chee-ah)
with rosemary and Parmesan cheese

Everyone's nose knows the smell of freshly baked bread. But toss in some rosemary and Parmesan cheese, and you've found the stairway to *leaven*! Our flatbread is the best of the *scentury*!

2 tbsp dried rosemary
1 tbsp honey
1 pkg active dry yeast
1 tsp salt
1 tbsp + 2 tsp olive oil
6 oz potatoes, peeled, boiled, and mashed
    (1 cup total mashed)
2-1/2 cups all-purpose flour, plus extra
    for dusting work surface
3 tbsp grated Parmesan cheese
1/2 cup minced red onions

- Pour 1 cup boiling water over 1 tablespoon rosemary in a small bowl. Let cool to lukewarm, about 20 minutes. Strain water, discarding rosemary. Stir honey into water. Pour over yeast in a large bowl. Let stand for 5 to 10 minutes, until foamy.

- Stir salt and 1 tablespoon olive oil into yeast mixture. Add mashed potatoes and enough flour to make a kneadable dough. Generously flour your hands and work surface. Turn dough out of bowl and knead until smooth and elastic, about 5 minutes.

- Spray a large bowl with non-stick spray and place dough inside. Cover tightly with plastic wrap and let rise in a warm place until double in bulk, about 45 to 60 minutes. Punch down dough and return to floured work surface. Knead for 1 more minute, adding more flour if dough is very sticky.

- Place dough on a 17 x 11-inch baking sheet that has been sprayed with non-stick spray. Pat dough to edges of pan. Brush remaining 2 teaspoons olive oil over surface of dough using a pastry brush. Sprinkle with Parmesan cheese, followed by onions and remaining 1 tablespoon rosemary. Cover loosely with plastic wrap and let rise for 30 minutes.

- Meanwhile, preheat oven to 400°. Bake focaccia for 16 to 18 minutes, until puffed up and golden. Remove from pan and let cool slightly on a wire rack. Cut into 12 pieces and serve warm.

Makes 12 servings

What's in it for me?

Per serving: 141 calories, 2.8 g fat,
0.4 g saturated fat, 3.9 g protein,
25.2 g carbohydrate, 1.3 g fiber,
1.3 mg cholesterol, 225.8 mg sodium
% calories from fat: 18

Who'da Thunk?

Look! Up in the sky! It's a bird! It's a plane! No, it's a...leavening agent?
They say that if you're ever snowbound at home and in need of eggs for leavening in pancakes or other baked goods, there's no need to make the dangerous trek to the market. Rumor has it that freshly fallen snow can be used in place of eggs, and that even older snow from below the surface will work. Apparently, snow's ammonia content makes it a good substitute leavening agent in a pinch. Snow way, José!

What the heck is wheat bran and where can I buy it?

Wheat bran is the rough outer covering of a wheat kernel, and using it is an inexpensive way to add flavor and fiber to baked goods. Look for it in boxes or bags in the cereal aisle or in the bulk foods section of your grocery store.

THE E FILES

If you can walk, you can exercise. And what better way to begin burning fat, losing weight, and increasing your cardio-endurance than by strolling through the park? Walking is inexpensive, it's easy on the joints, it's enjoyable, and it's something you can do for the rest of your life. In fact, walking is probably the greatest form of exercise there is. Why not put on some headphones and listen to music, a book-on-tape, or the ball game? If you grab a friend, you can chat *and* burn fat. Stride, strut, stroll, or saunter— no matter how you move your body, you'll benefit. Remember, if you wanna burn some flab, you gotta walk around the block tonight, you gotta walk, walk, walk 'til broad daylight.

Pumpkin and Spice and Everything Nice

Pumpkin spice muffins

If you feed these tasty pumpkin muffins to your family, they sure won't be plump kin! That's because we've carved out the fatty ingredients and left in the yummy ones. No tricks. Just treats!

1-1/2 cups all-purpose flour
1/2 cup wheat bran
  (see tip in margin)
2 tsp each baking powder
  and pumpkin pie spice
1 tsp baking soda
1/2 tsp salt
1 cup canned
  pumpkin
1/2 cup grated carrots
1/2 cup each buttermilk and honey
1/4 cup butter or margarine, melted
1 egg
1 tsp each vanilla and grated orange zest
1/2 cup chopped walnuts (optional)

- Preheat oven to 375°. Spray a 12-cup muffin tin with non-stick spray and set aside.

- In a large bowl, combine flour, wheat bran, baking powder, pumpkin pie spice, baking soda, and salt. Set aside.

- In a medium bowl, whisk together pumpkin, carrots, buttermilk, honey, butter, egg, vanilla, and orange zest. Add wet ingredients to flour mixture and stir just until moistened. Batter will be thick. Gently fold in walnuts, if using.

- Divide batter among 12 muffin cups. Bake for 20 minutes, or until a toothpick inserted in center of muffin comes out clean. Remove muffins from pan and let cool on a wire rack.

Makes 12 large muffins

Per muffin: 144 calories, 4.7 g fat, 2.6 g saturated fat, 3.2 g protein, 23.9 g carbohydrate, 2.6 g fiber, 28.6 mg cholesterol, 277 mg sodium
% calories from fat: 28

What's in it for me?

Pie R²

What do you get when you divide the area of a pumpkin by its radius² ? Pumpkin pi.

The Rolling Scones

These delectable, cranberry-orange scones are perfect for tea time

Taste buds can't get no satisfaction? This old-time favorite treat will get them rockin'.

2 cups all-purpose flour
1/3 cup packed brown sugar
2 tsp baking powder
3/4 tsp baking soda
1/2 tsp salt
1 cup + 2 tbsp buttermilk
1/3 cup sweetened, dried cranberries (see Cooking 101)
2 tbsp butter, melted
2 tsp grated orange zest
1/2 tsp vanilla
1 egg

- Preheat oven to 400°. Spray a large baking sheet with non-stick spray and set aside.

- In a large bowl, combine flour, brown sugar, baking powder, baking soda, and salt. Set aside.

- In a medium bowl, whisk together buttermilk, cranberries, butter, orange zest, and vanilla. Add wet ingredients to dry ingredients. Stir until a soft dough is formed. Turn dough out onto a lightly floured surface. Divide into 2 pieces. Shape each piece into a ball. Roll out or pat dough to 3/4-inch-thick circles, about 6 inches in diameter. Transfer dough to baking sheet. Using a sharp knife, cut each circle into 6 wedges, but do not separate them.

- To make glaze, lightly beat egg and 1 tablespoon water in a small bowl. Brush glaze lightly over top of dough (you will use less than half of it). Bake for 15 to 17 minutes, until scones are puffed up and golden. Serve warm.

Makes 12 scones

What's in it for me? → Per scone: 130 calories, 2.5 g fat, 1.4 g saturated fat, 3.2 g protein, 23.6 g carbohydrate, 0.7 g fiber, 14.9 mg cholesterol, 267.5 mg sodium
% calories from fat: 17

COOKING 101

Cranberries are a relative newcomer to the dried fruit scene, but most supermarkets do carry them. They're usually sold sweetened to compensate for their natural tartness. You'll find them in the baking aisle beside the raisins.

TRIVIAL TIDBIT

Cranberries are almost 90% water, and the remaining 10% is carbohydrates and fiber. Because they're a good source of vitamin C, early New England sailing ships used to carry barrels of cranberries to supplement the sailors' nutrient-deficient diets of salt pork and crackers. Long before modern science confirmed the cranberry's role in preventing scurvy and treating urinary infections, Indian women believed the berries possessed special healing powers. They would often brew hot cranberry poultices to help draw out the poison from arrow wounds.

My wife cooks for fun. For food we go to a restaurant.

Chestnuts are the Bestnuts

People have been roasting chestnuts over fires for years, and it's not because they've had a few too many rum-laced eggnogs, either! Chestnuts are bite-sized nuggets of nutrition. Five chestnuts have as much fiber as a slice of whole wheat bread and contain a puny one gram of fat. An entire bowlful would barely put a dent in your daily fat budget. Compare that to other members of the nut family: peanuts get 76% of their calories from fat, almonds get 80%, and macadamias get 95%. That's nutty! Better stay away from those macarenas! Wait a second...that's macadamias. (The Macarena is a dance, and last time we checked, it was 100% fat-free.) One thing's for sure, if you're trying to stay slim, there are lots of reasons to sing and dance about chestnuts.

What is canola oil?

The canola plant is a genetic variation of rapeseed, an oilseed crop that's part of the mustard family and that's grown primarily in Western Canada. Although rapeseed has been grown for years for industrial oils, Canadian scientists were able to breed new varieties of rapeseed that were suitable for cooking. They named their creation in honor of their country. Canola stands for CANadian Oil, Low Acid. Interesting, eh?

Who'da Thunk?

The only thing that ever sat its way to success was a hen.

Sarah Brown

"Date a Nut" Bread

Perfect for Sunday brunch

Our delectable date bread is nutty, but nice. It's just the kind of sweet thing you could take home to mother.

- 1-1/2 cups all-purpose flour
- 1/2 cup each chopped, pitted dates and chopped pecans
- 1 cup graham cracker crumbs
- 2 tsp baking powder
- 1 tsp each baking soda and cinnamon
- 1/2 tsp salt
- 1/4 tsp nutmeg
- 1 cup packed brown sugar
- 1/2 cup fat-free egg substitute, or 2 whole eggs
- 1/2 cup buttermilk
- 1/3 cup unsweetened applesauce
- 1/4 cup canola oil
- 1 tsp each vanilla and grated orange zest

- Preheat oven to 350°. Spray a 9 x 5-inch loaf pan with non-stick spray and set aside.

- In a small bowl, combine 2 tablespoons of the flour with dates and nuts. Set aside.

- In a large bowl, combine remaining flour, graham crumbs, baking powder, baking soda, cinnamon, salt, and nutmeg.

- In a medium bowl, whisk together brown sugar, egg substitute, buttermilk, applesauce, oil, vanilla, and orange zest. Add wet ingredients to flour mixture and stir just until dry ingredients are moistened. Fold in dates and nuts. Spoon batter into prepared pan. Spread evenly. Bake for 45 to 50 minutes, or until a toothpick inserted in center of loaf comes out clean. Let cool in pan for 10 minutes. Remove loaf and cool completely on a wire rack.

- To serve, slice loaf into 10 large pieces, then cut each slice in half. For a special treat, serve with light cream cheese and apricot preserves.

Makes 1 large loaf, 20 pieces

Per piece: 161 calories, 5.4 g fat, 0.6 g saturated fat, 2.4 g protein, 26.7 g carbohydrate, 1.3 g fiber, 0.2 mg cholesterol, 205.4 mg sodium % calories from fat: 29

What's in it for me?

BRING HOME THE BAKIN'

Eats Without Meats

Vegetarian fare with flavor and flair

Jack and the Bean Stack

Monterey Jack cheese and black-bean salsa
layered between stacked tortillas

It's not just a hill of beans, you know. This multilevel Tex-Mex entree
is the bean-all and the end-all!

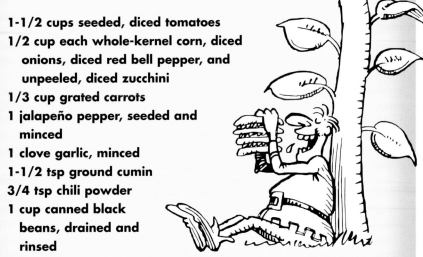

1-1/2 cups seeded, diced tomatoes

**1/2 cup each whole-kernel corn, diced
  onions, diced red bell pepper, and
  unpeeled, diced zucchini**

1/3 cup grated carrots

**1 jalapeño pepper, seeded and
  minced**

1 clove garlic, minced

1-1/2 tsp ground cumin

3/4 tsp chili powder

**1 cup canned black
  beans, drained and
  rinsed**

1/4 cup chopped, fresh cilantro

1 tbsp lime juice

4 7-inch flour tortillas

1 cup shredded, reduced-fat Monterey Jack cheese (4 oz)

1/4 cup chopped green onions

1/3 cup low-fat sour cream

1/2 cup chopped lettuce

- Preheat oven to 400°. Spray a medium, non-stick saucepan with
  non-stick spray. Add 1 cup tomatoes, plus next 9 ingredients.
  Cook and stir for 5 minutes, until vegetables are softened. Add
  beans and cook for 2 more minutes. Remove from heat and stir
  in cilantro and lime juice.

- Spray a baking sheet with non-stick spray. Place one tortilla in
  middle of tray. Spoon 1/3 bean mixture over tortilla, followed by
  1/4 cheese. Repeat layering 2 more times. Place final tortilla on
  top, and sprinkle with last bit of cheese and green onions.

- Bake for 15 to 20 minutes, or until cheese is melted and tortillas
  turn golden brown around edges. Remove from oven and slice
  into 4 wedges. Top with sour cream, remaining tomatoes, and
  lettuce. Serve immediately.

Makes 4 servings

What's
in it
for me?

Per serving: 271 calories, 8.7 g fat,
3.2 g saturated fat, 18.2 g protein,
38.1 g carbohydrate, 6.5 g fiber,
21.3 mg cholesterol, 460.5 mg sodium
% calories from fat: 26

EATS WITHOUT MEATS

66

Who'da Thunk?

Why are the rolls served on airplanes often as hard as bricks?

Actors and airline
passengers have the
same complaint: Good
rolls are hard to come
by. As for the hard rolls served on flights,
don't blame the catering company. At
least half the cabin's air pressure comes in
through the plane's superheated engines,
which suck all the moisture out of the air
before it's cooled for use in the cabin. The
overdry air zaps the moisture out of the
buns to the point that they could double
as hockey pucks. The simple solution
would be to stop serving rolls, but that
would leave an empty spot on all those
molded plastic trays.

THE E FILES

Most people know that eating a healthy,
varied diet can cut their risk of heart
disease, cancer, diabetes, stroke, and
osteoporosis. But while few of us could go
even one day without eating, it's easy to
go days, weeks, or even years without
exercising. Yet physical activity can help
prevent the same slew of illnesses. After
many years and hundreds of scientific
studies, the evidence is clear and
irrefutable: Exercise is the best preventive
medicine for the mind and body. Simply
put, it's the equivalent of a miracle drug
that's good for just about everything and
everybody. Live an active lifestyle and
you'll probably live longer and stronger.
Exercise adds years to your life and life to
your years. What are you waiting for?
Take a hike!

*Losing weight is a triumph
of mind over platter.*

What the heck are rice noodles and where can I buy them?

Rice noodles, also called rice sticks, are a staple of Thai cooking. Made from rice flour, water, and salt, they're categorized as either round or flat, and they're available fresh or dried. Look for dried, flat, fettuccine-like rice noodles that are about one-quarter-inch thick for this recipe. You'll find them in the Oriental-food aisle of your grocery store, or in Asian markets. They require very little cooking, so don't wander away from the stove while they're boiling.

TRIVIAL TIDBIT

At one time, baking soda was added to the cooking water of vegetables to preserve their color. This practice stopped, however, when it was discovered that baking soda destroys the vitamin C content of vegetables.

Pod's Pad Thai

Popular, spicy Thai noodle dish

If you like oodles of noodles, then *Thai* one on with this delectable, low-fat version of pad Thai.

8 oz rice noodles, uncooked (see tip in margin)
1/4 cup ketchup
2 tbsp each reduced-sodium soy sauce, lime juice, and brown sugar
1 tbsp seasoned rice vinegar
1 tsp sesame oil
1/2 tsp crushed red pepper flakes
1 tsp vegetable oil
1/2 cup diced red onions
2 cloves garlic, minced
1 cup bean sprouts
1/2 cup grated carrots
1/4 cup each chopped green onions and chopped, fresh cilantro
1/4 cup chopped peanuts

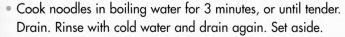

Come on— give it a thai!

- Cook noodles in boiling water for 3 minutes, or until tender. Drain. Rinse with cold water and drain again. Set aside.

- To make sauce, combine ketchup, soy sauce, lime juice, brown sugar, vinegar, oil, and crushed red pepper flakes in a small bowl. Set aside.

- Heat oil in a large, non-stick wok or skillet over medium heat. Add onions and garlic. Cook and stir until onions are tender, about 3 minutes. Add sauce and bring to a boil. Add cooked noodles, bean sprouts, carrots, green onions, and cilantro. Mix well. Cook until noodles are heated through, about 2 minutes. Sprinkle individual servings with chopped peanuts.

Makes 4 servings

Per serving: 320 calories, 6.3 g fat, 0.9 g saturated fat, 4.9 g protein, 60.9 g carbohydrate, 2.7 g fiber, 0 mg cholesterol, 420.3 mg sodium
% calories from fat: 18

What's in it for me?

Did you hear what happened to the peanut when he walked through the park? He was a salted.

Garden of Eatin'

Warm vegetable salad with rosemary and feta

If you don't know a good salad from Adam, then take our word for it: This mouthwatering vegetable medley is so tasty, it's sure to lead you into temptation. No need to worry, though—it's sin-free.

6 medium red potatoes, unpeeled, cut into 1-inch cubes
3 cups whole medium mushrooms
2 medium carrots, peeled and coarsely chopped
2 medium zucchini, cut into bite-sized chunks
1 medium red onion, cut into rings
1 large red bell pepper, cut into bite-sized chunks
1 large yellow bell pepper, cut into bite-sized chunks
2 cloves garlic, minced
1 tbsp olive oil
1 tbsp fresh or dried rosemary
1 tbsp chopped, fresh oregano, or 1 tsp dried
1 tbsp balsamic vinegar
1/4 tsp each salt and black pepper
1/2 cup crumbled light feta cheese (2 oz)

It's s-s-s-sinfully delicious!

- Spray a large roasting pan with non-stick spray. Add vegetables, garlic, oil, and herbs. Mix well. Roast, uncovered, at 425° for 30 minutes. Stir once or twice during cooking time. Turn on the broiler and broil vegetables for about 5 minutes, until edges start to brown.

- Remove vegetables from oven and transfer to a serving bowl. Toss with vinegar, salt, and pepper. Sprinkle crumbled feta over top. Serve warm.

Makes 4 meal-size servings

What's in it for me? ⇨ Per serving: 292 calories, 6.7 g fat, 1.7 g saturated fat, 10.7 g protein, 51.5 g carbohydrate, 8.5 g fiber, 10 mg cholesterol, 502.9 mg sodium
% calories from fat: 20

Strength-training causes weight gain.

FAT OR **FICTION?**

Muscle weighs more than fat, so if you lose fat while adding muscle, your weight may climb. But that's no reason to get your knickers in a knot. You'll probably look thinner, since muscles are firmer, take up less space, and are more pleasing to the eye than fat. And even though your weight may go up, your waist measurement may go down, so your knickers may actually fit better! Remember, having less muscle than fat is one reason why people on restricted diets who don't exercise reach a plateau—they stop losing weight even though they're eating very little. You can starve all you want, but to lose weight, you gotta move weight! To win the battle of the bulge, you need to be a calorie-burning machine 24 hours a day, and having adequate muscle mass is the *weigh* to go.

I'd highly recommend the 89 octane unleaded. It's an unpretentious little fuel with a surprising kick. Care to sniff the nozzle?

All aboard the Orient Express! You're in for a non-stop, high-speed, fat-filled journey down the digestive track! Final destination: Arteryville. Oriental instant noodles, like Japanese ramen, are pre-cooked, then dried and packaged with seasonings. All you have to do is add water. Couldn't be more convenient— and couldn't be less nutritious. Harmless as it may seem, this noodle concoction is usually deep-fried in saturated fat such as lard or palm oil, and it's high in salt to boot. Just one cup packs in 15 grams of fat and 400 calories, and you can bet that'll be stowed away in your caboose! If you want to stay on the right track toward Healthy City, then moderation is the ticket.

YOU DO THE MATH

Traditional salad dressings are loaded with fat, so on your next trip to the salad bar, avoid the *oil-you-can-eat* buffet. Try substituting two tablespoons of low-fat Italian dressing for the same amount of the high-fat kind just once a week. You'll save 3,120 calories and 416 grams of fat in a year—more than six days' worth of fat! With so many low-fat options now available, dressing your salads doesn't have to be *oil-or-nothing*.

If a parsley farmer is sued, can they garnish his wages?

Quiche Me, You Fool!

Crustless, roasted pepper and potato quiche

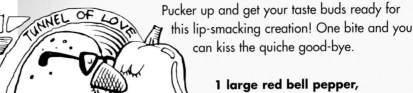

Pucker up and get your taste buds ready for this lip-smacking creation! One bite and you can kiss the quiche good-bye.

1 large red bell pepper, seeded and halved
1 large yellow or orange bell pepper, seeded and halved
1 small red onion, thinly sliced into rings
1 tsp olive oil
1 clove garlic, minced
2 tbsp chopped, fresh basil leaves
3 medium potatoes
1 cup shredded, reduced-fat sharp cheddar cheese (4 oz)
1 cup fat-free egg substitute
1/2 cup evaporated 2% milk
1/2 tsp each dried thyme and salt
1/4 tsp black pepper

- Spray 1 medium and 1 small baking pan with non-stick spray. Place peppers, cut side down, in medium pan. Combine onions, olive oil, and garlic in small pan. Place both pans under broiler. Broil onions for 5 minutes and peppers until they begin to blister and char.

- Reduce oven temperature to 375°. Transfer onion mixture to a medium bowl and set aside. Let peppers sit until cool enough to handle. Using a paring knife, peel off and discard skins. Slice into strips. Add peppers to bowl with onions, along with basil. Mix well.

- Peel potatoes and slice into 1/4-inch-thick rounds. Steam potatoes for 10 to 12 minutes, until tender.

- To assemble quiche, spray an 8-inch round quiche pan or cake pan with non-stick spray. Layer 1/2 potatoes over bottom. Top with 1/2 pepper mixture, followed by 1/2 cheese. Repeat layering.

- In a medium bowl, whisk together egg substitute, milk, thyme, salt, and pepper. Pour over vegetables. Bake, uncovered, for 35 to 40 minutes, until quiche is firm to touch and cheese is golden brown. Let stand for 10 minutes before slicing.

Makes 6 servings

Per serving: 194 calories, 4.8 g fat, 2.4 g saturated fat, 13 g protein, 26.3 g carbohydrate, 2.6 g fiber, 15 mg cholesterol, 424.2 mg sodium
% calories from fat: 22

What's in it for me?

EATS WITHOUT MEATS

69

It's a Little Pizza Heaven

Colorful vegetable pizza with pesto and feta

You'll experience supreme happiness when you bite into our flavorful veggie pizza. It's like heaven on earth!

2 cups sliced, mixed mushrooms (see p. 106)
1 cup broccoli florets, cut small
3/4 cup thinly sliced zucchini
1/2 cup each thinly sliced red and yellow bell peppers
1 small red onion, thinly sliced into rings
1 tbsp pesto sauce (see tip in margin)
1/3 cup pizza sauce
1 12-inch unbaked pizza crust (see p. 56)
2 tbsp grated Romano or Parmesan cheese
1/2 cup crumbled light feta cheese (2 oz)
1/2 cup shredded, part-skim mozzarella cheese (2 oz)

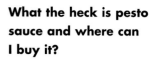

- Spray a large, non-stick skillet or wok with non-stick spray. Add mushrooms, broccoli, zucchini, red and yellow peppers, and onions. Cook and stir over medium heat until vegetables are tender, about 6 minutes. Remove from heat and stir in pesto sauce. Mix well.

- Spread pizza sauce evenly over unbaked pizza crust. Sprinkle with Romano cheese. Top with vegetable mixture. Sprinkle feta and mozzarella cheese over top.

- Bake at 450° for 13 to 14 minutes, until crust is lightly browned and cheese is completely melted. Serve immediately.

Makes 1 12-inch pizza, 6 large slices

Hint: If using a store-bought, pre-cooked pizza shell, reduce baking time by 4 minutes. Sliced olives and/or sun-dried tomatoes make a nice addition to this pizza.

What's in it for me?

Per slice: 214 calories, 7.1 g fat,
2.7 g saturated fat, 10.5 g protein,
27.8 g carbohydrate, 2.4 g fiber,
14.1 mg cholesterol, 517 mg sodium
% calories from fat: 29

What the heck is pesto sauce and where can I buy it?

Pesto sauce is a dark green, fresh-tasting, uncooked sauce that originated in Genoa, Italy. It's a combination of fresh basil, garlic, pine nuts, Parmesan cheese, and olive oil. The ingredients are usually pureed in a food processor until they reach the consistency of a thick paste. Pesto sauce is most commonly tossed with pasta, but it also makes a tasty pizza sauce. It's sold both refrigerated and unrefrigerated in small tubs or jars.

The Carbs are on the Table

Do you crave pasta, bread, and pizza? Cravings once thought to be "all in your mind" are actually triggered by changes in brain chemistry. (So, they're "all in your mind," after all!) Today we know that these cravings are linked to the brain's release of serotonin, a natural chemical that induces a sense of calm and well-being. High-carbohydrate foods such as bread and pasta stimulate the production of serotonin, leaving you pleasantly drowsy and relaxed. That's why they're called comfort foods. And that's why you might find yourself yearning for an after-lunch siesta if you overdo it on the carbs at noon hour. But you can slough off that midday slump if you balance lunchtime carbohydrates with low-fat, high-protein foods such as lean fish, chicken, beans, or lentils. Unless you're employed as a mattress merchant, you might want to save the pasta for supper, when the sleepy aftereffect is more welcome.

I like long walks, especially when they're taken by people who annoy me.

Fred Allen

Bye-Bye Burgie

Broiled portobello "burgers" with sweet peppers, red onions, and a spicy, chickpea spread

You'll put on a happy face when you bite into these succulent mushroom burgers—and say "farewell" to the thought of any leftovers!

Chickpea Spread

1 cup canned chickpeas, drained and rinsed
2 tbsp low-fat sour cream
2 tbsp minced onions
1 tbsp chopped, fresh cilantro
2 cloves garlic, minced
2 tsp lemon or lime juice
1 tsp brown sugar
3/4 tsp ground coriander
1/2 tsp ground cumin

1 tbsp each olive oil and balsamic or red wine vinegar
1/2 tsp dried basil
4 medium portobello mushrooms, wiped clean
1 large red bell pepper, seeded and cut into wide strips
1 medium red onion, sliced into thick rings (do not separate)
4 multi-grain buns
1 cup whole baby spinach leaves

- To make chickpea spread, combine all ingredients in a blender or food processor and whirl until smooth. Refrigerate until ready to use.

- In a small bowl, combine olive oil, vinegar, and basil. Brush oil mixture over both sides of mushrooms, pepper strips, and onion rings. Arrange vegetables in a baking pan and place under the broiler, about 5 inches from heat source. Broil for 3 minutes. Remove pan from oven, turn vegetables over, baste with any remaining oil mixture, and return to oven. Broil for 3 to 4 more minutes, until vegetables are tender.

- To serve, line bottom of bun with spinach leaves. Place one whole mushroom over top. Spread chickpea mixture over mushroom. Top with peppers, onions, and top half of bun. Serve immediately.

Makes 4 servings

Per serving: 267 calories, 6.8 g fat, 0.1 g saturated fat, 10.4 g protein, 44.9 g carbohydrate, 3.9 g fiber, 0.5 mg cholesterol, 422.9 mg sodium % calories from fat: 22

What's in it for us?

Who'da Thunk?

If you're "ridin' the gravy train," couldn't things get a little messy?

What is a gravy train, anyway? Is someone actually hauling gravy by rail? Are crowds gathering around huge mounds of mashed potatoes waiting for the 5:15 gravy to show up? Sauciness aside, "to ride the gravy train" was an expression coined by railroad workers in the 1920s. They used the phrase to describe a run on which there was good pay and little labor. The words were quickly adopted into general speech to describe any easy job that paid well, or more commonly, living prosperously with little work.

TRIVIAL TIDBIT

During times of battle, British navy ships used to carry a supply of limes to help prevent scurvy. That's why the British were tagged with the nickname "Limeys."

What's the best way to introduce a hamburger? Meat Patty.

Eggplant Parmesan

Layered eggplant casserole with
mozzarella and Parmesan cheeses

Dear reader: Alas, we arrive at the unnameable recipe. Not even the queens of corn (that's us) could come up with a clever title for this one. Any ideas? Please call us at 1-800-470-0738. Signed, Brain-drained in Cookbookland.

1 cup unseasoned, dry bread crumbs
1/3 cup grated Parmesan cheese
2 tsp dried basil
4 egg whites
1/2 tsp salt
2 medium eggplants (about 2 pounds),
   unpeeled, each cut crosswise into
   8 slices
Olive oil cooking spray
3 cups low-fat, tomato-based pasta
   sauce
1 cup shredded, part-skim mozzarella
   cheese (4 oz)
2 tbsp chopped, fresh parsley

- In a shallow bowl, combine bread crumbs, Parmesan cheese, and basil. Mix well.

- In another shallow bowl, lightly beat together egg whites and salt. Working one at a time, dip eggplant slices into egg whites, then into crumb mixture. Turn to coat both sides with crumbs. Place slices on 1 large or 2 small baking sheets that have been sprayed with non-stick spray.

- Spray tops of slices lightly with olive oil cooking spray. Bake at 400° for 15 minutes. Remove eggplant slices from oven, turn them over, and spray again with cooking spray. Return to oven and bake for 15 more minutes.

- To assemble casserole, spoon 1 cup pasta sauce over bottom of a 9 x 13-inch baking dish. Top with 1/2 eggplant slices. Spoon another 1 cup sauce over eggplant, followed by 1/2 mozzarella. Repeat layering with remaining eggplant slices, sauce, and mozzarella. Sprinkle parsley over top.

- Return to oven and bake, uncovered, for 20 minutes, until cheese is completely melted and sauce is bubbly. Serve immediately.

Makes 8 servings

What's in it for me?

Per serving: 194 calories, 4.4 g fat,
2.3 g saturated fat, 12.6 g protein,
27.1 g carbohydrate, 4.8 g fiber,
10.1 mg cholesterol, 751.4 mg sodium
% calories from fat: 20

FAT OR FICTION?

If your relatives are plump, you might as well give up on efforts to control your weight.

Studies show that the weights of adults who were adopted as children closely resemble the weights of their biological parents, not their adoptive parents. But that's no reason to summon the Gene Genie and wish for a more favorable bloodline. Although heredity strongly influences body size and shape, you don't inherit fatness. Having overweight relatives makes you more susceptible—but not destined—to obesity. He ain't heavy just 'cause he's your brother! To gain weight, you still have to consume more calories than you burn. Heredity can also influence the health risks associated with obesity, such as heart disease, high blood pressure, and diabetes. So, by all means, don't give up on your efforts to lose weight, especially if your *genes* are feeling a little snug.

YOU DO THE MATH

Let's be candid about canned tuna. One measly tin of tuna packed in oil holds a whopping 14 grams of fat. But if you swap a can of oil-packed tuna for the water-packed kind once a week, you'll save 6,396 calories and 686 grams of fat in a year—more than 10 days' worth of fat! When you eat tuna that's swimming in oil, you'll be sorry, Charlie.

After lunch, rest awhile.
After supper, walk a mile.

Arabian proverb

What the heck are dried currants and where can I buy them?

There are two different types of fruits that we call currants. The first is a tiny berry related to the gooseberry. It's mainly used to make syrups, sauces, liqueurs, and preserves. The second is a dried Zante grape that looks like a tiny raisin. This is the type you want for this recipe. You'll find dried currants in plastic bags right beside the raisins at your supermarket.

THE E FILES

Just sittin' around? Then be afraid. Be very afraid. Inactivity is an eerie and unnatural state for human beings. In fact, the body is biologically designed for movement, and when you're not moving, your body gets spooked into *scaredy-fat* mode. Whenever you're inactive for more than an hour, it's likely that your body is sending a signal to your brain to put the brakes on fat-burning and accelerate fat-storing. Without activity, we gain weight, our muscles atrophy, our cardiovascular systems suffer, and to make matters worse, we feel depressed and anxious. The longer we sit still, the more we feel ill. Exactly how much time do you spend just sitting 'round? (Did someone say "round"?)

I guess my eyes were bigger than my stomach

Itsy-Bitsy Teeny-Weeny Colored Polka-Dot Rotini

Tricolored rotini with currants and green peas cooked in a spicy coconut broth

Heavens to bitsy! This rotini isn't weeny in the flavor department. You'll *be-keeny* to make it again and again.

1-1/2 cups vegetable broth
1 cup light coconut milk
1 tsp each sugar and ground coriander
1/2 tsp each ground cumin and chili powder
1/4 tsp each curry powder and ground ginger
8 oz tricolored rotini, uncooked (about 3 cups dry)
1 cup frozen green peas, thawed
1/2 cup finely chopped red bell pepper
1/4 cup dried currants (see tip in margin)

- In a medium, non-stick saucepan, combine vegetable broth, coconut milk, sugar, coriander, cumin, chili powder, curry powder, and ginger. Bring to a boil. Add rotini. Reduce heat to medium-low. Cover and simmer for 6 minutes, stirring occasionally.

- Add peas, red pepper, and currants. Simmer for 6 to 7 more minutes, until liquid has been absorbed and pasta is tender. Remove from heat and let stand for 5 minutes before serving.

Makes 4 servings

Note: You can substitute 1 cup cooked lentils for the green peas.

Per serving: 326 calories, 4.4 g fat, 2 g saturated fat, 11.1 g protein, 60.1 g carbohydrate, 5 g fiber, 0 mg cholesterol, 311.1 mg sodium % calories from fat: 12

 What's in it for me?

TRIVIAL TIDBIT

It takes 20 times more land to feed a person on a meat-based diet than it does to feed someone who is fully vegetarian.

Rockin' Moroccan Stew

Moroccan vegetable stew with
sweet potatoes, chickpeas, and ginger

This unique recipe came right
out of Africa! Say "yes, please"
to chickpeas and you can eat
to the beat!

2 tsp olive oil
1 cup chopped
   onions
1/2 cup each diced
   celery and
   chopped green
   bell pepper
1 clove garlic, minced
3 cups vegetable broth
3 cups peeled, cubed sweet potatoes
1 can (14-1/2 oz) tomatoes, drained and cut up
1 can (15 oz) chickpeas, drained and rinsed
1 tbsp lemon juice
2 tsp grated gingerroot
1 tsp each ground cumin, curry powder,
   ground coriander, and chili powder
1/2 tsp salt
1/4 tsp black pepper
1/4 cup raisins
2 tbsp each light peanut butter and chopped, fresh cilantro

- Heat olive oil in a large, non-stick saucepan over medium-high
  heat. Add onions, celery, green pepper, and garlic. Cook and stir
  until vegetables begin to soften, about 3 minutes.

- Add all remaining ingredients, except raisins, peanut butter, and
  cilantro. Bring to a boil. Reduce heat to low and simmer, covered,
  for 20 minutes.

- Stir in raisins, peanut butter, and cilantro. Mix well. Simmer for
  5 more minutes. Serve hot.

Makes 6 servings

Per serving: 232 calories, 5 g fat,
0.5 g saturated fat, 7.9 g protein,
41.4 g carbohydrate, 4.1 g fiber,
0 mg cholesterol, 708.5 mg sodium
% calories from fat: 18

EATS WITHOUT MEATS

Body-Fat Chat

Goodness gracious! Great balls of fat!
If a pound of body fat represents
3,500 calories, how big would that be
if you shaped it into a ball? The answer:
About the size of a softball. Or, you could
imagine it as four sticks of
butter. Since butter is
100% fat, that's a
realistic comparison.
So, why doesn't a
person who's 15 pounds
overweight have a mound
of fat the size of a beach
ball around his middle?
Well, some people do! But
generally speaking, fat
doesn't accumulate in just one area. It's
dispersed throughout the body, and not
just beneath the skin, either. It surrounds
and cushions organs, too.

Don't be lured into thinking you're a
dietary do-gooder just because you're
hooked on fast-food fish sandwiches. You
might as well have the burger you
really want, because the average breaded
fish sandwich tips the scales at 400 to
500 calories and 25 grams of fat! *Buoy,
oh buoy*—breaded can be dreaded!

My doctor told
me that my
liver is
10 inches long.

Well, that shows
you come from
a line of long livers!

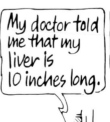

COOKING 101

Though dried wild mushrooms can be quite expensive, a tiny amount can go a long way to liven up a sauce. Look for dried porcini or shiitake mushrooms in small plastic bags in the produce department of your grocery store. You can substitute two cups of sliced regular white button mushrooms in this recipe if you prefer. Cook them with the onions and garlic until tender. Decrease boiling water to a half cup when soaking sun-dried tomatoes.

Who'da Thunk?

What popular vegetable was once thought to be poisonous?

There's nothing quite like the taste of a plump, ripe, freshly picked tomato. Though classified as a vegetable since 1893, tomatoes are actually the fruit of a vine native to South America, and our love affair with them is fairly recent. Brought to Europe from Central America by the Spanish in the early 1500s, tomatoes were grown strictly as decorative plants because it was feared they were poisonous. Colonists emigrating from northern Europe brought their tomato suspicions to the New World. In fact, records show that one brave American publicly ate a tomato on the courthouse steps in Salem, New Jersey, in 1820 to disprove the poison theory. When he suffered no ill effects, others were encouraged to indulge. Still, it wasn't until the 1900s that the tomato gained some measure of popularity. Today, North Americans eat roughly 18 pounds of tomatoes per person each year, in some form or other—more than any other vegetable except potatoes and lettuce.

It's-a-bella Tortellini

Cheese-filled tortellini with sun-dried tomato and wild-mushroom sauce

This beautiful Italian dish has star quality! It's the belladonna of tortellinis, and that's why the *pastarazzi* are in such a frenzy.

10 sun-dried tomatoes (not oil-packed)
1/2 oz dried wild mushrooms (see Cooking 101)
1 tsp olive oil
1 cup chopped red onions
2 cloves garlic, minced
1 can (28 oz) diced tomatoes, undrained
1 can (6 oz) tomato paste
1/4 cup chopped, fresh oregano, or 1 tbsp dried
1/2 tsp dried mint
1/4 tsp each salt and black pepper
1/4 tsp crushed red pepper flakes (optional)
1-1/2 pounds fresh or frozen cheese-filled tortellini
Grated Parmesan cheese (optional)

- Place sun-dried tomatoes and wild mushrooms in a small bowl. Pour 1 cup boiling water over top and let stand for 30 minutes.

- To prepare sauce, heat olive oil in a large, non-stick saucepan over medium-high heat. Add onions and garlic. Cook and stir until vegetables begin to soften, about 3 minutes. Add diced tomatoes and their liquid, tomato paste, oregano, mint, salt, pepper, and crushed red pepper flakes (if using). Bring to a boil. Reduce heat to low. Cover and simmer for 10 minutes, stirring occasionally.

- Add soaking liquid from sun-dried tomatoes and mushrooms to tomato sauce. Chop tomatoes and mushrooms and add to sauce. Simmer, covered, for 10 more minutes.

- While sauce is simmering, cook tortellini according to package directions. Drain well. Toss hot tortellini with sauce and sprinkle with Parmesan cheese, if desired. Serve immediately.

Makes 6 servings

Per serving: 407 calories, 7.7 g fat, 3.1 g saturated fat, 17 g protein, 67.3 g carbohydrate, 5.2 g fiber, 40.5 mg cholesterol, 767.5 mg sodium % calories from fat: 17

What's in it for me?

Piled-High Veggie Potpie

Vegetable potpie with a colossal sweet-potato biscuit crust

It's a potpie piled to the sky! And it's so darn tasty, you'll be begging for a second heaping helping.

1 cup each chopped onions and chopped red bell pepper
2 cloves garlic, minced
2-1/2 cups vegetable broth
2 cups peeled, cubed potatoes
1 cup sliced carrots
1-1/2 tsp dried rosemary
1/2 tsp dried thyme
1/4 tsp each salt and black pepper
1 cup sliced asparagus pieces or sliced green beans
1/2 cup frozen green peas, thawed
3 tbsp all-purpose flour
1/4 cup chopped, fresh parsley

Sweet-Potato Biscuit Crust
1-1/2 cups all-purpose flour
1 tbsp baking powder
1/2 tsp salt
3 tbsp butter or margarine, softened
3/4 cup cooked, mashed sweet potatoes
3/4 cup 1% milk, plus extra for brushing top of crust

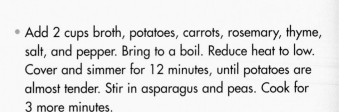

- Spray a large, non-stick saucepan with non-stick spray. Add onions, red pepper, and garlic. Cook and stir over medium-high heat until vegetables begin to soften, about 4 minutes.

- Add 2 cups broth, potatoes, carrots, rosemary, thyme, salt, and pepper. Bring to a boil. Reduce heat to low. Cover and simmer for 12 minutes, until potatoes are almost tender. Stir in asparagus and peas. Cook for 3 more minutes.

- In a small bowl, mix 3 tablespoons flour with remaining 1/2 cup vegetable broth until smooth. Add to vegetable mixture. Cook until bubbly and thickened. Stir in parsley. Transfer to a 2-quart casserole dish. Set aside.

- Preheat oven to 425°. In a large bowl, combine flour, baking powder, and salt. Cut in butter until mixture resembles coarse crumbs. Whisk together sweet potatoes and milk, then add to flour mixture. Stir until a soft ball forms. Transfer dough to a lightly floured surface and roll or pat out to fit top of casserole. Place dough over vegetables. Brush with milk. Bake for 20 minutes, until crust is puffed up and golden brown. Let cool for 5 minutes before serving.

Makes 6 servings

Per serving: 320 calories, 7.1 g fat, 3.9 g saturated fat, 9.4 g protein, 55.7 g carbohydrate, 5.2 g fiber, 16.8 mg cholesterol, 628.3 mg sodium
% calories from fat: 20

So many people spend their health gaining wealth, and then have to spend their wealth to regain their health.

A.J. Reb Materi
Our Family

EATS WITHOUT MEATS

A staple throughout much of the Middle East and India, lentils are tiny, dried, lens-shaped seeds. They're a valuable source of protein and fiber, and have long been used as a meat substitute. You'll need cooked lentils for this recipe, so look for them in cans beside the canned beans at your grocery store. Drain the lentils well, then rinse them with cold water to remove the added salt.

Getting Canned

You know, it seems like frozen and canned foods often get a bad rap for being high in calories, fat, and sodium. And nutrients? Naaah. Couldn't possibly come close to the fresh stuff! Well, truth be told, that's not the truth. Sometimes canned fruit and frozen vegetables actually provide more nutrition than their fresh counterparts. Up to 60% of nutrients can be lost as fresh produce makes its journey to grocery stores, sits on store shelves, and then lingers in home refrigerators. But when fruits and veggies are frozen, nutrient loss is usually less than 20%. If fresh items aren't in season, you can use canned fruits in muffins, pancakes, and frozen-yogurt shakes. Add frozen veggies to soups, stews, casseroles, and pasta. When it comes to taste, there's no doubt that fresh is best, but in a pinch, food from a can ain't nothin' to *freeze* at.

Lentili Chili

Zesty vegetarian chili with lentils

If you're longin' for a different kind of chili that's sure to please your palate, our spicy, meatless creation is the best you'll find this side of the *contilentil* divide.

1 tsp olive oil
1 cup each diced onions, diced celery, diced green bell pepper, and diced carrots
1 clove garlic, minced
1 tbsp chili powder
2 tsp ground cumin
1-1/2 tsp dried oregano
1/4 tsp ground cinnamon
1 can (14-1/2 oz) diced tomatoes, undrained
1 can (15 oz) cooked lentils, drained and rinsed (see Cooking 101)
1 cup tomato sauce
1/2 cup unsweetened pineapple juice
1/4 cup chili sauce (see hint below)
1 tbsp brown sugar
1/4 cup chopped, fresh cilantro
Low-fat sour cream for garnish (optional)

- Heat olive oil in large pot over medium heat. Add onions, celery, green pepper, carrots, and garlic. Cook and stir for 5 minutes, until vegetables begin to soften.

- Add chili powder, cumin, oregano, and cinnamon. Cook and stir for 1 more minute. Add all remaining ingredients, except cilantro and sour cream. Bring to a boil. Reduce heat to medium-low. Cover and simmer for 15 minutes, stirring occasionally.

- Stir in cilantro. Remove from heat. Ladle into serving bowls and top with a dollop of sour cream, if desired.

Makes 6 servings

Hint: Bottles of chili sauce (Heinz) can be found in the ketchup aisle at your grocery store. For a milder chili, use ketchup in place of the chili sauce.

Per serving: 171 calories, 1.9 g fat, 0.1 g saturated fat, 8.6 g protein, 33.1 g carbohydrate, 8.2 g fiber, 0 mg cholesterol, 382.5 mg sodium % calories from fat: 9

What's in it for me?

Pasta la Vista, Baby

Say good-bye to hunger with these delicious pasta entrees

Mr. Bowjangles

Bow-tie pasta with chicken, broccoli, and sun-dried tomatoes in a light broth

The zest and zing of this pasta dish will make your heart sing and your taste buds dance for joy!

1/4 cup reduced-sodium
  soy sauce
2 tbsp each honey and lime juice
1 tbsp each olive oil, Dijon
  mustard, and balsamic vinegar
1 clove garlic, minced
4 boneless, skinless chicken breast halves,
  cut into 1-inch cubes
1/2 cup sun-dried tomatoes (not oil-packed)
8 oz bow-tie pasta, uncooked (about 5 cups dry)
3 cups broccoli florets
1/2 cup chopped green onions

- In a small bowl, whisk together soy sauce, honey, lime juice, olive oil, mustard, vinegar, and garlic. Pour marinade over chicken cubes in a shallow, glass baking dish. Stir until all chicken pieces are coated with marinade. Cover and refrigerate for 30 minutes.

- Pour 1 cup boiling water over sun-dried tomatoes and let soak for 5 minutes. Drain tomatoes and chop. Set aside.

- Prepare pasta according to package directions. Add broccoli florets to pasta cooking water for last 3 minutes. Drain pasta and broccoli and return to pot. Keep warm.

- Transfer chicken and marinade to a large, non-stick skillet. Cook over medium-high heat until chicken is cooked through. Remove from heat. Add chicken, sauce, sun-dried tomatoes, and green onions to pasta and broccoli. Mix well. Serve immediately.

Makes 4 servings

What's in it for me?

Per serving: 477 calories, 7.2 g fat, 0.5 g saturated fat, 43.6 g protein, 57 g carbohydrate, 0.9 g fiber, 82.4 mg cholesterol, 939.8 mg sodium
% calories from fat: 14

Who'da Thunk?

Why is a speech proposing to someone's health called a toast?

In 17th century England, the wine wasn't quite as good as it is now. In order to improve its flavor, pieces of spiced toast were floated in the goblet before the wine was drunk. When people raised their glasses in the tradition of drinking to wish someone good health, it was considered rude not to finish every drop, and so the toast was consumed along with the wine. The custom came to be called "toasting," but eventually the toast was tossed.

Physical activity shouldn't be a shortcut to losing weight; it should become part of the fabric of your life, as natural a part of your day as your morning shower. And making it a habit is a lot easier if you aim for frequency, not duration. Instead of exercising for one hour, three times a week, try to incorporate simple, small bouts of activity into your everyday life. Fifteen minutes here and 10 minutes there seems like a cinch compared to cramming your entire week's worth of exercise into one marathon torture session. You wouldn't brush your teeth 21 times in one day and say, "There. That'll do it 'til next week!" If you want physical activity to become routine, learn to do it in short, frequent bursts. 'Cause it's better to exercise in short bursts than burst shorts!

Instead of using plain ol' white mushrooms in this recipe, try a mixture of shiitake and cremini mushrooms. Almost all grocery stores carry them. While you're there, look for jars of roasted red peppers and pimentos near the pickles.

Giving Up is Hard to Do

Name your vice. C'mon, fess up. Is it chocolate? Potato chips? Could it be ice cream? How about steak? We all have a weakness for one type of food or another, and there's no reason we can't enjoy the occasional tryst with a burger and fries. Healthy eating doesn't mean giving up your favorite foods, but it does mean cutting back on them. For instance, instead of having steak once a week, have it once every two weeks. Treat yourself to ice cream for dessert only on the weekends. *Halve* your cake, and eat it, too! Modest sacrifices like these are a lot easier to stomach than the total deprivation called for by most "diet plans," don't you think? Remember, if you're trying to lose weight, you can't do it overnight. You'll have more success by making simple, gradual changes that will add up to a healthier you in the long run. When putting on your weight-loss face, slow and steady wins the race.

In 1878, one of the first so-called anti-fat diet drinks featured iodine on its ingredient list. And the first diet pill combined arsenic or strychnine with a thyroid extract, raising the user's metabolism, but depleting muscle tissue. Talk about dying to lose weight!

Lanky Noodle Dandy

Chicken and mushroom cream sauce
served over egg noodles

Lanky Noodle really went to town when he created this mildly flavored, super-satisfying pasta dish.

12 oz large no-yolk egg noodles, uncooked (about 5 cups dry)
2 tsp butter or margarine
1 clove garlic, minced
3 cups sliced mixed mushrooms (see Cooking 101)
1-1/2 cups 2% milk
2 tbsp all-purpose flour
1/2 cup low-fat chicken broth
1/2 cup grated Romano or Parmesan cheese
1/2 cup low-fat sour cream
1/2 tsp each dried thyme and dried basil
1/4 tsp white or black pepper
3 cups chopped, cooked chicken breast
1 cup frozen green peas, thawed
1/3 cup chopped, fresh parsley
1/4 cup chopped, roasted red peppers or pimentos (see Cooking 101)

- Cook noodles according to package directions. Drain well and keep warm.

- Meanwhile, melt butter in a large, non-stick saucepan over medium-high heat. Add garlic and mushrooms. Cook and stir for 3 to 4 minutes, until mushrooms are tender.

- Whisk together milk and flour until smooth. Add to mushrooms, along with chicken broth. Cook until sauce has thickened, stirring constantly. Add cheese, sour cream, thyme, basil, and pepper. Stir until cheese is melted. Add cooked chicken, peas, parsley, and red peppers. Cook until chicken and peas are heated through. Serve over hot noodles.

Makes 6 servings

Per serving: 455 calories, 9 g fat, 4 g saturated fat, 39.2 g protein, 53.3 g carbohydrate, 1.9 g fiber, 75.4 mg cholesterol, 329.3 mg sodium % calories from fat: 18

What's in it for me?

PASTA LA VISTA, BABY

Thai a Yellow Ribbon

If you love Thai food, this recipe is a must

The idea for this sumptuous fettuccine dish came to us while sitting under an old oak tree in Orlando. It was dawn. Yup, that was the exact moment we decided to give it a Thai twist, and it's been three long years since that day.

Sauce

1/2 cup low-fat chicken broth
1/4 cup reduced-fat peanut butter
2 tbsp each chopped, fresh cilantro
and chopped, fresh basil leaves
1 tbsp sugar
2 tsp each grated gingerroot and
lemon zest
1 tsp each sesame oil and
cornstarch
1 clove garlic, minced
1/2 tsp each ground cumin and
crushed red pepper flakes

12 oz uncooked fettuccine
4 boneless, skinless chicken breast halves, cut into thin strips
1 large red pepper, cut into thin strips
2 cups snow peas, cut in half diagonally
1 large carrot, cut into thin strips

- Combine all sauce ingredients in a blender and whirl until smooth. Set aside.

- Cook fettuccine according to package directions. Drain well and keep warm.

- While pasta is cooking, spray a large, non-stick wok or skillet with non-stick spray and place over medium-high heat. Add chicken and cook until no longer pink. Add red pepper, snow peas, and carrots. Cook and stir for 3 more minutes, until vegetables are tender-crisp. Add sauce. Cook until bubbly and thickened. Remove from heat, stir in cooked fettuccine, and serve immediately.

Makes 4 servings

What's in it for me?

Per serving: 543 calories, 11.5 g fat,
0.6 g saturated fat, 43 g protein,
70.5 g carbohydrate, 4 g fiber,
66 mg cholesterol, 235 mg sodium
% calories from fat: 19

FAT OR FICTION?

Cholesterol-free labels on vegetable oils aren't all they're cracked up to be.

Blood cholesterol is a waxy substance that contributes to the formation of many of the body's essential compounds, including vitamin D, bile acid, estrogen, and testosterone. Your liver makes all the cholesterol you'll ever need. But cholesterol also comes from the foods you eat (dietary cholesterol), and only animal-related foods contain it: meat, poultry, fish, egg yolks, cheese, and milk. Plant-based foods do not contain cholesterol. Not grains. Not fruit. Not vegetables. Not nuts and seeds. Not oils. You read it correctly—oils never had cholesterol to begin with!

Manufacturers could just as well put "no plutonium" on the label. It's all marketing hype. You're better off ignoring the cholesterol-free propaganda and, instead, start scouring food labels for saturated fat, the artery-clogging culprit that really gets your body's blood-cholesterol factory working overtime. Translation: eating shrimp, which are naturally higher in cholesterol but contain unsaturated fat, is better for you than eating some types of cholesterol-free cookies. If those cookies are made with hydrogenated margarine, vegetable oil, or shortening, they're packed with saturated fat and its evil counterpart, trans fatty acid. Unfortunately, many people mistake the cookies for a healthy, low-fat snack just because of the label.

The most difficult part of a diet isn't watching what you eat. It's watching what other people eat.

The Six-Million-Dollar Manicotti

When we set out to revamp plain, ol' everyday manicotti, they said it couldn't be done. We replied, "Nonsense. We can rebuild it. We have the technology." The result: creamy, chicken-stuffed manicotti that's so scrumptious, its flavor is bionic!

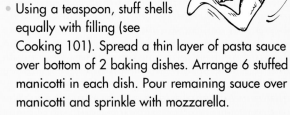

1 clove garlic, minced

1/2 cup finely chopped onions

**3 boneless, skinless chicken breast halves,
cut into small pieces (see hint below)**

**1 cup each grated carrots, grated zucchini,
and finely chopped mushrooms**

**3 tbsp minced, fresh basil, or
1-1/2 tsp dried**

**1 tbsp minced, fresh oregano, or
1 tsp dried**

1/4 tsp black pepper

4 oz light cream cheese, cut into cubes

1 cup part-skim ricotta cheese

1/4 cup grated Parmesan cheese

12 manicotti shells, uncooked

**2 cups of your favorite low-fat, tomato-based
pasta sauce**

**1/2 cup shredded, part-skim mozzarella
cheese (2 oz)**

Chopped, fresh parsley for garnish (optional)

- While filling is chilling, cook manicotti according to package directions. Rinse with cold water and drain well.

- Using a teaspoon, stuff shells equally with filling (see Cooking 101). Spread a thin layer of pasta sauce over bottom of 2 baking dishes. Arrange 6 stuffed manicotti in each dish. Pour remaining sauce over manicotti and sprinkle with mozzarella.

- Cover with foil and bake at 350° for 40 minutes. Let cool for 5 minutes before serving. Garnish with chopped parsley, if desired.

Makes 6 servings

- To make filling, spray a large, non-stick skillet with non-stick spray. Add garlic and onions. Cook and stir over medium heat until softened, about 2 minutes. Be careful not to burn them.

- Add chicken, increase heat to medium-high, and cook until no longer pink. Add carrots, zucchini, mushrooms, basil, oregano, and pepper. Cook for 3 more minutes. Add cream cheese and stir until melted. Remove from heat. Stir in ricotta and Parmesan cheeses. Transfer filling to a large bowl and refrigerate for 20 minutes.

Hint: Chicken is easier to cut into small pieces if it's partially frozen.

Per serving: 404 calories, 10.8 g fat, 6.1 g saturated fat, 33.3 g protein, 43.6 g carbohydrate, 1.4 g fiber, 65.6 mg cholesterol, 586.8 mg sodium % calories from fat: 24

What's in it for us?

It's easier to stuff manicotti shells if they're slightly undercooked. This also makes them less likely to tear. Drain the cooked shells and rinse them with cold water to stop the cooking process and to keep them from sticking together. Use a teaspoon to stuff them. If you prefer, you can substitute lasagna noodles in this recipe and make lasagna roll-ups, or you can use 24 jumbo pasta shells.

COOKING
101

Tubes and Cubes

Rigatoni tubes with chicken cubes
and barbecue sauce

It takes two to tango, and
chicken and rigatoni do make
a fabulous couple. But when
smooth-talking barbecue
sauce is permitted to cut in,
things really get swingin'.

1 tsp olive oil
1/2 cup chopped red
  onions
1 clove garlic, minced
4 boneless, skinless
  chicken breast halves,
  cut into 1-inch cubes
2 cups sliced mushrooms
1 cup chopped green bell pepper
1 cup of your favorite low-fat spaghetti sauce
1/3 cup barbecue sauce (see hint below)
8 oz rigatoni, uncooked (about 5 cups dry)
1/2 cup shredded, reduced-fat Monterey Jack cheese (2 oz)
Chopped, fresh cilantro or parsley for garnish

- Heat oil in a large, non-stick saucepan over medium-high heat. Add onions and garlic. Cook and stir for 1 to 2 minutes, until onions are softened. Add chicken and cook until no longer pink. Add mushrooms and green pepper. Continue to cook for 3 to 4 minutes, until vegetables are tender. Add spaghetti sauce and barbecue sauce. Stir well. Reduce heat, cover, and simmer for 5 minutes.

- Meanwhile, prepare rigatoni according to package directions. Drain well. Add rigatoni to chicken and vegetables and mix well. Spoon pasta mixture onto serving plates and sprinkle with cheese and cilantro. Serve immediately.

Makes 4 servings

Hint: Any type of bottled barbecue sauce will do, but we prefer the kind that says "for chicken and ribs." If you like your pasta really saucy, increase spaghetti sauce to 1-1/2 cups and barbecue sauce to 1/2 cup.

What's
in it
for me?

Per serving: 454 calories, 6.8 g fat,
1.9 g saturated fat, 40.2 g protein,
57.4 g carbohydrate, 1.5 g fiber,
75.8 mg cholesterol, 627.6 mg sodium
% calories from fat: 14

SAY IT AIN'T SO!

Here are the cold, hard facts on cold cuts: Many popular luncheon meats now come in a turkey version, but that doesn't mean you should gobble them up like there's no tomorrow. In fact, turkey roll, turkey bologna, and turkey salami may be as high in fat as their beef counterparts. That's because they're often made with dark meat and skin, and some cuts contain turkey hearts and gizzards, which are high-fat, high-cholesterol no-nos. If you want to cut down on the killer cuts, you've gotta go cold turkey: Plain, ol' turkey breast is leaner than the rest.

Supercalifragilisticexithalitosis

Garlic, sometimes called "the stinking rose," is a member of the lily family and a cousin of onions and chives. As early as 3000 BC, Chinese scholars had good things to say about garlic's health-giving properties, and modern medicine has been following suit. Garlic may help to lower blood cholesterol and blood pressure, can relieve asthma, and may prevent certain cancers. Not bad for a stinkin' rose! But what about garlic breath, you say? There are plenty of remedies, from sipping coffee, red wine, or a glass of milk, to eating honey or yogurt. Then there's the old standby—chewing parsley. It's like nature's mouthwash. Some people even suggest that putting garlic in your pooch's food will stop fleas from bothering him, doggone it!

What the heck are pimentos and where can I buy them?

Pimentos are sweet, red, heart-shaped peppers. They're most commonly used as a stuffing for green olives. Look for them in small jars near the pickles and olives at your grocery store. If you can't find pimentos, roasted red peppers make a good substitute.

THE E FILES

Want to burn fat 24 hours a day—even while sleeping? Wait! Don't touch that dial! This is not a paid advertisement for the ACME Rubber Blubber-Burning Suit or the latest girth-control pill. We're advocating exercise here. Good, ol' movement. It won't cost you a dime, but you'll reap huge health benefits if you buy into it. Why bother? Well, exercise boosts your metabolism, your body's fat-burner. When you move, it's like turning up the thermostat on your personal furnace. You burn more fuel, fat included. What's more, exercise keeps the fuel-burning fire stoked even after you stop. Imagine! Walk briskly for 30 minutes, then flake out on the couch while your calorie-burning engine works overtime. The more muscle mass you build, the more calories you're able to burn around the clock—yes, even while you catch some zzz's! So, if you want to give new meaning to the phrase "you snooze, you lose," then just move it!

Does drinking make your liverwurst?

Tickle Me Elbows
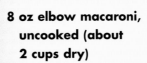

Our Mom's simple and delicious tuna noodle casserole with elbow macaroni

Revamped tuna noodle casserole that's so easy to make, it'll tickle your fancy. And if you have finicky kids, it's guaranteed to tickle their taste buds, too.

8 oz elbow macaroni, uncooked (about 2 cups dry)
1 can (6 oz) water-packed tuna, drained
1 cup sliced celery
1/3 cup chopped green onions
1/4 cup diced green bell pepper
1/4 cup diced pimento (see tip in margin)
1 can (10-3/4 oz) reduced-fat cream of celery soup, undiluted
1/2 cup 1% milk
1 cup shredded, reduced-fat sharp cheddar cheese (4 oz)
1/2 cup low-fat mayonnaise
1/4 tsp black pepper

- Cook macaroni according to package directions. Drain. Rinse with cold water and drain again. In a large bowl, combine cooked macaroni, tuna, celery, onions, green pepper, and pimento. Mix well.

- In a small saucepan, combine soup and milk. Heat over medium heat until smooth. Add cheese and continue to cook until cheese is melted. Remove from heat and stir in mayonnaise and pepper.

- Pour sauce over macaroni mixture. Mix well. Pour into a 1-1/2-quart casserole dish that has been sprayed with non-stick spray. Bake at 350°, uncovered, for 30 minutes. Serve hot.

Makes 6 servings

Per serving: 280 calories, 5.4 g fat, 2.4 g saturated fat, 18.2 g protein, 40.6 g carbohydrate, 1.3 g fiber, 23.5 mg cholesterol, 637.4 mg sodium
% calories from fat: 17

What's in it for me?

Lawrence of Arrabbiata

Penne pasta topped with a spicy, oven-roasted tomato sauce

It's no mirage. Penne that's simple to make, yet bursting with flavor. Tasting is believing!

2 pounds plum tomatoes, quartered
1-1/2 cups chopped red onions
4 slices raw bacon, chopped
2 cloves garlic, minced
1 tbsp red wine vinegar
1-1/2 tsp each dried basil
  and dried oregano
12 oz penne pasta,
  uncooked (about
  4 cups dry)
2 tbsp tomato paste
1 tsp salt
1/2 tsp each black pepper
  and crushed red pepper flakes
1/4 cup grated Parmesan cheese
Chopped, fresh parsley for garnish

- Spray a roasting pan with non-stick spray. Add tomatoes, onions, bacon, and garlic. Mix well and spread evenly in pan. Roast, uncovered, at 400° for 15 minutes. Remove pan from oven. Add vinegar, basil, and oregano. Stir well and return pan to oven. Roast for 15 more minutes.

- Meanwhile, prepare pasta according to package directions. Drain well and keep warm.

- Transfer roasted vegetable mixture to a blender or food processor. Work in batches if necessary. Puree until smooth. Transfer mixture to a medium saucepan. Add tomato paste, salt, pepper, and crushed red pepper flakes. Bring sauce to a boil, then reduce heat and simmer, uncovered, for 5 minutes. Spoon hot sauce over cooked pasta. Sprinkle with Parmesan cheese and parsley. Serve immediately.

Makes 4 servings

What's in it for me?

Per serving: 468 calories, 7.8 g fat,
2.6 g saturated fat, 18.5 g protein,
80.1 g carbohydrate, 4.1 g fiber,
9.9 mg cholesterol, 897.8 mg sodium
% calories from fat: 15

"The sign said 'Free Weights,' so I took a couple."

Where did mayonnaise get its name?

Who'da Thunk?

Mayonnaise originated in the 18th century when a Frenchman, Duc de Richelieu, was taking part in a battle against the British at Mahón, a port on the Mediterranean island of Minorca. It was there that he first tasted the interesting combination of egg yolks, oil, and vinegar, so he dubbed it the Sauce of Mahón. Later, it was renamed mahonnaise, which means "after the manner of Mahón." Other egg-yolk-based sauces have "aise" endings, too, including hollandaise, "after the manner of Holland," and béarnaise, "after the manner of Béarn." As far as fat goes, these sauces are no yolking matter. Mayo weighs in at close to 100% fat! Over *aisey* now!

YOU DO THE MATH

If you drink two cups of coffee a day, you can save almost 16,000 calories and close to 2,000 grams of fat in a year just by using 2% milk instead of cream. That's more than 29 days' worth of fat! So, if you wanna hava some java, don't pop a seam. Just limit your cream!

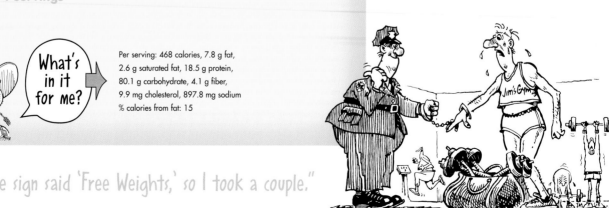

On average, wine drinkers are slimmer than beer drinkers.

In a recent study, researchers at the University of North Carolina measured the bellies of men who drank a beer a day, as well as men who averaged a glass of wine a day, and a third group of non-drinkers. They found that the waistlines of the wine drinkers were the smallest, and the beer drinkers the largest. Does that mean that wine prevents our belts from busting? Well, that wasn't proven. It may not be the type of alcohol that affects your waistline, but instead, what you eat along with it. It's hard to pack away the nacho chips while sipping on a nice Merlot. On the other hand, beer is often guzzled alongside potato chips, chicken wings, or hot dogs. If that's the case, it may be better to wine and dine than chug from a mug!

TRIVIAL TIDBIT

Bill Haskell of Stanford University calculated that an office worker who spends two minutes an hour sending e-mails to colleagues day after day would burn about 38,000 more calories a decade if he simply walked down the hall to speak to them. That's the energy equivalent of 11 pounds of fat! It's a tiny amount each hour, and not much each day, but it sure adds up.

Minutes at the table don't make you put on weight—it's the seconds.

The Yellow Bows of Texas

Zesty chili with ground turkey and black beans served over bow-tie pasta

Deep in the heart of Texas, the locals ranked this spicy masterpiece the best pasta dish this side of the Alamo.

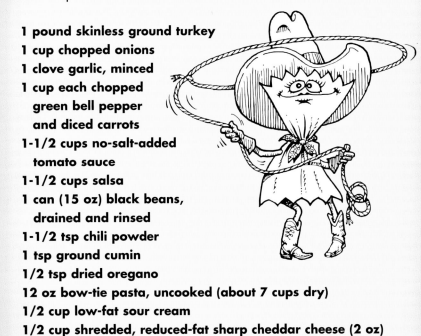

1 pound skinless ground turkey
1 cup chopped onions
1 clove garlic, minced
1 cup each chopped green bell pepper and diced carrots
1-1/2 cups no-salt-added tomato sauce
1-1/2 cups salsa
1 can (15 oz) black beans, drained and rinsed
1-1/2 tsp chili powder
1 tsp ground cumin
1/2 tsp dried oregano
12 oz bow-tie pasta, uncooked (about 7 cups dry)
1/2 cup low-fat sour cream
1/2 cup shredded, reduced-fat sharp cheddar cheese (2 oz)
1/2 cup chopped green onions

- Spray a large, non-stick skillet with non-stick spray. Add ground turkey and cook over medium-high heat until no longer pink. Break up any large chunks with a fork. Add onions, garlic, green pepper, and carrots. Cook and stir for 4 to 5 minutes, until vegetables have softened. Stir in tomato sauce, salsa, beans, chili powder, cumin, and oregano. Bring mixture to a boil, then lower heat and simmer for 10 minutes, stirring occasionally.

- Meanwhile, prepare pasta according to package directions. Drain well. Divide pasta among six serving plates. Ladle chili over pasta. Place a dollop of sour cream in the center, then sprinkle with cheese and onions. Serve immediately.

Makes 6 servings

Per serving: 439 calories, 6 g fat, 1.4 g saturated fat, 34.3 g protein, 65 g carbohydrate, 4.7 g fiber, 43.3 mg cholesterol, 465.7 mg sodium
% calories from fat: 12

What's in it for me?

Thai for Two

Linguini, shrimp, and vegetables in a spicy plum sauce

And two for Thai. How romantic! Embark on a delightfully spicy journey, a *Thaitanic* pasta voyage that you can sink your teeth into. Your heart will go on...longing for a second helping.

4 oz uncooked linguini
1/2 cup each plum sauce and low-fat chicken broth
1 tbsp seasoned rice vinegar
2 tsp grated gingerroot
1 tsp each reduced-sodium soy sauce and sesame oil
1 clove garlic, minced
1/4 tsp crushed red pepper flakes
1 cup each carrots, zucchini, and red bell pepper,
   cut into thin strips
8 oz uncooked jumbo shrimp, peeled
1/4 cup chopped green onions

- Prepare linguini according to package directions. Drain well and keep warm.

- In a small bowl, combine plum sauce, chicken broth, vinegar, gingerroot, soy sauce, sesame oil, garlic, and crushed red pepper flakes. Set aside.

- Spray a large, non-stick wok or skillet with non-stick spray. Add carrots, zucchini, and red pepper. Cook over medium heat until vegetables begin to soften, about 4 minutes. Stir often. Add shrimp, green onions, and sauce. Increase heat to medium-high. Cook and stir until mixture is hot and bubbly, and shrimp is cooked through, about 3 to 4 minutes. Add cooked linguini to wok or skillet and mix well. Remove from heat and serve immediately.

Makes 2 servings

What's in it for me?

Per serving: 518 calories, 6.3 g fat, 0.8 g saturated fat, 33.8 g protein, 80.8 g carbohydrate, 4.7 g fiber, 172.3 mg cholesterol, 345.7 mg sodium
% calories from fat: 11

COOKING 101

Shrimp is the most popular shellfish in North America. As with all shellfish, shrimp should be cooked very briefly or it becomes tough and rubbery. Cook just until the flesh turns opaque and the shrimp starts to curl. Because the intestinal vein of large shrimp contains grit, it should always be removed before cooking.

A Root Worth Taking

Suffering from motion sickness? Next time you're en route, make sure you pack some of the "in" root—ginger, that is. Tests have shown that gingerroot, either fresh or preserved, can counteract the nausea and vomiting of motion sickness. It's as effective as Dramamine, but it doesn't make you drowsy like the drug can. And sipping flat gingerale or sucking candied ginger may help to quell nausea from morning sickness and food poisoning, too. According to folk medicine, ginger is also a supposed cure for fever, diarrhea, coughing, and stomach pains. In New Guinea, it's considered a contraceptive, and in Africa, an aphrodisiac. On *Gilligan's Island*, Ginger's a castaway, and in pop music, an ex-Spice Girl. A root for all reasons, ginger cures what *ales* ya!

I'm on a strict diet. I'm only allowed to eat tiny portions the size of a postage stamp.

Then stick to it!

It's divine!

Penne from Heaven

Shrimp, scallops, black olives, feta, and a zesty tomato sauce, served over penne noodles

This miraculously delicious Mediterranean-style pasta dish was created with the help of some divine intervention. Okay, okay, so we're telling a fib. Greta actually concocted the recipe in her kitchen, all by herself, without assistance from the heavens. Just a little white lie. Not like we broke a commandment or anything.

1 cup chopped red onions
2 cloves garlic, minced
1-1/2 cups chopped zucchini
1 can (28 oz) diced tomatoes, undrained
1 cup no-salt-added tomato sauce
2 tbsp tomato paste
2 tbsp each chopped, fresh oregano and basil,
**   or 1-1/2 tsp each dried**
1/2 tsp black pepper
1/4 tsp crushed red pepper flakes
12 oz penne pasta, uncooked (about 4 cups dry)
8 oz uncooked jumbo shrimp, peeled
8 oz uncooked bay scallops
1/4 cup sliced black olives
1 cup crumbled feta cheese (4 oz)
Chopped, fresh parsley for garnish

- Spray a large, non-stick saucepan with non-stick spray. Add onions and garlic. Cook and stir over medium heat for 3 minutes, until onions are softened. Add zucchini and cook for 3 more minutes. Add diced tomatoes and their liquid, tomato sauce, tomato paste, oregano, basil, pepper, and crushed red pepper flakes. Bring to a boil. Reduce heat to medium-low and simmer, uncovered, for 10 minutes.

- While sauce is simmering, prepare pasta according to package directions. Drain well and keep warm.

- Add shrimp, scallops, and olives to sauce. Increase heat to medium-high and cook for 3 to 4 minutes, until shrimp and scallops are cooked through.

- To serve, spoon cooked penne onto serving plates. Top with sauce, followed by crumbled feta and chopped parsley. Serve immediately.

Makes 4 servings

Who'da Thunk?

Why are onions found in so many recipes?

The obvious answer is that they taste good. But it's not just the way onions taste, it's the way onions make other foods taste. Like hot peppers, onions contain astringent oils that irritate the mouth's membranes, making the taste buds more sensitive to flavor. Not only that, those oils carry the aroma and flavor of the food to the real taste center of the body—the nose.

YOU DO THE MATH

One potato, two potato, three potato, four...How many baked potatoes do you have in a week? Suppose you have just one. If you top that tater with two tablespoons of low-fat sour cream rather than the regular, full-fat kind, you'll save almost 2,000 calories and 291 grams of fat in a year. That tiny change amounts to more than four days' worth of fat. Can't top that!

Per serving: 547 calories, 9.6 g fat,
4.5 g saturated fat, 30.5 g protein,
81.8 g carbohydrate, 2.9 g fiber,
111.4 mg cholesterol, 459.2 mg sodium
% calories from fat: 16

What's in it for me?

PASTA LA VISTA, BABY

Blast from the Pasta

Old-fashioned, one-pot hamburger noodle casserole

Fusilli with far-out flavor, man! Whether you're cooking dinner for *My Three Sons*, lunch for the Partridges, or brunch for the Bradys, this recipe will feed an army. Any leftovers? Just leave them to Beaver.

1-1/2 pounds extra-lean ground beef
1 cup each chopped green bell pepper and chopped onions
2 cups sliced mushrooms
1 can (28 oz) diced tomatoes, undrained
1 can (10-3/4 oz) reduced-fat cream of tomato soup, undiluted
1 can (10-3/4 oz) reduced-fat cream of celery soup, undiluted
1/2 cup 1% milk
1-1/2 tsp dried oregano
1 tsp chili powder
1/2 tsp paprika
1/4 tsp each black pepper and crushed red pepper flakes
8 oz fusilli pasta, uncooked (about 3 cups dry)

These noodles are really groovy.

HAVE A NICE DAY

BLESS THIS PAD

- Spray a large, non-stick skillet or electric fry pan with non-stick spray. Add beef and cook over medium-high heat until no longer pink. Break up any large pieces using a wooden spoon. Add green peppers, onions, and mushrooms. Continue to cook until vegetables begin to soften, about 3 to 4 minutes.

- Stir in diced tomatoes and their liquid, tomato soup, and celery soup. Cook and stir until mixture is well blended. Add all remaining ingredients. Bring to a boil. Reduce heat to low. Cover and simmer for 30 minutes, stirring occasionally. Serve hot.

Makes 8 servings

According to the Beef Information Centre, ground beef is the most popular form of meat eaten in Canada. It's no wonder, considering how economical, easy to prepare, and delicious it is! As far as your waistline goes, your best option is the extra-lean kind, which, by law, cannot contain more than 10% fat. Regular ground beef can have up to 30 grams of fat in a three-and-a-half ounce serving. Why beef up on beef when you don't have to?

Eat Green to Feel in the Pink

What you see is what you get. And when it comes to vegetables, the more color you see, the better. Brightly colored fruits and vegetables like carrots, yams, cantaloupe, spinach, broccoli, and kiwi are the richest in nutrients. A wide array of colors means you're getting the full spectrum of phytochemicals that these foods have to offer. Phytochemicals is just a fancy name for plant chemicals. Some lower cholesterol, some slow the aging process, others guard against cancer. All are great reasons to create a palette for your palate. How about a little lycopene found in tomatoes or a dash of lutein from spinach? Then there's chlorogenic acid from green pepper, and, of course, sulphorophane, compliments of good, ol' broccoli. Who cares if you can't pronounce them? Just eat them!

What's in it for me?

Per serving: 327 calories, 8 g fat, 2.7 g saturated fat, 24.4 g protein, 37.9 g carbohydrate, 1.9 g fiber, 47.4 mg cholesterol, 638.9 mg sodium
% calories from fat: 22

The Un-Known Cowmic

If a cow laughed, would milk come out of its nose?

Less-On-Ya Lasagna

Roasted vegetable lasagna with four kinds of cheese

Translation: You'll end up with less fat on ya since there's less fat in your lasagna. But you'll actually have more healthy stuff in ya, given the heaping layers of veggies hidden under the cheese and noodles. Just don't drop any on ya!

3 cups sliced portobello mushrooms
2 medium zucchini, unpeeled, sliced
1 large red bell pepper, seeded and chopped
1 large yellow bell pepper, seeded and chopped
1 large red onion, thinly sliced
1 tbsp olive oil
1 tsp balsamic or red wine vinegar
2 cloves garlic, minced
1 tsp each dried rosemary and dried oregano
1 cup part-skim ricotta cheese
1 cup low-fat (1%) cottage cheese
1/3 cup chopped, fresh parsley
1/4 cup grated Parmesan cheese
1 egg white
12 lasagna noodles, uncooked
3 cups of your favorite low-fat spaghetti sauce
1-1/2 cups shredded, part-skim mozzarella or
    Swiss cheese (6 oz)

- Spray a large roasting pan with non-stick spray. Add mushrooms, zucchini, bell peppers, onion, olive oil, vinegar, garlic, rosemary, and oregano. Mix well, until vegetables are coated with seasonings. Roast, uncovered, at 400° for 25 minutes, stirring once halfway through cooking time.

- While vegetables are roasting, prepare cheese filling and cook pasta. In a medium bowl, combine ricotta and cottage cheeses, 1/4 cup parsley, Parmesan cheese, and egg white. Mix well. Refrigerate until ready to use. Prepare lasagna noodles according to package directions. Drain well. Rinse with cold water and drain again.

- To assemble lasagna, spray a 9 x 13-inch baking dish with non-stick spray. Spread 1/4 spaghetti sauce over bottom of pan. Arrange 4 lasagna noodles, 3 lengthwise and one crosswise, over sauce. Spread 1/2 cheese filling over noodles, followed by 1/3 roasted vegetables. Sprinkle vegetables with 1/3 mozzarella. Repeat layering: 4 noodles, 1/2 cheese filling, 1/3 roasted vegetables, and 1/3 mozzarella. Layer final 4 noodles over mozzarella, followed by remaining spaghetti sauce. Top sauce with remaining roasted vegetables.

- Cover with foil and bake at 375° for 35 minutes. Remove lasagna from oven, sprinkle with remaining mozzarella and parsley, and return to oven, uncovered, for 5 more minutes. Let cool for 10 minutes before serving.

Makes 8 servings

Per serving: 353 calories, 9.1 g fat, 3.1 g saturated fat, 22.9 g protein, 47.1 g carbohydrate, 2.2 g fiber, 19 mg cholesterol, 618.6 mg sodium % calories from fat: 23

What's in it for me?

Mincing your words makes it easier if you have to eat them later.

Franklin P. Jones

Clamborguini

Linguini with red clam sauce

Rev up your engine with this high-performance, high-flavor pasta entree. The taste will drive you wild!

1 tsp olive oil
1 cup chopped red onions
2 cloves garlic, minced
1 can (28 oz) diced tomatoes, undrained
3 tbsp tomato paste
1 tbsp each red wine vinegar
  and brown sugar
2 tsp dried basil
1 tsp dried oregano
1/2 tsp salt
1/4 tsp each black pepper and crushed red pepper flakes
12 oz linguini, uncooked
1 can (6-1/2 oz) whole baby clams, drained
1/4 cup chopped, fresh parsley
1/4 cup grated Parmesan cheese

- Heat olive oil in a large, non-stick saucepan over medium heat. Add onions and garlic. Cook and stir for 3 to 4 minutes, until onions are softened. Add diced tomatoes and their liquid, tomato paste, vinegar, brown sugar, basil, oregano, salt, black pepper, and crushed red pepper flakes. Bring to a boil. Reduce heat to medium-low. Simmer, uncovered, for 20 minutes, until sauce has thickened.

- Meanwhile, prepare linguini according to package directions. Drain well and keep warm.

- Add drained clams and parsley to sauce. Simmer for 5 more minutes. Serve hot sauce over linguini. Sprinkle with Parmesan cheese.

Makes 4 servings

What's in it for me?

Per serving: 489 calories, 5.6 g fat,
1.3 g saturated fat, 25.6 g protein,
82.9 g carbohydrate, 2.3 g fiber,
28.7 mg cholesterol, 474.2 mg sodium
% calories from fat: 10

THE E FILES

Today's labor-saving devices are bordering on the ridiculous. Do we really need Rototillers for our petunia gardens? We blow our leaves out of the yard rather than rake them, we send e-mail to our co-workers instead of walking down the hall, we drive up to the bank machine rather than—heaven forbid—get out of our cars. We even have automatic toilet flushers! Well, you'd be doing your body a big favor by flushing technology down the toilet every now and then. Looking for opportunities to be on your feet and moving is one of the best fitness strategies going. Refuse to take the elevator unless you're going up more than three floors, and avoid other "people movers" like escalators and moving sidewalks, too. C'mon! Turn off that noisy leaf blower and use a rake, broom, and some elbow grease. Your heart, your waistline, and your neighbor will thank you.

TRIVIAL TIDBIT

Did you know that Americans eat more on Super Bowl Sunday than on any other day of the year except Thanksgiving? After 3,000 calories, your tight end might look more like a fullback!

According to a new scientific theory, lifting weights actually kills germs. Sounds great, but how do you get the germs to lift weights?

Chicken Worth Pickin'

Keeping you abreast of chicken trends

Fee, Fie, Faux Fried Chicken

Oven "fried" chicken pieces with a crispy herb coating

Fee, Fie, Foh Yum! I smell the scent of chicken with crumbs! If you love fried chicken, but hate all the fat, our healthier rendition is a *giant* step in the right direction.

2/3 cup all-purpose flour
1 tsp dried oregano
1/2 tsp each dried thyme, paprika, and salt
1/4 tsp garlic powder and black pepper
1-1/2 cups crushed cornflake cereal
2 tbsp grated Parmesan cheese
1 cup buttermilk
3 pounds skinless chicken thighs and drumsticks
    (about 12 pieces)

• Spray a large roasting pan with non-stick spray and set aside.

• In a shallow bowl or pie plate, combine flour, oregano, thyme, paprika, salt, garlic powder, and pepper. In a separate bowl or pie plate, combine cornflake crumbs and cheese. Pour buttermilk into another bowl.

• Rinse chicken and pat dry. Working one at a time, dip chicken pieces in buttermilk and moisten all sides. Place chicken in bowl with flour mixture and turn to coat. Dip in buttermilk again, then coat with cornflake mixture. Arrange chicken in roasting pan, leaving some space between pieces. This process can get a bit messy, but hang in there.

• Bake, uncovered, at 425° for 40 minutes, until chicken is no longer pink and juices run clear. Serve immediately.

Makes 6 servings

What's in it for us?

Per serving: 277 calories, 6 g fat, 1.8 g saturated fat, 30.8 g protein, 23.4 g carbohydrate, 0.8 g fiber, 108.4 mg cholesterol, 507.5 mg sodium
% calories from fat: 20

Quibbling Over Nibbling

In the midst of the nation's low-fat, no-fat craze, consumers are making a lot of silly snack choices. Because the package descriptions of a product make it sound like it's good for you—bran, all-natural, made with real fruit—consumers assume they'll get skinny or healthy eating what's inside. Take cookies, for example. An Oreo has two grams of fat and 50 calories. A Pepperidge Farm Wholesome Choice Apple Oatmeal Tart cookie has the same amount of fat but 20 more calories! Perhaps we should turn to some old favorites that really are low in fat: gingersnaps, vanilla wafers, animal crackers, graham crackers, and Fig Newtons. You can't always judge a food by its cover, so to make smarter choices, read the numbers, not the names.

SAY IT AIN'T SO!

Chicken nugget. Nugget. Little lump o' chicken. How can something that sounds so small end up making your waistline so large? Easy. Just six of these little lumps are a gold mine of fat and calories—28 grams of fat and 500 calories to be exact! You'll be the lumpy one if you don't curb your appetite for these fat-filled, fast-food gems.

Are you making a meal of those fireflies?

Yup, I'm having a light supper tonight.

What piece of cookware was originally a Mongol warrior's hat?

Who'da Thunk?

If the wok resembles an Oriental helmet of sorts, it's no accident. During the Bronze Age, invading Mongolian warriors wore a wok-shaped metal helmet. The helmet not only protected the head, but could also be turned over and used as a cooking pan. No kidding! Imagine the infomercial potential: Act now! Don't delay! The Mongolian Miracle Wok. Fight hunger AND the enemy at the same time! Joking aside, nothing beats the wok for rapid cooking and efficient use of oil—the perfect kitchen tool for health-conscious, time-pressured folks.

THE E FILES

Does the mere mention of the word "exercise" send your blood-pressure levels into another stratosphere? If you approach exercise with the same air of expectation that's usually reserved for scouring your toilet bowl, fat chance you'll make time for it (and that gives fat a chance). Try thinking of *lifestyle* physical activity rather than structured exercise. Consider walking your dog, washing your car, or playing with your kids as opposed to sweating it out at aerobics class, jogging five miles (ugghh!), or "going for the burn" on a rowing machine. Abs of steel, buns of whatever—it can be intimidating. What the heck is Tae Bo, anyway? *Tie a Yellow Ribbon 'Round the Old Oak Tree*, if that's what turns your crank. As long as it involves movement, it counts. Change the way you think about exercise and soon you'll be marching to the beat of a different drummer. See, you're movin' already!

To Stir, With Love

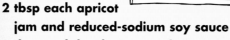

Quick, colorful, and delicious chicken and vegetable stir-fry

Eat to your heart's content! One taste of this Oriental stir-fry and it's love at first bite!

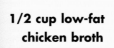

1/2 cup low-fat chicken broth
2 tbsp each apricot jam and reduced-sodium soy sauce
1 tbsp each ketchup, grated gingerroot, and cornstarch
1 tsp sesame oil
1 clove garlic, minced
1/4 tsp crushed red pepper flakes
1 tsp olive or canola oil
4 boneless, skinless chicken breast halves, cut into thin strips
1 cup sliced red bell pepper
1 cup whole mini corncobs
1 cup sliced water chestnuts
2 cups packed, whole baby spinach leaves
1/2 cup chopped green onions
8 whole basil leaves, coarsely chopped
4 cups hot, cooked brown rice or noodles

- To make sauce, combine broth, jam, soy sauce, ketchup, gingerroot, cornstarch, sesame oil, garlic, and crushed red pepper flakes in a small bowl. Set aside.

- Heat oil in a large, non-stick wok over high heat. Add chicken. Cook and stir until chicken is no longer pink. Continue to cook until chicken is lightly browned. Add red pepper and cook for 2 more minutes. Add corncobs, water chestnuts, spinach leaves, and green onions. Cook for 3 more minutes, until spinach is wilted and corncobs are heated through. Add basil leaves and sauce. Cook and stir until sauce is bubbly and has thickened. Serve chicken and vegetables over hot rice or noodles.

Makes 4 servings

Per serving (with rice): 458 calories, 6 g fat, 1 g saturated fat, 35.2 g protein, 65.8 g carbohydrate, 7.2 g fiber, 65.8 mg cholesterol, 618.5 mg sodium % calories from fat: 12

What's in it for me?

CHICKEN WORTH PICKIN'

Mom's Famous No-Peek Chicken

Simple, creamy, chicken and rice casserole

"Look under the foil and the chicken will spoil." Or so our Mother told us. Don't ask us why. Ask our Mother!

1 can (10-3/4 oz) reduced-fat cream of celery soup, undiluted
1 can (10-3/4 oz) reduced-fat cream of mushroom soup, undiluted
1-1/2 cups skim milk
1-1/4 cups uncooked brown rice
4 whole chicken legs, skin removed
1/2 envelope dry onion soup mix

- Spray a 9 x 13-inch baking dish with non-stick spray. Set aside.
- In a medium bowl, whisk together celery soup, mushroom soup, and milk until smooth. Stir in rice. Pour rice mixture over bottom of baking dish. Arrange chicken legs over rice. Sprinkle top of chicken and rice with onion soup mix.
- Cover with foil and bake at 350° for 1-1/2 hours. DO NOT PEEK! Remove from oven and let stand for 10 minutes before serving.

Makes 4 servings

What's in it for me?

Per serving: 516 calories, 9.8 g fat, 2.8 g saturated fat, 36.3 g protein, 67.1 g carbohydrate, 3.5 g fiber, 112.8 mg cholesterol, 1236.5 mg sodium
% calories from fat: 18

The Hydrogenated Bomb

It hides in cookies, crackers, potato chips, and other snacks. In margarine, peanut butter, pastries, and sauces it takes refuge. Deep-fried foods are its sanctuary. If you care about your health—and your family's health—you'd better beware. A cholesterol-raising, artery-clogging creature is lurking beneath the surface of many popular name-brand foods. Look out! It's trans fatty acid! Trans fats are created when hydrogen is added to vegetable oil. The process, called partial hydrogenation, gives products longer shelf lives and prevents oils from breaking down and becoming rancid. Hydrogenation is what makes margarine and peanut butter spreadable. Great idea, huh? Maybe for food manufacturers, but not for your body. Studies show that trans fatty acids not only raise LDL ("bad" cholesterol), as saturated fat does, but can also lower a person's HDL ("good" cholesterol), too. That spells disaster for your arteries and heart. Let's face it, trans fatty acids can be difficult to avoid, with packaged and processed foods being so convenient and inexpensive. But don't take hydrogenation lightly. Read the label before you buy and practice moderation.

Honey, you've never asked me to go to the gym with you before!

Well, the doctor told me to start exercising with dumbbells.

The average woman goes on 15 diets in her lifetime and loses about 100 pounds. Unfortunately, she regains 125!

TRIVIAL TIDBIT

You've probably seen the ads: Electric muscle stimulators! Zap the fat but don't move an inch! Equivalent to doing 2,000 sit-ups, without even leaving the comfort of your La-Z-Boy! Sound too good to be true? That's because it is. Electric muscle stimulators pass a current through electrodes applied to your skin. (Yee-oouuch!) That causes muscles to contract. But studies show that muscle stimulators don't reduce fat. In fact, researchers have found they burn only six calories in 30 minutes! Shocking, huh? And even if they burned a lot more calories, they still wouldn't chisel the fat from the treated areas. That's because you can't spot-reduce fat. Your body doesn't selectively draw energy from fat stores in the part being zapped by electrodes. It draws on fat from all areas. Instead, try the high-voltage fat zapper that really works: a healthy, varied diet along with regular exercise. 'Cause when it comes to weight loss, if it calls for a shock then it's likely a crock!

YOU DO THE MATH

If you like to start your day with a bowl of cereal, try making a simple switch from 2% to 1% milk. You'll save almost 12,000 calories and over 900 grams of fat in a year—more than 13 days' worth of fat! (Enough to snap, crack, and pop a seam.) Remember, small changes can pay big health dividends.

On a diet? Go to the paint store. You can get thinner there.

The Thigh Who Loved Me

Easy-to-make, extra-tasty, oven-barbecued chicken thighs

As sisters and double agents, we risked life and limb to uncover the secret formula for zesty, gooey, barbecued chicken thighs. You can deliver the goods to your dinner table knowing they're sure to please a crowd. Psst! They make great leftovers, too.

3 pounds boneless, skinless chicken thighs (about 12 pieces)
3/4 cup ketchup
1/2 cup salsa
1/4 cup honey
1 tbsp Dijon mustard
1 tsp chili powder
1/2 tsp ground cumin
1 tbsp cornstarch

- Trim off any visible fat from chicken. Arrange thighs in a single layer in a 9 x 13-inch baking dish. Set aside.

- In a medium bowl, whisk together ketchup, salsa, honey, Dijon mustard, chili powder, and cumin until well blended. Pour sauce over chicken. Turn pieces to coat both sides with sauce.

- Bake, uncovered, at 400° for 45 minutes. When chicken is done, arrange thighs on a serving platter and keep warm. Pour sauce into a small saucepan, skimming off as much fat as possible. In a small bowl, mix cornstarch with 1 tablespoon water until smooth. Add to sauce. Bring to a boil, and cook until sauce thickens, stirring constantly. Pour extra sauce over chicken or serve it on the side as a dipping sauce.

Makes 4 to 6 servings

Hint: Chicken breasts or drumsticks can be used in place of thighs. If using chicken breasts, bake them for 30 minutes instead of 45.

Per serving (based on 6 servings): 287 calories, 7.3 g fat, 2 g saturated fat, 33.4 g protein, 20.1 g carbohydrate, 0.8 g fiber, 140 mg cholesterol, 586.2 mg sodium
% calories from fat: 23

What's in it for me?

Celine Dijon Chicken

Mildly flavored Dijon chicken
with a creamy herb sauce

Even if you have 13 siblings, a grandpa, and a Grammy, this *Titantilizing* dish is sure to make everyone's taste buds sing.

1 cup unsweetened apple juice
1 tbsp each Dijon mustard and
   lemon juice
1 large shallot, minced
   (see Cooking 101)
1/2 tsp dried thyme
1/4 tsp dried rosemary
1/8 tsp black pepper
2 tsp olive oil
4 boneless, skinless
   chicken breast halves
1/4 cup low-fat sour cream
1 tsp each honey and
   cornstarch

- Combine apple juice, Dijon mustard, lemon juice, shallot, thyme, rosemary, and black pepper in a small bowl. Set aside.

- Heat olive oil in a medium skillet over medium-high heat. Add chicken breasts and cook for 2 to 3 minutes on each side, until lightly browned. Add apple juice mixture. Reduce heat to medium. Simmer, covered, for 5 to 7 minutes, until chicken is no longer pink. Remove chicken from skillet and keep warm.

- Gently boil remaining liquid for 3 minutes, until slightly reduced in volume. Mix sour cream, honey, and cornstarch in a small bowl. Add to skillet. Cook and stir until sauce is bubbly and has thickened. Pour sauce over warm chicken and serve immediately.

Makes 4 servings

Shallots are mild-flavored members of the onion family, though they look like oversized cloves of garlic wrapped in thin, papery brown skins. Because of their delicate, sweet flavor, shallots are a good choice for light sauces. Dry shallots are available year-round in the produce section of your supermarket, sold in mesh bags or in bulk. Look for shallots that are plump and sprout-free. They should be stored like onions in a cool, dry, well-ventilated place. They'll keep for about a month.

Don't dine and drive! A recent survey showed that North Americans are eating more meals in cars, and that French fries, hamburgers, and chicken nuggets are the most popular choices for four-wheel diners. Maybe that's one reason that more than a third of us are overweight—one of the highest rates in the world. So, you'd better watch what you eat when you're behind the wheel...uh...figuratively speaking, that is. Keep your eyes on the road, of course.

What's in it for me?

Per serving: 203 calories, 4.4 g fat,
0.5 g saturated fat, 27.2 g protein,
11.5 g carbohydrate, 0.2 g fiber,
66.8 mg cholesterol, 188.1 mg sodium
% calories from fat: 20

People tell me not to lose weight—I might lose my personality. I tell them, "Honey, my personality ain't in my thighs."

Oprah Winfrey

SAY IT AIN'T SO!

Join the club! Just don't eat one. If you were to order a typical turkey club sandwich for lunch...oh...let's say twice a week, you'd be gobbling up a feather-ruffling 1,470 calories and 68 grams of fat! Now, don't have a bird! Just go for the Health Club: A toasted turkey sandwich with tomatoes, lettuce, and mustard has half the calories, one-fifth the fat, and just as much taste as its bacon-loaded, mayo-laced cousin.

What soft drink once contained lithium?

Down in the dumps? How about a quick pick-me-up? Try a nice refreshing bottle of Bib-Label Lithiated Lemon-Lime Soda. The soda with the antidepressant was introduced to supermarkets just before the stock market crash in 1929. (And that's no bull!) Its inventor, C.L. Griggs, shortened the soda's name to 7-Up, but he left in the lithium carbonate until the 1940s. The 7-Up name was inspired by a cattle brand that Griggs particularly liked and by the soda's seven ingredients. Today's 7-Up contains no caffeine, no artificial flavors or colors, and most importantly, no lithium.

So I sez, 'To get to the other side, Frankie Boy'

The Whole Chick and Caboodle

Simple, roasted whole chicken

You'll want to propose a toast to this succulent roast! Lotsa *cluck* to ya!

4-pound whole roasting chicken
1 tsp seasoned salt
1 tsp honey
1/2 tsp dried thyme
1/2 tsp ground cumin

- Rinse chicken well and pat dry. In a small bowl, combine seasoned salt, honey, thyme, and cumin. Using a small, sharp knife, make several slits in the chicken skin. Do not cut into meat. Using your fingers, rub chicken all over (underneath skin) with spice mixture. (Leaving the skin on during roasting keeps the chicken moist.) Use all of the spice mixture.

- Set chicken on a rack in a small roasting pan. Use the smallest roasting pan that will comfortably hold the chicken. Cover loosely with foil and roast at 400° for 45 minutes. Remove foil and continue to roast for 40 to 45 more minutes, until juices run clear.

- Before removing chicken from pan, tilt it to let juices from bird's cavity run into roasting pan. If juices are red, roast for another 5 minutes or so. Let chicken rest for 5 minutes before carving. Remove skin before serving.

Makes 4 servings

Per serving (white and dark meat): 187 calories, 6.1 g fat, 1.6 g saturated fat, 29.6 g protein, 1.8 g carbohydrate, 0.1 g fiber, 86.8 mg cholesterol, 402.5 mg sodium
% calories from fat: 30

What's in it for me?

What do you get when you throw a grenade into a kitchen in France? Linoleum Blown-apart.

One Flew Over the Couscous Nest

Malaysian chicken and sweet-potato stew on a bed of couscous

Tired of the same old dinnertime fare? Spice things up with this uniquely flavored chicken stew. It's as good as it gets!

1 tsp olive oil
4 boneless, skinless chicken breast halves, cut into 1-inch cubes
1 tbsp grated gingerroot
2 cloves garlic, minced
1 cup each chopped onions and chopped red bell pepper
1 tsp each ground coriander and curry powder
1/2 tsp ground cumin
1/4 tsp cinnamon
1-1/2 cups low-sodium, low-fat chicken broth
3 cups peeled, cubed sweet potatoes
1 cup couscous (see Cooking 101)
2 tbsp frozen orange juice concentrate, thawed
3/4 cup light coconut milk
2 tbsp each cornstarch and chopped, fresh cilantro

- Heat olive oil in a large, non-stick saucepan over medium-high heat. Add chicken, gingerroot, and garlic. Cook and stir until chicken is no longer pink. Add onions and red pepper and cook for 3 more minutes. Stir in coriander, curry powder, cumin, and cinnamon. Cook for 1 more minute. Add broth and sweet potatoes. Bring to a boil. Reduce heat to medium-low. Cover and simmer for 12 minutes, or until potatoes are tender.

- Meanwhile, prepare couscous. In a medium bowl, combine couscous and orange juice concentrate. Pour 1 cup boiling water over couscous and mix well. Cover and set aside until liquid is absorbed, about 5 minutes.

- Combine coconut milk and cornstarch until smooth. Add to chicken and vegetables, along with cilantro. Increase heat to medium-high and cook until stew is bubbly and has thickened.

- Fluff couscous with a fork. Make a "nest" of couscous in individual serving bowls. Ladle stew over top. Serve immediately.

Makes 4 servings

What's in it for me?

Per serving: 531 calories, 6.4 g fat, 2.2 g saturated fat, 42.6 g protein, 74.3 g carbohydrate, 7.3 g fiber, 82.2 mg cholesterol, 555.9 mg sodium
% calories from fat: 11

Couscous is a tiny pasta of North African origin. It doesn't have a lot of flavor on its own, but can be dressed up in a salad, sweetened and mixed with fruits as a dessert, or piled high with a savory stew, as in this recipe. It takes less than 10 minutes to cook and comes in white or whole wheat varieties. It's often classified as a grain, not a pasta, so you're likely to find it near the rice at your grocery store.

THE E FILES

C'mon, baby! Do the locomotion! If you love to boogie, you're making great strides toward a longer, healthier life. That's because dancing is a far-out fatburner, a magnificent muscle toner, and a hip-hop heart helper. Vigorous dancing burns upwards of 400 calories an hour and elevates your heart rate as much as running or cross-country skiing. Even moderate ballroom dancing burns about 250 calories an hour. Maybe that's why folks all over the map are dancing to their heart's content: There's the waltz in Tennessee, the polka in Pennsylvania, the last tango in Paris, and the cha-cha in Chattanooga. Um, excuse the jive talking...that's choo choo. Even square dancing qualifies as a top-notch aerobic activity. In fact, it's been estimated that square dancers often travel as far as three miles a night. (You'd think they could find a closer hall.) Swing yer partner round and round, get your heart rate up and your fat way down!

You can't plow a field by turning it over in your mind.

Adventures in Food

From now on, every time you grocery shop, embark on a shopping safari! Wallet in hand, set out to explore the unknown depths of your supermarket shelves. Bravely venture into uncharted territory and search for one new fruit, vegetable, grain, or legume to add to your cart. Your local supermarket probably offers a vast array of foods you've never heard of, let alone eaten. Buy some of them, then take them home and figure out what to do with them. (Sounds like fun, huh?) There's a world of exotic choices to replace these old, tired standbys. And any new fruit or vegetable is bound to be a boon to your diet, right? The key is to think opportunity, not oppression. For every food you're better off without, there's a new, healthy one just waiting to be discovered!

♪ One of these things is not like the others. One of these things is not the same. ♫

TRIVIAL TIDBIT

According to an old wives' tale, cumin is said to inspire fidelity in men. In Europe, when young men went off to war, their sweethearts would bake bread sprinkled with cumin seeds to send with them. The soldier would return faithful and full-bellied, thanks to his wife's *doughnation* to the war cause.

Sesame Sweet Chicken

Oriental, grilled chicken thighs basted with a sticky, sweet sesame sauce

Can you tell me how you get, how you get your chicken so sweet? These grilled chicken thighs are as easy as 1-2-3. Feeding the whole street? Don't be a grouch—it's a big bird!

3 pounds skinless chicken thighs (about 12 pieces)
1/2 cup hoisin sauce (see p. 111)
1/4 cup honey
3 tbsp lime juice
2 tbsp reduced-sodium soy sauce
1 tbsp grated gingerroot
1 tbsp toasted sesame seeds (see tip below)
1/2 tsp each ground cumin and paprika

- Arrange chicken pieces in a shallow glass dish. Combine all remaining ingredients in a small bowl and pour over chicken. Turn pieces to coat both sides with marinade. Cover with plastic wrap and marinate in the refrigerator for 1 hour. (You can marinate chicken overnight if you have the time.)

- Prepare grill. Remove chicken pieces from marinade and grill over medium-hot coals for about 10 minutes per side. Be careful not to burn them. Brush frequently with extra marinade. Serve hot.

Makes 6 servings

Tip: To toast sesame seeds, place them in a small skillet over medium heat. Cook until seeds turn golden brown, shaking pan frequently. Cool before using.

Per serving: 256 calories, 6.8 g fat,
1.6 g saturated fat, 28.5 g protein,
18.8 g carbohydrate, 0.8 g fiber,
115.2 mg cholesterol, 665.6 mg sodium
% calories from fat: 24

What's in it for me?

He who eat too much sweet, have too much seat.

I Got Stew, Babe

Chicken stew with balsamic roasted vegetables

Stew that's so irresistibly savory, you'll want to Cher it with everyone!

**4 cups unpeeled, cubed
   red potatoes**
2 cups whole baby carrots
1 cup chopped red onions
2 tbsp balsamic vinegar
1 tbsp olive oil
1 clove garlic, minced
1-1/2 tsp dried thyme
1-1/2 tsp dried rosemary
1 tsp dried tarragon
1/2 tsp each salt and black pepper
1 cup sliced green beans
1/2 cup dry white wine
**6 boneless, skinless chicken breast halves,
   cut into 1-inch cubes**
3 cups low-sodium, low-fat chicken broth
3 tbsp all-purpose flour

- Spray a large roasting pan with non-stick spray. Add potatoes, carrots, onions, vinegar, oil, garlic, 1 teaspoon thyme, 1 teaspoon rosemary, tarragon, salt, and pepper. Mix well. Roast, uncovered, at 425° for 30 minutes. Stir once, halfway through cooking time. Add green beans and roast for 10 more minutes.

- Meanwhile, pour wine into a large saucepan. Add remaining 1/2 teaspoon thyme and 1/2 teaspoon rosemary. Bring to a boil. Add chicken pieces and reduce heat to medium-high. Cook, uncovered, until chicken is cooked through, about 12 minutes.

- Add roasted vegetables to chicken and wine. Stir in 2-1/2 cups of broth. In a small bowl combine flour with remaining 1/2 cup broth and stir until lump-free. Add flour mixture to chicken and vegetables. Cook until stew is bubbly and has thickened, about 3 minutes. Serve hot.

Makes 6 servings

What's in it for me?

Per serving: 298 calories, 4.6 g fat,
0.5 g saturated fat, 31 g protein,
29.5 g carbohydrate, 3.8 g fiber,
65.8 mg cholesterol, 362 mg sodium
% calories from fat: 15

The cholesterol content of chicken is similar to that of beef.

FAT OR FICTION?

All animal meat products have 20 to 25 milligrams of cholesterol per ounce. So, a three-and-a-half-ounce serving of chicken breast (with or without skin) has about 75 milligrams, 25% of the recommended daily intake of 300 milligrams and only slightly less than a similar serving of beef. The good news for poultry lovers: The fat in chicken is highly monounsaturated, while the fat in red meat is highly saturated. However, eating chicken skin doubles your trouble, more than doubling the amount of saturated and total fat. And as most people know, white meat is lower in fat than dark meat. So, breast is best, but sometimes it's OK to be a leg man!

YOU DO THE MATH

There's no need to pig out at breakfast when you can substitute lean Canadian bacon for the regular high-fat kind. Switching from a two-ounce serving of regular bacon to a two-ounce serving of Canadian bacon once a week will save you an astonishing 11,440 calories and 1,196 grams of fat in a year. That's more than 17 days' worth of fat! A simple swap can make a *pig* difference.

If it's called a fast, why does it go so darn slow?

Lemon zest is the yellow, outermost skin layer of a lemon. The oil in the zest gives a distinctive lemon taste and scent to all sorts of dishes. To grate lemon zest, first wash the lemon well, then rub it against the small holes of a cheese grater. Avoid grating the white pith beneath the skin, since it's quite bitter.

Chicks on Sticks

Fragrant chicken skewers in an Asian marinade

Let's hear it for these flavorful, marinated chicken cubes grilled to perfection. Chick-chick-hooray!

You're too busy to exercise. Or too out of shape. Or your (pick one) knees, back, hips, or feet hurt. You have children to care for, increasing job demands, house chores, and obligations to friends and to the community. But are those the things that really get in the way of exercise, or is it more likely to be what's happening on TV? How about swapping 30 minutes of TV-watching for 30 minutes of walking? Hey, it's just one lousy sitcom, and most likely a rerun, anyway. Once and for all, it's time to put an end to the intimate, Velcro-like affair you've had going with your sofa. Yes, breaking up is hard to do, but you can begin severing ties by jumping to your feet during commercials (without heading for the kitchen!). Don't sit if you can stand. Don't stand if you can walk. If all of your previous attempts at fitting exercise into your oh-so-busy schedule have failed, perhaps you should ask yourself: TV or not TV? That is the question.

2 tbsp each reduced-sodium soy sauce and brown sugar

1 tbsp each olive oil and grated lemon zest (see Cooking 101)

2 cloves garlic, minced

1 large shallot, minced

1-1/2 tsp grated gingerroot

1 tsp each ground cumin and ground coriander

4 boneless, skinless chicken breast halves, cut into 1-inch cubes

8 wooden or metal skewers

- To make marinade, combine all ingredients except chicken in a small bowl. Pour marinade over chicken pieces in a large, heavy-duty, resealable plastic bag. Make sure all pieces are coated with marinade. Marinate overnight in the refrigerator.

- If using wooden skewers, soak them in water for at least 20 minutes before using to prevent burning. Prepare grill. Thread chicken cubes onto skewers. Grill for 4 to 5 minutes per side, turning often. (If you prefer, cook chicken under the broiler, 4 inches from heat, for about 4 minutes per side.) Serve immediately. You can dip chicken pieces in plum sauce (see p. 21), or eat them just as they are.

Makes 8 skewers, 4 servings

Per serving: 225 calories, 5.6 g fat, 0.5 g saturated fat, 33.6 g protein, 8.8 g carbohydrate, 0.6 g fiber, 82.3 mg cholesterol, 399.4 mg sodium % calories from fat: 23

What's in it for me?

The dentist told me I grind my teeth at night. So, now before I go to sleep, I fill my mouth with hot water and coffee beans and set my alarm for 7:30.

Do Re Mi Fa So La-sagna

Layers of roasted chicken with creamy ricotta and spinach filling

Yo! It's here. It's really here. Yay! It's full of chicken, yum! Me. I eat it all myself...OK. You get the drift. Our chicken lasagna is Do Re Mi Fa Sooo delicious!

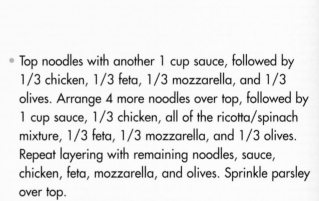

1 cup part-skim ricotta cheese
3/4 cup low-fat (1%) cottage cheese
1/2 pkg (5 oz) frozen spinach, thawed,
  squeezed dry, and chopped
1 egg white
1/2 tsp dried oregano
12 lasagna noodles, uncooked
1 small, store-bought, whole roasted chicken
  (about 2 pounds net weight)
4 cups low-fat, chunky vegetable pasta sauce
1 cup crumbled light feta cheese (4 oz)
1-1/2 cups shredded, part-skim
  mozzarella cheese (6 oz)
1/4 cup chopped black olives
1/4 cup chopped, fresh parsley

- In a medium bowl, combine ricotta cheese, cottage cheese, spinach, egg white, and oregano. Cover and refrigerate until ready to use.

- Prepare lasagna noodles according to package directions. Drain. Rinse with cold water and drain again. While noodles are boiling, remove skin from chicken and chop meat into bite-sized pieces. You should end up with roughly 3-1/2 cups chicken. Set aside.

- Spray a 9 x 13-inch baking pan with non-stick spray. To assemble lasagna, spoon 1 cup sauce over bottom of pan. Arrange 4 lasagna noodles, 3 lengthwise and 1 crosswise, over sauce.

- Top noodles with another 1 cup sauce, followed by 1/3 chicken, 1/3 feta, 1/3 mozzarella, and 1/3 olives. Arrange 4 more noodles over top, followed by 1 cup sauce, 1/3 chicken, all of the ricotta/spinach mixture, 1/3 feta, 1/3 mozzarella, and 1/3 olives. Repeat layering with remaining noodles, sauce, chicken, feta, mozzarella, and olives. Sprinkle parsley over top.

- Cover loosely with foil and bake at 375° for 45 minutes. Remove foil for last 5 minutes of baking time. Let cool for 10 minutes before serving.

Makes 8 servings

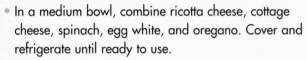

What's in it for us?

Per serving: 467 calories, 12.1 g fat, 5 g saturated fat, 43.4 g protein, 43.9 g carbohydrate, 0.6 g fiber, 87.8 mg cholesterol, 727.7 mg sodium
% calories from fat: 24

Did you hear about the man who used counterfeit money to pay his lunch bill? He had been served decaffeinated coffee with non-dairy creamer and artificial sweetener.

Grill of a Lifetime

Grilled chicken breasts in a mango-curry marinade

At one time, kings were fearful of being poisoned by their cooks, so it was vital that their food be prepared only by a trusted member of the royal household. When the chef had proved his worth, a *toque blanche* was placed on his head. The hat's pleats represented the vertical bars of the monarch's golden crown. Legend says the tall hat was originally designed to keep the head cool, but modern cooks say that's just a lot of hot air.

These zesty grilled chicken breasts earned top-flavor honors at the annual Spice Grill competition. Ginger Spice failed to make an appearance.

4 boneless, skinless chicken breast halves
1/3 cup mango chutney (see p. 29)
3 tbsp honey
2 tbsp lemon juice
1 tbsp reduced-sodium soy sauce
1 tsp curry powder
1/2 tsp ground cumin

- Arrange chicken breasts in a glass baking dish. Combine remaining ingredients in a small bowl and pour over chicken. Turn pieces to coat both sides with marinade. Cover and marinate in the refrigerator for 1 hour.

- Prepare grill. Remove chicken from marinade and grill over medium-hot coals for about 5 minutes per side, until chicken is no longer pink. Baste often with leftover marinade. Serve immediately.

Makes 4 servings

Per serving: 263 calories, 2.6 g fat, 0.5 g saturated fat, 33.2 g protein, 25.8 g carbohydrate, 0.2 g fiber, 82.2 mg cholesterol, 802.1 mg sodium
% calories from fat: 9

What's in it for me?

Don't Get Waisted

If you're wondering where those love handles came from, ever consider the possibility that more weight could be accumulating from booze than from burgers? Here's proof: Research has shown that meals consumed with alcohol may contain 350 to 500 more calories than those consumed without. Plus, alcohol, although fat-free, has almost twice as many calories per gram as carbohydrates and protein. In addition to the calorie wallop, drinking also whittles away at your ability to control your eating. It's been shown that diners spend nearly three times longer at the table when they're drinking. Here's the last call on alcohol: Two or more drinks at one sitting can dramatically increase insulin levels, shifting your body's fat-forming processes into overdrive and reducing its ability to burn fat by about one-third. One-third! Holy Brown Cow!

BUTTWIDER BEER

TRIVIAL TIDBIT

The number of taste buds and the way they're distributed in the mouth is different from person to person. This may explain the discriminating palates of some, but it doesn't offer an explanation for poor taste.

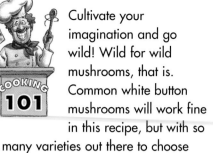

Barbecutie Patootie Chicken Pizza

Hungry-man pizza that's perfect for your next party

Our pizza has pizazz! Make this tasty pizza-pie for your cutie-pie when he's in a *fowl* mood.

1/4 cup barbecue sauce
1/4 cup pizza sauce
2 boneless, skinless chicken breast halves
2 cups sliced mixed mushrooms (see Cooking 101)
1 medium red onion, sliced thinly into rings
1/2 tsp dried oregano
1 12-inch unbaked pizza crust (see hint below)
1 cup shredded, reduced-fat Monterey Jack cheese (4 oz)
1 to 2 tbsp chopped, fresh cilantro or parsley

- Combine 2 tablespoons barbecue sauce with pizza sauce in a small bowl. Set aside.

- Grill chicken breasts over medium-hot coals for about 5 minutes per side, until juices run clear and chicken is no longer pink inside. Brush generously with remaining barbecue sauce during cooking. Remove from grill and let cool slightly. Slice into thin strips and set aside.

- Spray a medium, non-stick skillet or wok with non-stick spray. Add mushrooms and onions. Cook over medium-high heat until vegetables are tender, about 5 to 6 minutes. Add oregano and cook for 1 more minute. Remove from heat.

- Spread sauce evenly over unbaked pizza crust. Top with mushroom-onion mixture, followed by chicken. Sprinkle with cheese and cilantro. Bake at 450° for 13 to 14 minutes, until crust is lightly browned and cheese is melted. Serve immediately.

Makes one 12-inch pizza, 6 large slices

Hint: If using a store-bought, pre-cooked pizza shell, reduce baking time by 4 minutes.

What's in it for me?

Per slice: 244 calories, 6.7 g fat,
2.4 g saturated fat, 17.8 g protein,
28.2 g carbohydrate, 2 g fiber,
34.6 mg cholesterol, 547.4 mg sodium
% calories from fat: 25

COOKING 101

Cultivate your imagination and go wild! Wild for wild mushrooms, that is. Common white button mushrooms will work fine in this recipe, but with so many varieties out there to choose from, why not have a little *fungus* and try something new? Look for fresh Japanese shiitake mushrooms next time you're at the supermarket. When cooked, they're meaty and silky with a woodsy flavor. They have tough stems, however, which need to be removed completely before cooking. Or how about some cremini mushrooms? They're a dark brown, slightly firmer variation of the everyday white mushroom, with a fuller flavor, too. (The extremely large portobello is just a fully matured cremini mushroom.) Then there's the white, fan-shaped oyster mushroom, with its chewy texture and mild flavor. The young, small ones (one-and-a-half-inch diameter) are considered best. Try the different varieties of mushrooms alone or in combination to give our delectable chicken pizza maximum mushroom taste.

Where did the chicken go on her vacation? Sandy Eggo.

Fishful Thinking

Seafood dishes for those who love fishes

Salmon and Dillilah

Baked shell pasta with salmon in a lemon-dill sauce

If preparing dinner for the kids is a hair-raising experience, and you can barely muster the strength to cook for a finicky family, then this baked pasta entree is the perfect mealtime solution.

12 oz medium shell pasta, uncooked (about 5 cups dry)
1 can (10-3/4 oz) reduced-fat cream of chicken soup, undiluted
3/4 cup 1% milk
3/4 cup shredded, reduced-fat Swiss cheese (3 oz)
1-1/2 tbsp chopped, fresh dill
2 tsp grated lemon zest
1/2 tsp dry mustard powder
1/4 tsp black pepper
1 can (7-1/2 oz) skinless, water-packed pink salmon, drained
1 tbsp each grated Parmesan cheese and chopped, fresh parsley

Now, if I only had the strength to get up!

- Cook shells according to package directions. Drain. Rinse with cold water and drain again. Set aside.

- In a large saucepan, combine soup, milk, cheese, dill, lemon zest, mustard powder, and black pepper. Cook over medium-high heat until cheese is melted. Stir in salmon. Remove from heat. Add pasta shells to sauce in pot and mix well.

- Spray a 2-quart casserole dish with non-stick spray. Add shells and sauce and spread evenly. Sprinkle with Parmesan cheese and parsley. Cover with foil and bake at 350° for 20 minutes. Remove foil and bake for 5 more minutes. Stir before serving.

Makes 4 to 6 servings

Hint: Instead of canned salmon, you can use chopped, cooked salmon steaks or fillets.

What's in it for me?

Per serving (based on 6 servings): 343 calories, 6.1 g fat, 2.9 g saturated fat, 20.2 g protein, 48.5 g carbohydrate, 1.1 g fiber, 23.6 mg cholesterol, 445.9 mg sodium
% calories from fat: 17

Who'da Thunk?

What fish's name means "leaper"?

The Romans called salmon "salmo," which means "leaper." But salmon was a staple of man's diet well before Roman times. As long as 10,000 years ago, an unknown caveman carved a picture of a salmon on a reindeer bone. Back then, man probably caught salmon the way bears did—by snatching them out of the water as they swam upstream to spawn. Salmon is leaps and bounds ahead of most other animal sources of protein. It contains all the essential amino acids, it's high in calcium, and it's low in saturated fat and calories. Best of all, its oils are swimming with omega-3 fatty acids. Despite the old "fat is bad" rule, these fatty acids are good for you. They help lower cholesterol and reduce the risk of heart disease. So, it's a good idea to get hooked on salmon.

Here's some girth-shattering news for those of you who thought that carob was a low-fat, healthy alternative to chocolate. Carob is made from the sweet, edible pulp of a Mediterranean tree pod. Once the pulp is dried, it's ground into a powder and used to flavor baked goods and candies. Sounds innocent enough, don't you think? Yet a measly ounce of plain carob has a surprising 153 calories and 8.9 grams of fat. Compare that to milk chocolate's 145 calories and 8.7 grams of fat per ounce. The worst news: 92% of carob's fat grams are saturated. Obviously, if you *carobout* your heart, you'd better not overindulge.

To minimize moisture loss when grilling, baking, or sautéing fish, it's important to use a relatively high heat and cook the fish for a short time. When you cook fish longer than necessary, the juices and flavors are lost, leaving the fish dry and chewy. Plus, overcooked fish is prone to falling apart.

Don't eat this. Cut back on that. So much of the weight-loss process involves limiting or cutting out. But exercise is the exception—the more you get up and move, the more you're doing your body some good. Being active not only produces tremendous physical gains, but it also leads to dramatic psychological benefits. And we're not just talking about a runner's high or an endorphin buzz, either. Exercise can relieve depression, anxiety, and stress, improve self-esteem, and better your outlook on life in general. Think about how great you feel when someone compliments the way you look, or when you slip into the jeans that haven't fit for years. When it comes to exercise, it's OK to have the urge to splurge!

Just for the Halibut

Baked halibut steaks topped with tomatoes, zucchini, and feta

Put some fish on your dish! When you pop these simple but sensational halibut steaks into the oven, you'll be waiting with *baited* breath for them to cook.

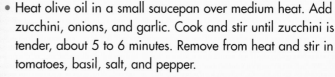

Why did the fisherman cross the ocean?

1 tsp olive oil
1 cup diced zucchini
1/2 cup minced onions
1 clove garlic, minced
2 cups diced tomatoes
2 tbsp chopped, fresh basil leaves
1/4 tsp each salt and black pepper
4 halibut steaks, about 5 to 6 oz each
1/3 cup crumbled feta cheese

- Heat olive oil in a small saucepan over medium heat. Add zucchini, onions, and garlic. Cook and stir until zucchini is tender, about 5 to 6 minutes. Remove from heat and stir in tomatoes, basil, salt, and pepper.

- Rinse fish steaks and pat dry with paper towels. Spray a medium baking pan with non-stick spray and place fish in pan. Spoon 1/4 tomato-zucchini mixture over each fish steak. Top with feta cheese. Bake at 450° for 12 to 15 minutes, depending on thickness of fish. Serve immediately.

Makes 4 servings

Per serving: 276 calories, 8.4 g fat, 2.5 g saturated fat, 41.2 g protein, 8.2 g carbohydrate, 2 g fiber, 69.1 mg cholesterol, 391.6 mg sodium
% calories from fat: 28

What's in it for me?

Tip for eating on the road: Bring a tablecloth and watch out for speeding cars!

FISHFUL THINKING

Cod Up in the Moment

Breaded fish sticks with tartar sauce

Coddle your taste buds with these breaded fish sticks—you'll fall for them hook, line, and sinker.

Tartar Sauce

1/2 cup low-fat mayonnaise
1 tbsp minced, fresh dill, or 1 tsp dried
1 tbsp sweet green relish
2 tsp each prepared horseradish and lemon juice

2/3 cup unseasoned, dry bread crumbs
3 tbsp grated Parmesan cheese
1 tbsp chopped, fresh parsley
3/4 tsp dried thyme
1/2 tsp paprika
1/4 tsp each salt and black pepper
3 egg whites
1-1/2 pounds cod fillets, at least 1/2-inch thick
6 lemon wedges (optional)

- To make tartar sauce, combine mayonnaise, dill, relish, horseradish, and lemon juice in a small bowl. Refrigerate until ready to use.

- In a shallow bowl, combine bread crumbs, Parmesan cheese, parsley, thyme, paprika, salt, and pepper. Lightly beat egg whites in another shallow bowl. Spray a baking sheet with non-stick spray and set aside.

- Rinse fish and pat dry with paper towels. Cut fish into thick strips. Working one at a time, dip pieces in egg whites, then in crumb mixture, coating both sides with crumbs. Place on baking sheet. Allow some space between pieces.

- Bake at 450° for 8 to 10 minutes, depending on thickness of fish. Fish is ready when it flakes easily with a fork. Serve with tartar sauce and lemon wedges, if desired.

Makes 6 servings

What's in it for me?

Per serving: 203 calories, 2.7 g fat, 0.6 g saturated fat, 30.7 g protein, 15.3 g carbohydrate, 0.9 g fiber, 55.3 mg cholesterol, 578.1 mg sodium
% calories from fat: 12

The only way to lose weight is to eat less.

FAT OR **FICTION?**

Actually, you may be doing your body a favor by pumping up the volume—of the right foods, that is. Which snack would you consider the superior hunger-quencher: a puny handful of peanuts or six cups of low-fat microwave popcorn? Both have roughly 150 calories, but the big differences are in the portion size and the amount of fat and fiber. The peanuts have 14 grams of fat and register a big goose egg on the fiber meter. The popcorn, on the other hand, contains six grams of fat and six grams of fiber, making it the unanimous fiber-grammy award winner. The popcorn is also more likely to fill you up, so you'll probably consume fewer calories over the course of the day than if you popped down the paltry portion of peanuts. Gram for gram, fat has more than twice as many calories as carbohydrates and protein. Translation: A little bit of fat goes a long *weigh*!

YOU DO THE MATH

Having a *Gouda* day? It seems that everyone likes one kind of cheese or another. But if you're trying to lose weight, you need to play your *curds* right. If you trade two ounces of regular cheddar cheese for two ounces of the reduced-fat variety once a week, you'll save 3,120 calories and 416 grams of fat in a year. That's more than six days' worth of fat! If you skim down on cheese, you won't be too big for your *brieches*.

What the heck is hoisin sauce and where can I buy it?

Hoisin sauce is a thick, sweet, and spicy sauce used widely in Chinese cooking. It's made from a mixture of soybeans, garlic, chili peppers, and various spices. Look for it in a jar in the Oriental-food aisle of your grocery store. It'll keep for about one year in your refrigerator.

Twinkie, Twinkie, Little Star

After dieting for a while, you can get obsessed with the idea of eating. Ever try singing to take your mind off food? Go ahead. Try it. *Gumdrops keep fallin' on my head...Ain't nothin' but a hot dog... The farmer in the deli...* It just doesn't work. And dieting doesn't work, either—in fact, diets stink. They're unrealistic and temporary, putting us in a voluntary state of famine. Funny that we'd starve ourselves to death, hoping we'll live longer. And how about those diet programs with the boot-camp mentality? You know, they say you have to eat their food, they tell you what time of day to eat it, and that you have to eat all of it. This isn't a diet, it's living with your parents! No wonder 95% of diets fail. It's time to forget about dieting and get on with living! Changing your eating habits doesn't always mean eating less, it means eating better. Now that's something to sing about.

HOW CAN YOU BE GAINING WEIGHT? YOU EAT NECKS TO NOTHING!

Tuna Turner

Grilled tuna steaks with a tropical fruit marinade

What's lime got to do, got to do with it? Well, lime is *diva-vine*—especially when it's grouped with tropical friends. These grilled tuna steaks are sure to top the flavor charts!

1/2 cup mixed tropical fruit jam
   (a pineapple-mango-orange combination works well)
1/4 cup hoisin sauce (see tip in margin)
2 tbsp lime juice
1 tbsp chopped, fresh cilantro
1 tsp grated gingerroot
1 tsp sesame oil
4 tuna steaks, about 6 oz each and 1-inch thick

- To prepare marinade, combine jam, hoisin sauce, lime juice, cilantro, gingerroot, and sesame oil in a small bowl. Stir well.

- Rinse tuna steaks and pat dry with paper towels. Arrange steaks in a glass baking dish. Pour marinade over fish. Turn pieces to coat both sides. Cover with plastic wrap and refrigerate for 1 hour.

- Brush grill with a little oil to prevent fish from sticking. Heat to medium-high. Grill steaks for 4 to 5 minutes per side. Baste with extra marinade during cooking. Be careful not to overcook. Tuna should be lightly browned on outside, but still slightly pink in middle. (Overcooked tuna is very dry, so pay attention!) Serve immediately.

Makes 4 servings

Per serving: 336 calories, 3.3 g fat, 0.7 g saturated fat, 40.4 g protein, 31.8 g carbohydrate, 0.5 g fiber, 77 mg cholesterol, 321.6 mg sodium % calories from fat: 9

What's in it for me?

Can you tell me how to get to Sesame Street? Just look for the golden arches. McDonald's sprinkles a total of 2,500 tons of sesame seeds on its buns over the course of a year.

TRIVIAL TIDBIT

Hootie and the Swordfish

Grilled swordfish steaks with a cucumber and cantaloupe relish

If your family usually doesn't give a hootie about eating fish, this easy-to-prepare and mildly flavored recipe will make them hoot and holler for more.

Cucumber and Cantaloupe Relish

1 cup peeled, seeded, and diced cucumber

1 cup diced cantaloupe

1/4 cup each chopped green onions and minced red bell pepper

2 tbsp seasoned rice vinegar

2 tsp sugar

1/2 tsp salt

1/8 tsp black pepper

1 tbsp each honey and lime juice

1 tsp canola oil

4 swordfish steaks, about 6 oz each and 1-inch thick

- Combine all relish ingredients in a medium bowl. Cover and refrigerate until ready to use.
- Prepare grill. Combine honey and lime juice in a small bowl. Set aside. Lightly brush swordfish steaks on both sides with oil. Grill for 4 to 5 minutes per side, until fish flakes easily with a fork. Brush fish with honey-lime mixture several times during cooking. Serve fish topped with cool relish.

Makes 4 servings

What's in it for me?

Per serving: 277 calories, 8.6 g fat, 2 g saturated fat, 36.8 g protein, 11.9 g carbohydrate, 0.9 g fiber, 70.9 mg cholesterol, 459.7 mg sodium % calories from fat: 29

French fries account for a whopping 25% of all vegetables consumed by Americans.

TRIVIAL TIDBIT

SAY IT AIN'T SO!

They're armed and dangerous! Fried, breaded calamari—a popular item on menus everywhere—is cooked in enough oil to make Exxon jealous. A typical, three-cup serving has 70 grams of fat—more than three large orders of French fries! You already know that fatty cuts of beef and fat-filled butter normally make a beeline for your arteries, but you just don't expect that kind of behavior from seafood. And that's just the appetizer! What are you having for your main course?

A Full Plate at Home Plate

Take me out to the ball game,
Take away my restraint,
Buy me some hot dogs and
    fattening snacks,
I don't care if I fit in my slacks,
It's just eat, eat, eat, for the whole game,
I'm feeling sick—what a shame,
I've gained one, two, three extra pounds,
At the old ball game.

You'll have to admit, the snacks at stadium concession stands don't exactly qualify as health foods. But what's a ball game without a hot dog and a beer? It's not like they're going to blow your dietary record in the long run, especially if you keep the following two tips in mind: (1) Sometimes a single is better than a triple. Do you really need that second or third slice of pizza? Why not opt for one of those big, baked pretzels or unbuttered popcorn when hunger strikes? (2) You don't have to get loaded just because the bases are. When your friend declares, "We sure could use a new pitcher," do you head straight for the draft taps? Downing three jugs of beer might increase your *chugging* percentage, but it won't help your waistline. A wiser choice would be bottled water, diet soda, or some fruit juice.

You'll have to can the canned tuna for this recipe and pick up some fresh tuna steaks at the fish counter instead. Fresh tuna has a firm-textured, rich-flavored flesh—perfect for making burgers! Refrigerating the fish before forming it into patties helps hold it together. When barbecuing fish burgers, you may need to brush a light coating of oil on the grill to prevent them from sticking.

Who'da Thunk?

Why do we say someone "drinks like a fish"?

There's something fishy going on here, because fish don't actually drink water. Most of the water they appear to be drinking while swimming is actually passing through their gills to supply them with oxygen. But they certainly do seem to be drinking continually, as many fish swim with their mouths open. That's how the idiom "drinks like a fish" came to mean someone who drinks excessively, especially alcohol.

My dentist told me I had too much tartar, so I asked him what he recommended. He said 'fish sticks.'

Low-Fatty Patties

These tender, Thai tuna patties make tasty, unique burgers

Patty-cake, patty-cake, here's the plan: Grill me a burger as fast as you can! Pull your *patty-o-chair* up to the *patty-o-table* and dig in.

1-1/2 pounds fresh tuna steaks (see Cooking 101)
1/2 cup unseasoned, dry bread crumbs
1/4 cup each minced green onions and grated carrots
1 tbsp each reduced-sodium soy sauce, ketchup, grated gingerroot, and chopped, fresh cilantro
1 egg
1 tsp sesame oil
1/2 tsp ground cumin
1/4 tsp each salt and black pepper
6 hamburger rolls
Lettuce, sliced tomatoes, and your favorite burger toppings (optional)

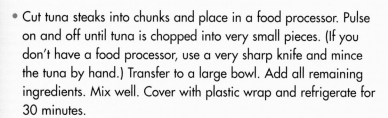

• Cut tuna steaks into chunks and place in a food processor. Pulse on and off until tuna is chopped into very small pieces. (If you don't have a food processor, use a very sharp knife and mince the tuna by hand.) Transfer to a large bowl. Add all remaining ingredients. Mix well. Cover with plastic wrap and refrigerate for 30 minutes.

• Form mixture into 6 patties, about 1/2-inch thick. Grill or broil patties for about 4 minutes per side, until cooked through. Be careful not to overcook. Serve on hamburger rolls with low-fat burger toppings such as lettuce, tomatoes, honey mustard, and ketchup.

Makes 6 burgers

Hint: Try these burgers topped with Sammy Salsa (p. 134).

Per burger: 338 calories, 9.5 g fat, 1.7 g saturated fat, 32.2 g protein, 29.4 g carbohydrate, 1.6 g fiber, 77.5 mg cholesterol, 580.3 mg sodium % calories from fat: 26

What's in it for me?

FISHFUL THINKING

Nouveau Quiche

Crustless crab and mushroom quiche

If you like living on easy street, this rich-tasting crab quiche is as simple as it gets. And when you have the good fortune to sample it, you'll see it's loaded with flavor.

3 cups sliced mushrooms
1 cup each diced onions
  and diced red bell
  pepper
2 cloves garlic,
  minced
1-1/2 cups fat-free
  egg substitute
3/4 cup evaporated 2% milk
1/4 cup grated Parmesan cheese
1/2 tsp dry mustard powder
1/4 tsp each salt and black pepper
8 oz canned, fresh, or frozen lump crabmeat
  (see note below)
3/4 cup shredded, reduced-fat sharp cheddar cheese (3 oz)
1/4 cup chopped green onions

- Spray a large, non-stick saucepan with non-stick spray. Add mushrooms, onions, red pepper, and garlic. Cook and stir over medium heat until vegetables are tender, about 6 to 7 minutes. Remove from heat and let cool slightly.

- In a large bowl, whisk together egg substitute, milk, Parmesan cheese, mustard powder, salt, and pepper. Stir in crabmeat, mushroom mixture, cheddar cheese, and green onions. Pour into a 9-inch deep-dish quiche pan or pie plate that has been sprayed with non-stick spray.

- Bake quiche at 350° for 40 to 45 minutes, until firm to touch. Let stand 10 minutes before slicing.

Makes 6 servings

Note: If using canned crabmeat, drain well before adding to other ingredients. Thaw frozen crabmeat before using.

What's in it for me? →

Per serving: 160 calories, 5 g fat, 2.8 g saturated fat, 20.1 g protein, 9.5 g carbohydrate, 1.6 g fiber, 48.6 mg cholesterol, 490.5 mg sodium
% calories from fat: 27

Fish and guests smell after three days.

Ben Franklin

FAT OR FICTION?

If you're trying to speed up weight loss, then fasting is the ticket.

Starvin' Marvins take note: Fasting is not the answer to controlling weight. Not only does it deprive your body of the nutrients and energy it needs for normal functioning, but also most of the weight you lose during a fast is actually water. This occurs as your body rids itself of ketones, the substances that your body turns to for energy when its number-one source of fuel—carbohydrates—isn't available. This process of metabolizing ketones can also lead to dehydration. Other side effects include dizziness, loss of muscle mass, irregular heartbeat, dangerously low blood pressure, and even bad breath! If that doesn't leave a sour taste in your mouth, then this will: Fasting causes your body to slam the brakes on its metabolic rate to prevent what it thinks is imminent starvation. So, when you start to eat again, that sluggish metabolism will make it easier to gain weight, even if you're eating less. See! Pulling a fast one on your body actually slows it down!

Would you like your eggs scrambled, sir?

No. At $3.00 an egg, I'd like to count them!

OLAF'S OVERPRICED OUEFS

The name gumbo comes from the African word *kingombo*, which means "okra." In gumbo-making, a browned roux (pronounced roo) is an essential ingredient. It serves to thicken the gumbo and give it a nutty flavor. Traditionally, roux is made by combining flour and oil, then cooking the mixture until brown. This can add a ton of fat and calories to an otherwise healthy meal. In our recipe, we toast the flour to achieve a heart-healthier result.

We're all hung up on the duration of our workouts, how many days a week we should exercise, and reaching our optimal heart rate. But what we should be doing is thinking about what exercise really is. It's simply physical activity. And what's the best activity? It's the one you'll do! If kick-boxing looks painful to you, it probably will be. If you've never skied before, that cross-country ski machine will likely double as a clothes hanger. If your eyes glaze over when you hear terms like "repetitions" and "intensity loads," bet you won't like lifting weights at the gym. It's important to find activities you enjoy and just do them. Maybe you could ride a bike down a tree-lined road or dance to old 70s tunes. Heck, dance naked if you think it'll be more fun! That's what Greta does, and the neighbors love her!

The trouble with dieting is that you don't eat what you like and you don't like what you eat.

Life is like a pot of gumbo.

Forrest Gumbo

Hearty, stew-like shrimp gumbo served over rice

If you're *hankerin'* for a hearty helping of gumbo, then run for Forrest Gumbo, run!

1/4 cup all-purpose flour
1 tbsp butter
1 cup each chopped onions and chopped green bell pepper
1/2 cup diced celery

2 cloves garlic, minced
3 cups low-fat chicken broth
1 can (14-1/2 oz) tomatoes, drained, cut up
1 cup diced okra or zucchini (see hint below)
1 tsp ground cumin
1/2 tsp each paprika, dried thyme, and dried oregano
1/4 tsp each salt and black pepper
1/8 tsp cayenne pepper
1 pound uncooked large shrimp, peeled
4 cups hot, cooked brown or white rice

- Sprinkle flour over bottom of a small pie plate. Toast at 400° for 15 to 20 minutes, until golden brown. Stir once or twice during cooking time. Remove from oven, transfer to a small bowl, and let cool.

- Melt butter in a large, non-stick saucepan over medium-high heat. Add onions, green pepper, celery, and garlic. Cook and stir until vegetables begin to soften, about 3 minutes. Stir in toasted flour and cook for 1 more minute. Add broth and mix well. Add drained tomatoes, okra, cumin, paprika, thyme, oregano, salt, pepper, and cayenne. Bring to a boil. Reduce heat to low. Cover and simmer for 20 minutes, stirring occasionally.

- Add shrimp and simmer for 5 more minutes, until shrimp is cooked through. To serve, spoon rice over bottom of individual serving bowls. Ladle gumbo over top. Serve hot.

Makes 6 servings

Hint: Using okra will result in a thicker gumbo.

Per serving: 304 calories, 4.3 g fat, 1.7 g saturated fat, 22.9 g protein, 42.5 g carbohydrate, 4.7 g fiber, 152.5 mg cholesterol, 630.4 mg sodium % calories from fat: 13

What's in it for us?

Heart and Sole

Baked sole fillets drizzled with a lemon-ginger sauce

Let's get to the heart of the matter: This lemony baked-sole recipe will become dear to your heart when you realize how wonderfully delicious it is. Bonus: You can make it in a heartbeat!

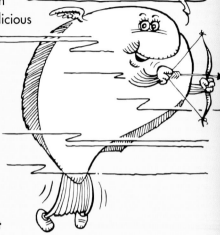

Your taste buds are about to fall in love!

1 pound sole fillets
1/2 tsp salt
1/4 tsp black pepper
1/3 cup lemon juice
1/4 cup low-fat chicken
  or vegetable broth
3 tbsp sugar
2 tsp each grated gingerroot
  and cornstarch
1 tsp grated lemon zest
1 clove garlic, minced
1 tbsp chopped, fresh parsley

- Spray a medium baking pan with non-stick spray. Set aside.
- Rinse fish with cold water and pat dry with paper towels. Sprinkle with salt and pepper. Roll up fish and place seam-side down in baking pan. Bake at 425° for 15 to 20 minutes, until fish is cooked through and flakes easily with a fork.
- While fish is cooking, prepare sauce. Combine lemon juice, broth, sugar, gingerroot, cornstarch, lemon zest, and garlic in a small saucepan. Cook over medium-high heat until mixture is bubbly and has thickened.
- Arrange fish on serving plates and drizzle with sauce. Sprinkle with parsley and serve immediately.

Makes 4 servings

What's in it for me?

Per serving: 149 calories, 2.1 g fat, 1 g saturated fat, 22.4 g protein, 12.5 g carbohydrate, 0.3 g fiber, 35 mg cholesterol, 430.2 mg sodium
% calories from fat: 12

Thirst Come, Thirst Served

Whether we realize it or not, we're all half-sloshed. That's because water makes up more than 50% of our bodies. It's the ultimate nutrient and is essential to human health. We could survive for weeks without food, but we'd last only a few days without H$_2$O. Our bodies need water for almost everything: to regulate hunger and body temperature, burn fat, tone muscles, keep blood volume up, and get rid of wastes and toxins. Plus, water is energizing. Feeling energetic makes you want to move, and moving burns calories. When you're dehydrated, you feel sluggish and tired, which usually leads you to eat. So, if you want to stay well-irrigated—go with the flow! Sneak in some extra water during the day by downing a glassful before each meal and another one each time you brush your teeth. Make water more appealing by adding a slice of lemon, lime, or orange, or a splash of cranberry juice. And don't worry about getting waterlogged. In the battle of *water-loo,* your kidneys will flush out the extra.

TRIVIAL TIDBIT

Number of hours of free time the average American reports having each week: less than 20. Number of hours the average American reports watching television each week: 21.

I've been in bed all day with a hot water bottle and a thermometer in my mouth.

Well, there's certainly room for both!

What makes our stomachs growl?

Who'da Thunk?

Some people find stomach rumbling embarrassing, but it's actually a normal part of digestion. It happens when muscles in the stomach or upper intestine contract to "clean house," moving food and digestive juices down the digestive tract (a *chew-chew* train, of sorts). Rumbles are more common after you've gone several hours without eating, which is why many people associate a growling stomach with hunger. But growls also occur when there's incomplete digestion of food, which can lead to excess gas in the intestine. (This is called "borborygmus," just in case you were looking for a new Scrabble word.) In rare cases, excessive abdominal noise may be a sign of other digestive conditions or diseases. Whatever the cause, there's no foolproof way to silence a stomach.

YOU DO THE MATH

You'll be flabbergasted when you hear the stats on creamy, buttery alfredo sauce. A typical three-quarter-cup serving packs in almost 52 grams of fat! Next time you chow down on pasta, make Mamma Mia proud and top your noodles with low-fat tomato sauce instead. If you make the swap once every two weeks, you could save 12,480 calories and 1,339 grams of fat in a year. That's almost 20 days' worth of fat! With a healthier sauce, there's no need to be *afraido*.

Fish for no compliments. They are generally caught in shallow water.

On Golden Prawns

Succulent shrimp simmered in a curry-coconut broth, served over rice

If you're looking for a sensational seafood recipe to serve at a dinner party, here's one the whole gang will be *fonda*.

1 tsp canola oil
1/2 cup each
   minced onions and minced red bell pepper
1 clove garlic, minced
1 tsp ground cumin
3/4 tsp ground coriander
1/2 tsp curry powder
1 cup light coconut milk
1 tsp sugar
1/4 tsp crushed red pepper flakes (optional)
1 pound uncooked jumbo shrimp, peeled
1 tbsp cornstarch
2 tbsp chopped, fresh cilantro
4 cups hot, cooked brown rice

- Heat oil in a large, non-stick saucepan over medium heat. Add onions, red pepper, and garlic. Cook and stir until vegetables begin to soften, about 3 minutes.

- Add cumin, coriander, and curry powder. Cook for 1 more minute. Add coconut milk, sugar, and crushed red pepper flakes, if using. Bring to a boil. Reduce heat and simmer, uncovered, for 2 minutes.

- Stir in shrimp. Increase heat to medium-high. Cook and stir until shrimp is cooked through, about 4 minutes.

- In a small bowl, combine cornstarch with 1 tablespoon water. Add to shrimp mixture. Cook until sauce is bubbly and has thickened, about 1 minute. Stir in cilantro and remove from heat. Serve shrimp and sauce over hot rice.

Makes 4 servings

Per serving: 393 calories, 7.4 g fat, 2.8 g saturated fat, 26.7 g protein, 53.9 g carbohydrate, 4.7 g fiber, 193.4 mg cholesterol, 381.6 mg sodium
% calories from fat: 17

What's in it for me?

Salmon Davis Jr.

Broiled salmon steaks marinated
in a spicy tomato sauce

Tap into heart-healthy salmon with this
show-stopping, crowd-pleasing recipe.

1 tsp butter or margarine
1/2 cup diced red onions
1 clove garlic, minced
1-1/2 cups diced plum
   tomatoes (fresh)
3 tbsp each ketchup and
   brown sugar
2 tbsp each lime juice and
   Dijon mustard
1 tbsp chili powder
2 tsp Worcestershire sauce
1 tsp paprika
1/4 tsp each ground cumin and cayenne pepper
6 salmon steaks, about 6 oz each

- Melt butter in a medium, non-stick saucepan over medium heat.
  Add onions and garlic. Cook and stir for 2 minutes, until onions
  begin to soften. Add all remaining ingredients except salmon.
  Mix well. Reduce heat to medium-low. Cover and simmer for
  20 minutes. Transfer mixture to a blender or food processor and
  puree until smooth. Let cool.

- Arrange salmon steaks in a single layer in a glass baking dish.
  Pour marinade over salmon. Turn pieces to coat both sides with
  marinade, or brush marinade all over salmon using a pastry
  brush. Cover and refrigerate for 1 hour.

- Remove salmon from marinade and place on a baking sheet.
  Broil about 4 inches from heat source for 3 minutes. Carefully
  turn salmon over and broil for another 3 to 4 minutes, until done.
  Be careful not to overcook salmon, or it will be dry. Serve
  immediately.

Makes 6 servings

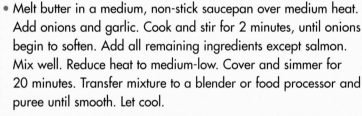

What's
in it
for me?

Per serving: 271 calories, 8.1 g fat,
2 g saturated fat, 34.6 g protein,
13.8 g carbohydrate, 1.5 g fiber,
79.6 mg cholesterol, 315.5 mg sodium
% calories from fat: 27

TRIVIAL TIDBIT

An old wives' tale suggests
that if a young girl were to
eat a herring that had
been preserved in salt
for three months, then
go to sleep without
drinking anything and
without speaking a word to anybody, her
future husband would appear to her in a
dream. (And hopefully he'll be carrying a
huge pitcher of water!)

Never-Never Land

"I'm *never* going to eat another pepperoni
pizza!" "I *always* pig out on potato chips,
so from now on, they're *off-limits*!" Sound
familiar? Well, if you're trying to embark
on a healthy eating journey that'll last a
lifetime, you'd better ban words like
"never," "always," and "off-limits" from
your vocabulary. These ultimatums put
you just a few nibbles away from failure.
That's the problem with dieting—you're
forced to label certain foods as off-limits
or taboo, and then these no-nos become
the foods you desperately crave. And
when your diet is "over," you'll fall back
into your old eating habits, gobbling up
all the forbidden foods you can get your
hands on and then some. Instead of
depriving yourself, follow the "80/20
rule," a more realistic and sensible
approach to healthy eating: Eighty
percent of the time, choose foods that are
nutritious, low in fat, and high in fiber;
twenty percent of the time, allow yourself
to have an indulgence. If you're dying
for French fries, have a small serving,
and enjoy every bite of it. Healthy
habits are forever when you learn to
never say never.

Ever notice how
the second day
of your diet
is easier?

Yeah, by
then I'm
off it!

The Meating Room

On the agenda: Delectable beef and pork recipes

The Roast of Christmas Past

Classic pot roast with vegetables
cooked in a savory cranberry sauce

Today's Specials
ROASTS FOR
GHOSTS
HUNGARIAN
GHOULISH

If it's a scrumptious pot roast
you want to be *goblin*, here's
a down-home dinner that'll
leave you in good spirits.

**1 tsp canola or
   vegetable oil**
**4-pound boneless top sirloin
   roast, trimmed of fat**
1/2 tsp salt
**1 can (10-3/4 oz) low-sodium,
   low-fat beef broth, undiluted**
1/2 cup cranberry sauce with whole cranberries
1/2 cup ketchup
1 envelope dry onion soup mix
2 cloves garlic, minced
1 tsp dry mustard powder
1/2 tsp each dried marjoram and dried thyme
1/4 tsp black pepper
8 medium potatoes, unpeeled, halved
4 large carrots, cut into quarters

- Heat oil in a large, non-stick skillet over medium-high heat.
  Sprinkle roast all over with salt. Add to skillet and brown roast on
  all sides. Transfer meat to a large roasting pan.

- In a medium bowl, whisk together broth, cranberry sauce,
  ketchup, onion soup mix, garlic, mustard powder, marjoram,
  thyme, and black pepper. Pour sauce over roast. Cover and roast
  at 350° for 2 hours, basting occasionally with sauce.

- Add potatoes and carrots to roasting pan. Spoon sauce over
  vegetables. Cover and roast for 1 more hour.

- Slice roast thinly and serve it on a platter surrounded by the
  vegetables. Skim off as much fat as possible from sauce in pan.
  Serve sauce on the side.

Makes 8 servings

**What's
in it
for me?**

Per serving: 508 calories, 11.9 g fat,
4.1 g saturated fat, 60.2 g protein,
38 g carbohydrate, 3.9 g fiber,
172 mg cholesterol, 884 mg sodium
% calories from fat: 21

In our long-ago hunting and gathering
past, food was sometimes hard to come
by. Plus, it was tough to find time to eat
while dodging spears or fighting saber-
toothed tigers. What was a poor soul to
do for energy? Actually, he drew down
from his fat stores. No wonder all those
caveman drawings were of stick people!
Even the chores that people did as
recently as a century ago—chopping
wood, pumping water, baling hay—have
gone out with the horse and buggy. Let's
face it—times have changed. Not only is
food readily available, but also today's
chores aren't exactly strenuous fat
burners. Struggling to program our VCRs
and changing the batteries in our remote
controls hardly constitute exercise. What's
needed is a good blast from the past.
Perhaps we should do as our ancestors
did and just move it! Unless we start
hunting for ways to be active, we'll surely
be gathering...fat, that is!

**Who'da
Thunk?**

**If an actor is
"hamming it up,"
does that mean he's
putting on weight?**

No sooo-eee!
"Hamming it up" has
nothing to do with
packing on the pounds
and everything to do with overacting.
Showboating actors have been called "big
hams" for generations. The term is
actually an abbreviation of "ham-fatter,"
the name audiences used in the 19th
century for amateur actors who
outrageously overplayed their scenes.
Ham-fatter implied second-rate, referring
to performers in minstrel shows who had
to remove their makeup with ham fat
because they couldn't afford cold creams.
But who needs cold cream when there's
Oink of Olay?

Rosemary, a member of the mint family, is native to the Mediterranean. It was originally called by the Latin name *ros marinus*, "sea dew," because it was often found on the sea cliffs in southern France. Its needle-shaped, silver-green leaves are highly aromatic, and their flavor hints of lemon and pine. This herb is widely available both fresh and dried, and either variety works well in this recipe. If using the dried herb, use about one-third of the amount called for of the fresh herb.

SAY IT AIN'T SO!

Wanna go skinny-dipping? C'mon, don't be shy. Take the plunge and try dunking your veggies in low-fat, homemade dips instead of the store-bought, high-fat varieties. Made with whole milk, mayonnaise, cream cheese, coconut oil, and/or hydrogenated vegetable oil, commercial dips may have three times more calories and 10 times more fat than the dips you can make at home. And since those kinds of figures certainly won't jibe with yours, be on the lookout for healthful recipes that use low-fat yogurt, low-fat cottage cheese, or light cream cheese in place of high-fat ingredients.

Love Me Tenderloin
Grilled pork tenderloin in a rosemary-apple marinade

Love me tenderloin,
Grill me true,
Never let me burn.

Though it looks like it ain't nothing but a grilled pork, it's really a fabulous dinner choice when you're having company. And it's so darn tasty, your guests will say, "Thank you! Thank you very much!"

**1/2 cup frozen apple juice
   concentrate, thawed**
2 tbsp honey mustard
2 tbsp minced, fresh rosemary (see Cooking 101)
1 tbsp olive oil
2 cloves garlic, minced
1 large shallot, minced
1/4 tsp black pepper
1-1/2 pounds pork tenderloin, trimmed of fat

- Combine all ingredients except pork in a small bowl. Pour marinade over pork in a glass baking dish or a large, heavy-duty, resealable plastic bag. Turn pork to coat it evenly with marinade. Marinate for 2 hours in refrigerator.

- Prepare grill. Remove pork from marinade and cook over hot coals for about 15 minutes, turning several times and basting frequently with reserved marinade. The outside should be nicely browned and the inside should still have a trace of pink. Let pork rest for 5 minutes before carving. Slice into 1/2-inch-thick slices and place on a serving platter. Bring any remaining marinade to a boil and drizzle over pork. Serve immediately.

Makes 6 servings

Per serving: 199 calories, 6.4 g fat, 1.4 g saturated fat, 24.2 g protein, 9.7 g carbohydrate, 0.1 g fiber, 73.7 mg cholesterol, 135.3 mg sodium % calories from fat: 30

What's in it for me?

Why didn't the hot dog star in the movies? Because the rolls weren't good enough.

For Goodness Steak

Grilled sirloin steak
with an Asian marinade

Goodness gracious—this steak's
bodacious! Our tasty marinade is good
to the last drop—and that's the
honest-to-goodness truth.

**1-1/2 pounds boneless top sirloin steak,
about 1-1/2 inches thick**
1/4 cup + 1 tbsp reduced-sodium soy sauce
3 tbsp steak sauce
2 tbsp each lime juice and packed brown sugar
1 tbsp grated gingerroot
2 cloves garlic, minced
1 tsp sesame oil
1/4 tsp black pepper

- Trim any excess fat from steak and pierce meat in several places with a fork. Combine all remaining ingredients in a small bowl and pour over steak in a large, heavy-duty, resealable plastic bag. Refrigerate for at least 2 hours, or overnight if possible.

- Prepare grill. Remove steak from marinade and grill over hot coals for 4 to 5 minutes per side, until desired "doneness" is reached. Brush steak occasionally with leftover marinade.

- Let meat rest for a few minutes before slicing. Cut against the grain into thin slices. Serve immediately.

Makes 6 servings

It's 2nd to nun.

What's in it for me?

Per serving: 262 calories, 8.5 g fat,
3.1 g saturated fat, 35.4 g protein,
8.3 g carbohydrate, 0.1 g fiber,
101 mg cholesterol, 661.2 mg sodium
% calories from fat: 30

As you get older, your metabolism inevitably declines.

FAT OR FICTION?

Experts tell us that as we age, we're going to suffer some memory loss, grow bigger ears, and put on weight. It's depressing—no wonder we're also expected to slouch! They predict that by age 55, we'll need about 150 to 200 fewer calories a day than younger folk, and that if we don't cut back on our food intake, we'll be walking around with a couple of bowling balls worth of blubber around our waistlines. Ah, the dreaded metabolic meltdown. A sluggish resting metabolism—the energy our bodies expend to sustain basic functions like breathing and heart rate—is due primarily to loss of muscle mass. It's not an "inevitable" metabolic decline as we age. The more muscle we have, the more calories we'll continue to burn, even when we're resting comfortably in our rocking chairs. Proposed solution to the meltdown crisis: Exercise. By conditioning our bodies, we can turn these so-called experts into false prophets (at least on the weight gain issue). Walk, swim, bike, or dance—and don't just do aerobic exercises, either. Lift something—anything! Weights, phone books, grandkids, whatever. Oh, by the way, exercise won't stop your ears from growing. But look at the bright side—you'll forget about them eventually!

He walks in his sleep so he can get his rest and exercise at the same time.

What the heck is apple butter and where can I buy it?

Apple butter is a thick, dark brown preserve made by slowly cooking apples, spices, sugar, and cider. It's most commonly used as a spread for muffins and breads, but it makes a great addition to sauces, too. Though its name sounds fattening, one cup of apple butter contains less than four grams of fat! Look for it in a jar near the jams and jellies at your grocery store.

Here's the scoop on ice cream: Just one measly half-cup serving of vanilla ice cream can pack in 260 calories and 17 grams of fat. For a healthier *scoop du jour*, why not give low-fat frozen yogurt a try? If you switch from ice cream to frozen yogurt just once a week, you'll save 7,956 calories and 743 grams of fat in a year. That's more than 11 days' worth of fat—enough reason to *lick* the habit!

In a 20-year study, men who walked nine or more miles a week had a 21% lower mortality rate than those who walked three miles or less—another reason to start accumulating those frequent walker miles.

Happily Ever Apple Pork Chops

Succulent pork chops topped with a sweet and spicy apple-mustard sauce

Once upon a time, there lived a *loinly* pork chop who was saddened because he had to go topless. Then along came a spicy apple and mustard sauce, and it was love at first sight. The end.

6 boneless pork loin chops (about 5 oz each), trimmed of fat
1 cup apple butter (see tip in margin)
2 tbsp mustard
1 tsp ground cumin
1/4 tsp salt
1/8 tsp black pepper
3 cups peeled and sliced Golden Delicious apples (about 3 large)
1/2 cup thinly sliced onions
2 tbsp cider vinegar

- Spray a large, non-stick skillet with non-stick spray. Cook chops over medium-high heat until browned on both sides, about 5 minutes.

- In a small bowl, combine apple butter, mustard, cumin, salt, and pepper. Spoon evenly over chops. Reduce heat to medium-low, cover, and cook until chops are just slightly pink in the center and juices run clear, about 10 minutes. Lift out chops, leaving sauce in skillet, and keep warm.

- Add apples, onions, and vinegar to skillet. Stir to coat apples and onions with sauce. Cover and cook over medium-high heat for 5 minutes, until apples are softened and onions are tender.

- To serve, spoon apple mixture over warm pork chops.

Makes 6 servings

Per serving: 291 calories, 8.2 g fat, 2.9 g saturated fat, 23.5 g protein, 23.1 g carbohydrate, 1.9 g fiber, 65.6 mg cholesterol, 200.4 mg sodium
% calories from fat: 28

What's in it for me?

Stew Good to Be True

Slow-cooked beef and vegetable stew

It's stew good to be true and too good to be stew, too. But it's true—it *is* stew. And a mighty good one at that! One bowlful and we guarantee your family will rock around the crock (pot)!

2 pounds stewing beef, trimmed of fat and cut into 1-inch cubes
3 cups peeled, cubed potatoes
2 cups chopped carrots
1-1/2 cups chopped onions
2 cups tomato sauce
1 can (10-3/4 oz) low-sodium, low-fat beef broth, undiluted
2 cloves garlic, minced
1 tbsp Dijon mustard
1 bay leaf
1-1/4 tsp each dried marjoram and dried thyme
1 tsp sugar
1/2 tsp each salt and black pepper
1 tbsp cornstarch
1/4 cup chopped, fresh parsley

- Combine all ingredients except cornstarch and parsley in a 3-quart or larger slow cooker. Cover and simmer on low setting for 9 hours. Stir occasionally.

- Combine cornstarch with an equal amount water and stir until lump-free. Add to stew and mix well. Cook for 1 more hour. Stir in parsley just before serving.

Makes 6 servings

What's in it for me?

Per serving: 335 calories, 8 g fat, 2.5 g saturated fat, 37.1 g protein, 28.5 g carbohydrate, 3.5 g fiber, 89.2 mg cholesterol, 811.6 mg sodium
% calories from fat: 22

It's all it's crocked up to be...

Have you ever noticed that all of the houseplants in a bachelor's apartment are dead, yet there's always something growing in the refrigerator?

Playing the Tuber

Did you know that the average North American eats 158 pounds of potatoes a year? In fact, one in every three meals includes potatoes, or at least some form of them. And that's a good thing, because potatoes are nutritional powerhouses, packed with vitamin C, fiber, potassium, and only a trace of fat. If only we could stick to potatoes in their original, uncorrupted form, but nooo!

Gut-bustin' potato chips and fat-drenched French fries also count in our overall intake. Look out hips, here come the chips! And French fries? With their fat content as high as the Eiffel Tower, you can say *au revoir* to your trim waistline. But don't stop savoring your spuds. Potatoes are a nutritious food as long as they're baked, boiled, or mashed, and topped with healthy stuff like dill, chives, salsa, low-fat sour cream, or low-fat tzatziki.

THE E FILES

Feel a snack attack mounting? Instead of resorting to your arsenal of peanuts, potato chips, and popcorn, try counter-attacking with exercise. That's right—snack on physical activity. Small amounts of activity multiplied throughout the day can pay huge dividends. Think about breaking up every hour of sitting with a short bout of activity, like climbing the stairs or going for a walk. Any kind of movement will do. Even just standing burns more calories than sitting. A mere half-hour of moderate exercise each day can lower your risk of dying prematurely by as much as a regimen of vigorous exercise. And it doesn't even have to be 30 consecutive minutes. You could walk for 10 minutes before work, at lunch time, and again in the evening. Still shaking your head? Well, that's a start!

SAY IT AIN'T SO!

It's *nacho* run-of-the-mill appetizer. No siree! Nachos are a definite standout when it comes to belt-busting snacks. A large order of beef and cheese nachos with the traditional toppings has roughly 89 grams of fat! Holy guacamole! Think of those *buenos nachos* as a huge plug headed straight for your arteries! To avoid the clog, don't be a hog! Share your nachos with a pal or two, and ask for salsa instead of high-fat sour cream and guacamole.

Who invented the sandwich?

Delicatessens of the world owe their livelihood to The Fourth Earl of Sandwich, John Montagu (1718-1792), who popularized his namesake in English high society. The story goes that the earl was a gambling man who hated to leave the card tables for any reason, dining included. To solve this problem, he ate his meal by placing it between two pieces of bread. This left one hand free, eliminated the need for a plate, knife, or fork, and allowed the earl to *butter* concentrate on his cards, which was especially helpful if he was on a *roll*. The sandwich concept spread swiftly!

The Wicked Sandwich of the West

Tender strips of sirloin steak, green peppers, and onions piled high on a soft roll

You'll be the wizard of oohs and aahs when you serve your family these bewitching steak sandwiches. They're TOTO-ly delectable!

- **1 pound sirloin tip steak, trimmed of fat and thinly sliced**
- **1/2 tsp paprika**
- **1/4 tsp each salt, black pepper, and garlic powder**
- **1 tbsp all-purpose flour**
- **1-1/4 cups low-fat beef broth**
- **2 tbsp barbecue sauce**
- **2 tsp brown sugar**
- **1/2 tsp dried thyme**
- **1 large green pepper, seeded and sliced into strips**
- **1 medium onion, thinly sliced into rings**
- **4 soft onion rolls**

- Place steak in a medium bowl and sprinkle with paprika, salt, pepper, and garlic powder. Add flour and toss to coat all sides.

- Spray a large, non-stick skillet with non-stick spray. Add steak and cook over medium-high heat until lightly browned and no longer pink. Add broth, barbecue sauce, brown sugar, and thyme. Stir and bring to a boil. Reduce heat to low. Cover and simmer for 15 minutes. Add green peppers and onions. Cover and simmer for 10 more minutes, stirring occasionally. If mixture is too saucy, continue to simmer, uncovered, until most of the liquid has evaporated.

- Serve on warm onion rolls.

Makes 4 servings

Hint: Try topping your sandwich with a slice of reduced-fat Swiss cheese.

Per serving: 393 calories, 9.5 g fat, 3.2 g saturated fat, 37.9 g protein, 37.9 g carbohydrate, 1.9 g fiber, 96 mg cholesterol, 661.9 mg sodium % calories from fat: 22

THE MEATING ROOM

125

The Big Chili

Spicy beef chili with two kinds of beans

You and your pals can chill out and pig out on this filling chili. Just don't fight for seconds, or you may end up with a chili concussion.

1-1/2 pounds stewing beef, cut into 1-inch cubes
1 cup each chopped red and green bell peppers
1 cup chopped red onions
2 cloves garlic, minced
3-1/2 cups low-sodium, low-fat beef broth
1-1/2 cups salsa (see Cooking 101)
1 can (14-1/2 oz) tomatoes, undrained, cut up
1-1/2 tbsp chili powder
1-1/2 tsp each ground cumin and dried oregano
1 tsp ground coriander
1/2 tsp ground black pepper
1 can (15 oz) black beans, drained and rinsed
1 can (15 oz) red kidney beans, drained and rinsed
1/4 cup chopped, fresh cilantro
2 tbsp lime juice
1 tbsp honey

- Spray a large saucepan or soup pot with non-stick spray. Add beef. Cook and stir over high heat until beef is browned all over. Add peppers, onions, and garlic. Reduce heat to medium. Cook and stir for 4 to 5 minutes, until vegetables begin to soften.

- Add broth, salsa, tomatoes and their juice, chili powder, cumin, oregano, coriander, and black pepper. Bring to a boil. Reduce heat and simmer, covered, for 1-1/2 hours, stirring occasionally.

- Add beans and simmer for 15 more minutes. Remove from heat. Stir in cilantro, lime juice, and honey. Serve hot.

Makes 8 servings

You can control the heat of this beef chili by choosing mild, medium, or hot salsa. The long, slow simmering is necessary to make the beef tender. If you're in a hurry, you can replace the stewing beef with extra-lean ground beef or cubed, boneless chicken breast, and simmer for 30 minutes instead of one-and-a-half hours. By the way, The Big Chili tastes great served with a batch of our delicious corn muffins on page 54.

Fiber Optics

Have high cholesterol? Want to reduce your risk of heart attack? Have we got something for you! No, you don't need to seek the advice of a medicine man, and you won't be required to massage a magic potion into your temples, either. This healer is conveniently found in carbohydrate-rich foods. It's fiber, one of the most valuable players in the healthy-living game. Soluble fiber from fruits, vegetables, dried beans and peas, barley, and oats has been shown to help decrease cholesterol, therefore reducing the risk of heart disease. Fiber also slows the absorption of blood sugar, which may, in turn, help control diabetes. Low-fiber diets have been associated with a host of health problems—from hemorrhoids, hypertension, and hiatus hernia to varicose veins, gallstones, and colitis. There. Now that we've spilled the beans, maybe you should eat some!

What's in it for us?

Per serving: 266 calories, 5.5 g fat, 1.4 g saturated fat, 27.1 g protein, 31.1 g carbohydrate, 4.7 g fiber, 50.2 mg cholesterol, 459.5 mg sodium
% calories from fat: 18

OLÉ!

That Mexican meal she cooked was so authentic, you couldn't even drink the water.

YOU DO THE MATH

Living in Genoa City is fine if you're a soap opera character, but not if you're a regular patron at the deli counter. That's because Genoa salami contains 220 calories and 20 grams of fat per two-ounce serving. How about swapping that high-fat salami for the same amount of roasted turkey breast once a week? You'll save 8,320 calories and 936 grams of fat in a year. That's almost two weeks' worth of fat! So, when it comes to luncheon meats, any way you slice it, turkey breast is best.

Vitamin supplements are all you need to stay healthy.

FAT or FICTION?

Some people wisely use vitamin supplements as nutritional insurance, while others mistakenly see them as a way of making up for poor eating habits. But, if you add the latest hot supplement to a poor diet, you'll still have a poor diet. You're much better off getting your nutrients from the food you eat. Real food contains hundreds of protective, health-giving substances. Pills don't. For instance, an orange contains vitamin C, plus about 150 other substances that may help protect your heart. A vitamin C pill contains only vitamin C. And food tastes better than pills (mind you—those Flintstones vitamins are pretty tasty!). Generally speaking, unless your doctor tells you that you need a little something extra, remember what Hippocrates prescribed: "Let your food be your medicine, and your medicine be your food."

Barbiechop Quartet

Spicy, marinated pork chops grilled on the barbie

This spicy number hits a high note where flavor's concerned. On the pork chop taste-o-meter, it rates a perfect *tenor*!

4 boneless pork loin chops (about 5 oz each), trimmed of fat
1/3 cup orange juice
3 tbsp each honey and ketchup
3 tbsp mango chutney (see p. 29)
1 tbsp lemon juice
2 tsp chili powder
3/4 tsp ground cumin

- Arrange pork chops in a single layer in a glass baking dish. Whisk together remaining ingredients in a small bowl. Pour over pork chops. Turn pieces to coat both sides with marinade. Cover with plastic wrap and refrigerate for at least 4 hours, or overnight if possible.

- Preheat grill. Cook pork chops over hot coals for 6 to 7 minutes per side, basting with leftover marinade. Serve immediately.

Makes 4 servings

Per serving: 297 calories, 8.7 g fat, 2.9 g saturated fat, 24.2 g protein, 30.6 g carbohydrate, 0.9 g fiber, 65.6 mg cholesterol, 353.5 mg sodium
% calories from fat: 26

What's in it for me?

The word barbecue comes from the Spanish *barbacoa*, meaning "frame of sticks." When early Spanish explorers landed on Haiti in the mid-17th century, they used this word to describe the Haitian Indians' method of grilling and smoking their meat outdoors on wooden racks over open fires.

TRIVIAL TIDBIT

Marla's Maple Pork

Roasted pork tenderloin drizzled with a zesty maple and orange sauce

You can't *trump* this recipe! Our roasted pork is so delectable, you'll shout, "*I vanna* some more!"

1-1/2 pounds pork tenderloin (see Cooking 101)
1/2 cup pure maple syrup
2 tbsp each reduced-sodium soy sauce and ketchup
1 tbsp Dijon mustard
2 tsp grated orange zest
1-1/2 tsp each curry powder and ground coriander
1 tsp Worcestershire sauce
2 cloves garlic, minced

* Trim pork of all visible fat. Place pork in a large, heavy-duty, resealable plastic bag. Whisk together all remaining ingredients in a medium bowl. Pour over pork in bag. Seal bag and allow pork to marinate in refrigerator for 1 hour.

* Transfer pork and marinade to a small roasting pan or baking dish. Roast, uncovered, at 350° for 40 minutes. Pork should still be slightly pink in middle.

* Let pork stand for 10 minutes before slicing. Slice thinly. Drizzle extra sauce over pork and serve immediately.

Makes 6 servings

What's in it for me?

Per serving: 236 calories, 5 g fat, 1.5 g saturated fat, 26.1 g protein, 20.5 g carbohydrate, 0.5 g fiber, 70.9 mg cholesterol, 624 mg sodium
% calories from fat: 19

He's so argumentative, he won't even eat food that agrees with him!

COOKING 101

If you're leaning toward more nutritious food choices, then take another look at today's fresh pork products, specifically, pork tenderloin. The pork industry has responded to public demand for more healthful products, and now many cuts of pork are as lean as chicken. Pork tenderloin, the leanest cut, contains only four grams of fat and 140 calories per three-ounce roasted serving. It's also one of the most convenient cuts. It's small—averaging around three-quarters of a pound—and has little waste.

Why is a frankfurter called a hot dog?

Who'da Thunk?

Because it resembles a dachshund—or at least that's what the famous sports cartoonist T.A. Dorgan thought. Around the turn of the century, a concessionaire at New York's Polo Grounds had his vendors yell out, "Get your red-hot dachshund sausages!" Dorgan liked this expression so much that he took to calling them hot dogs (as a pet name, perhaps). In 1900, he drew a cartoon frankfurter shaped like a dachshund in a bun, and doggone it, a new expression was born!

Today's UN-HAPPY MEAL: Sauerkraut with Hot Cross Buns

You're such a Sour Kraut!

I know.

What the heck is seasoned rice vinegar and where can I buy it?

Rice vinegar is a mild and slightly sweet vinegar made from fermented rice. Used widely in Japanese and Chinese cooking, you can buy it in both seasoned and unseasoned varieties. Seasoned rice vinegar has added salt and sugar. With the popularity of Asian cooking, you should have no trouble finding rice vinegar right beside the regular vinegars at your grocery store.

Red Meat, White Meat, Dark Meat, Light Meat

Have you ever wondered what makes some meats white and others dark? Well, we thought we'd tell you anyway! It's myoglobin—an oxygen-holding compound—that gives meat its red color. Without getting too complex, myoglobin in muscle cells receives oxygen from the blood and holds it for use in cell metabolism. The amount of myoglobin, and therefore the amount of redness, depends on how often the muscle is used. Since cattle are relatively active, roaming animals, and pigs are raised in pens that confine their activity, beef has more myoglobin than pork. Fish, on the other hand, have very little myoglobin. Their "fast" muscles are designed to burn glycogen, a process that uses less oxygen. That's why most fish meat is white. Chickens have both dark and light meat because their leg muscles are more active than their pectoral (breast) muscles. In contrast, game birds—which do use breast muscles to fly—have mostly dark meat. Looks like the more hustle, the more muscle! What color is *your* leg meat?

Hay fever is much achoo about nothing.

Stir Crazy

Orange-ginger pork stir-fry with broccoli and peppers

Our insanely delicious pork and ginger stir-fry will make your taste buds go gaga! The flavor's so irresistible, it's sure to cause a stir.

1/2 cup low-fat chicken broth
1/4 cup hoisin sauce (see p. 111)
1/4 cup orange marmalade
1 tbsp seasoned rice vinegar (see tip in margin)
1 tbsp cornstarch
1 tsp each sesame oil and grated gingerroot
1 clove garlic, minced
1/4 tsp Chinese five-spice powder
1 pound pork tenderloin
3 cups broccoli florets
1 cup each sliced red and yellow bell peppers
4 cups hot, cooked brown or white rice

- In a medium bowl, whisk together chicken broth, hoisin sauce, marmalade, vinegar, cornstarch, sesame oil, gingerroot, garlic, and five-spice powder. Set aside.
- Trim any visible fat from pork. Cut pork crosswise into 1/4-inch-thick slices.
- Spray a large, non-stick wok or skillet with non-stick spray. Add pork. Cook and stir over high heat until no longer pink. Add broccoli and peppers. Reduce heat to medium-high. Cook for 3 more minutes. Add sauce and cook until bubbly and thickened. Serve pork and vegetables over hot, cooked rice.

Makes 4 servings

Per serving: 493 calories, 7.7 g fat, 2 g saturated fat, 32.1 g protein, 74.6 g carbohydrate, 5 g fiber, 74.2 mg cholesterol, 411.1 mg sodium
% calories from fat: 14

What's in it for me?

Ham–Me–Down Dinner

Baked ham and pineapple with orange-mustard sauce

You'll pine over this simple ham and pineapple dinner that was handed down by our Mother. It makes great leftovers, too, so you can play it again, ham.

1 can (20 oz) pineapple rings in juice, undrained
2 tbsp frozen orange juice concentrate, thawed
1 tbsp each mustard and cornstarch
1 2-pound fully-cooked lean ham

- Drain juice from pineapple into a small saucepan. Set rings aside. You should have about 1 cup juice. Add orange juice concentrate, mustard, and cornstarch to juice in pan. Cook and stir over medium heat until mixture is bubbly and has thickened, about 2 minutes. Remove from heat.

- Slice ham into 8 pieces. Arrange pieces in a 9 x 13-inch baking dish, overlapping as necessary. Top each piece with a pineapple slice. Pour sauce evenly over ham and pineapple.

- Cover with foil and bake at 350° for 30 minutes, until ham is heated through and sauce is bubbly.

Makes 8 servings

What's in it for me?

Per serving: 209 calories, 5.6 g fat, 1.8 g saturated fat, 25.3 g protein, 13.7 g carbohydrate, 0.6 g fiber, 54.6 mg cholesterol, 1338.2 mg sodium
% calories from fat: 24

You don't stop laughing because you grow old.
You grow old because you stop laughing.

Michael Pritchard

If you ignore your health for long enough, it'll go away.

FAT OR FICTION?

Do you treat your car with the utmost care and respect? Tank filled with Ultra-Supreme? Regularly scheduled oil changes? Nothing like a little preventive maintenance to keep ol' Bessie's engine humming. But what about your own body's engine? You know, the one that's expected to give you unlimited mileage and last a lifetime? Run it on a steady stream of hamburgers, fries, potato chips, and beer, and it's bound to end up in the shop. Many people take their bodies for granted until something goes wrong, and then they expect a quick fix, just as they do with their cars. But, by the time your doctor tells you there's something seriously wrong "under the hood," it may be too late. Some parts can't be replaced. However, with 70% of illnesses having a dietary link, preventive maintenance may be as simple as making smarter food choices. So, fill your tank with nutritious, low-fat, high-fiber foods—premium-quality fuel to keep your engine running smoothly and your spare tire from inflating.

I'm thinking of getting my eggs frozen...but just the whites – I'm cutting back on cholesterol!

FERTILITY CLINIC

SAY IT AIN'T SO!

What's the name of that quaint, little Chinese restaurant you go to every week? You know, the one where they serve those heaping mounds of fried rice, and you always have a second helping? Can you think of it? Ah, yes. That's it...*Ah-so Fat!* Fried rice can have up to two tablespoons of oil per cup. That's 28 grams of fat just in your rice! Holy chow! Steamed rice is a smarter choice, and brown rice is even better because it has three times as much fiber. He who overeats Chinese food may not fit into his *Beijing* suit!

THE E FILES

Did you know your body comes with a lifetime warranty? It's true. Keep your muscles—your body's fat-burning engine—tuned and toned, and they'll remain strong, flexible, and well-balanced throughout your life. By creating a bigger, stronger engine through strength-training, you can postpone age-related weakness a decade or longer. Both men and women lose about a third of a pound of muscle each year after age 40, and they gain as much fat, if not more. But it doesn't have to be that way. In a study by Tufts University, a group of out-of-shape volunteers followed a high-intensity, strength-training regimen for eight weeks, and the results were quite impressive. Some achieved three- and fourfold increases in strength. Not bad, considering they were all in their nineties!

Those who indulge, bulge.

A Wok in the Pork

Stir-fried pork tenderloin, vegetables, and pineapple chunks in a sweet-and-sour sauce

You'll squeal with delight when you discover that this sweet-and-sour pork dish won't make you porky.

1 tsp olive oil
1-1/4 pounds pork tenderloin, cut into cubes or strips
2 tsp grated gingerroot
1 clove garlic, minced
1-1/2 cups each chopped green bell pepper and sliced carrots
1 cup chopped onions
2 cans (8 oz each) pineapple chunks, undrained
1/4 cup each ketchup and white or rice vinegar
3 tbsp brown sugar
2 tbsp reduced-sodium soy sauce
1 tbsp cornstarch
1/2 tsp chili powder
4 cups hot, cooked brown or white rice

- Heat olive oil in a non-stick wok or skillet over medium-high heat. Add pork, gingerroot, and garlic. Cook and stir for 6 to 7 minutes, until pork is cooked through and begins to brown. Remove pork from wok and keep warm. Add green pepper, carrots, and onions to wok. Cook and stir for about 5 minutes, or until vegetables are tender.

- Meanwhile, prepare sauce. Drain pineapple, reserving 1/2 cup juice. In a small bowl, combine reserved pineapple juice, ketchup, vinegar, brown sugar, soy sauce, cornstarch, and chili powder. Add sauce to vegetables in wok, along with cooked pork and pineapple chunks. Cook until sauce is bubbly and has thickened, and pork and pineapple are heated through. Serve over hot, cooked rice.

Makes 4 servings

Per serving: 565 calories, 8.5 g fat, 2.1 g saturated fat, 37.4 g protein, 84.6 g carbohydrate, 7.9 g fiber, 92.1 mg cholesterol, 571.1 mg sodium % calories from fat: 14

What's in it for me?

The Side Show

A crowd-pleasing circus of side dishes

Sammy Salsa

Mango salsa that makes an excellent topping for grilled fish or chicken

It's going, going, gone! Our mango salsa is a big hit—a real dinger! We think it's the best salsa you'll ever have cross your plate.

1 large mango, peeled and diced (see Cooking 101)
2/3 cup minced red bell pepper
1/2 cup minced red onions
1 jalapeño pepper, seeded and minced
2 tbsp each lime juice and chopped, fresh cilantro
2 tsp sugar
1 tsp olive oil
1/4 tsp ground cumin
1/8 tsp salt

- Combine all ingredients in a medium bowl. Mix well.
- Let salsa stand at room temperature for 30 minutes before serving. Cover and refrigerate any leftovers.

Makes 3 cups

What's in it for me?

Per serving (1/4 cup): 36 calories, 0.5 g fat, 0 g saturated fat, 0.4 g protein, 8.5 g carbohydrate, 1 g fiber, 0 mg cholesterol, 26.4 mg sodium
% calories from fat: 12

COOKING 101

The mango tree is considered sacred in India, where the fruit first appeared. This exceedingly juicy fruit is not only delicious, but also rich in vitamins A, C, and D. You need to be careful when eating mango, though—the juice can stain your clothing!

Familiarity Breeds Contempt

Have you packed the same lunch for the last 18 years? Do you order the same thing in the same restaurant day after day? Do you define the five basic food groups as McDonald's, Burger King, Wendy's, KFC, and Pizza Hut? Eating the same foods day in and day out supplies you with the exact same vitamins and minerals over and over again. Varying your food intake provides you with a much broader range of nutrients, and that breeds contentment as far as your body's concerned. Your attitude toward food should be the same as your attitude toward life. To get the most out of both, you have to be willing to try new things. So, gather a list of different fruits, vegetables, grains, and new low-fat products you've seen advertised, and challenge yourself to try something new each week. C'mon! Where's your sense of adventure? Every once in a while, go out on a limb. Isn't that where the fruit is?

TRIVIAL TIDBIT Back in the days of the manual typewriter, a typist burned an average of 15 more calories an hour than a person doing the same work today on a computer. For someone who does word processing four hours a day, that adds up to burning 60 calories less a day, or 300 calories over a five-day workweek.

Four nice chops please—and make them lean.

Certainly, ma'am. Which way?

SAY IT AIN'T SO!

Feel like a big, hearty breakfast? How about an omelette? At some diners, it's certainly big, and it's definitely *heart-attacky*. A ham and cheese omelette at one popular family restaurant (we don't like to name names, but let's just say you'll always smell the coffee *perkin'* there) weighs in at a belt-busting 644 calories and 51 grams of fat. Hmm. Maybe you should opt for the "healthier" mushroom and cheese omelette instead. Surprise! You'll be sending 687 calories and 60 grams of fat straight to your rear end! For a real coronary on a plate, order the "deluxe" model with a side of hash browns. It has an unthinkable 1,033 calories and 82 grams of fat. Oh, and make sure you leave a tip for the waitress: Omelettes are not recommended for the faint of heart.

THE E FILES

"If I don't exercise for at least 30 minutes at a time, I won't burn fat or get fit." True? Or a simple *mythunderstanding*? To burn an optimal number of calories, experts say we should exercise for at least 30 minutes, four or five times a week. Sure, that's ideal—but we don't live in an ideal world. Let's face it, sometimes our busy lives get in the way of our best fitness intentions. But don't throw in the exercise towel just because you can't make the half-hour commitment prescribed by health gurus. Remember this simple truth: A calorie burned is a calorie burned. Every little movement helps. Fifteen minutes of exercise is better than zero minutes. If you're pressed for time, try choosing activities that give you a lot of bang for your buck. Jumping rope, for instance, burns close to 10 calories a minute. Stair-climbing is another calorie-burning doozie. So, if you want to get fit, don't *myth* out on any opportunity to get your body moving.

De-lish Kebabs

Marinated, grilled shish kebabs, loaded with veggies

Invite your neighbors over for these delicious vegetable skewers! But be forewarned: They're so appetizing, there's sure to be a war over the leftovers.

6 small red potatoes, unpeeled, halved
1 medium zucchini, unpeeled, cut crosswise into 12 slices
12 whole, medium button mushrooms
1 large red bell pepper, cut into 12 chunks
3 tbsp each red wine vinegar and apple juice
2 tbsp chopped, fresh basil
1 tbsp each reduced-sodium soy sauce, Dijon mustard, and honey
2 tsp olive oil
2 cloves garlic, minced
1/4 tsp black pepper
6 metal skewers

- Steam potatoes for 6 to 7 minutes, until tender. Combine cooked potatoes with remaining vegetables in a large bowl.

- In a small bowl, whisk together vinegar, apple juice, basil, soy sauce, mustard, honey, olive oil, garlic, and pepper. Pour marinade over vegetables. Stir vegetables to coat them evenly with marinade. Cover and refrigerate for 2 hours.

- Thread vegetables onto skewers. Grill over medium-high heat for 10 to 15 minutes, or until vegetables are tender-crisp. Turn vegetables once or twice during cooking, and baste with extra marinade. (To broil, place kebabs on broiler pan and broil 4 to 6 inches from heat source for about 5 minutes per side.)

Makes 6 skewers

Per skewer: 134 calories, 2.2 g fat, 0.1 g saturated fat, 3.7 g protein, 26.1 g carbohydrate, 3.1 g fiber, 0 mg cholesterol, 168.7 mg sodium
% calories from fat: 14

What's in it for me?

Twice as Nice Coconut Rice

If you're tired of serving plain, ol' white rice with a meal, but don't have time to prepare anything too fancy, this doubly delicious recipe will *rice* to the occasion.

After you, I insist.

1 tsp canola or vegetable oil
2 tsp grated gingerroot
1 clove garlic, minced
1-1/2 cups uncooked, long-grain white rice
3/4 cup light coconut milk
1 tsp each honey and grated lemon zest
1/2 tsp salt

- Heat oil in a medium, non-stick saucepan over medium heat. Add gingerroot and garlic. Cook and stir for 1 minute. Add rice and cook for 1 more minute.

- Stir in coconut milk, 2-1/4 cups water, honey, lemon zest, and salt. Bring to a boil. Reduce heat to medium-low. Cover and simmer for 20 minutes, or until liquid is absorbed and rice is tender.

- Fluff rice with a fork and serve immediately.

Makes 6 servings

What's in it for me?

Per serving: 199 calories, 2.6 g fat, 1.1 g saturated fat, 3.5 g protein, 39.5 g carbohydrate, 0.7 g fiber, 0 mg cholesterol, 207.3 mg sodium
% calories from fat: 12

Why does orange juice taste terrible after you brush your teeth?

Who'da Thunk?

Have you ever taken a sip of orange juice right after giving your teeth a good brushing? Yuk! The foul taste is caused by a chemical detergent called sodium lauryl sulfate (SLS) that's present in your toothpaste. Any leftover SLS in your mouth reacts with the natural acids in orange juice, reducing its sweetness and producing an unpleasant, bitter taste. Fortunately, SLS dissipates quickly, so if you wait a few minutes, your OJ will taste OK.

Take Our Word For It

English is a crazy language. For instance, there are no grapes in grapefruit, no eggs in eggplant, no horse in horseradish, nor ham in hamburger. You won't find any pine or apples in pineapple. English muffins weren't invented in England and French fries didn't originate in France. And here's a little food for thought: If a vegetarian eats vegetables, what does a humanitarian eat?

I'm trying to get back to my original weight.

What? Eight pounds, six ounces?

Twenty years ago, 10% of children were overweight. Today, the figure is 20%. Statistics also show that the average American child younger than 11 watches almost 20 hours of television a week. A *remote* coincidence?

TRIVIAL TIDBIT

FAT OR FICTION?

For a healthy diet, you should buy and eat only foods that contain 30% or fewer calories from fat.

Most health experts recommend that we keep fat consumption to no more than 30% of total daily calories. But this pertains to our overall diet, not to individual food items. Just because a food contains more than 30% calories from fat, doesn't mean it's an unhealthy, high-fat food. Sound confusing? Consider the following examples: (1) A turkey sandwich made with three ounces of roasted turkey breast, two slices of bread, lettuce, tomato, and mustard: 270 calories, five grams of fat, 17% of calories from fat; (2) One cup of 2% milk: 120 calories, five grams of fat, 38% of calories from fat; (3) Salad made with mixed greens and two tablespoons of low-fat salad dressing: 50 calories, five grams of fat, 90% of calories from fat. All three food items are equally low in fat at five grams per serving, but vary considerably in percentage of calories from fat. Most importantly, all are nutritious foods that can be part of a healthy eating plan. Even truly high-fat foods such as chicken wings don't need to be eliminated altogether from your diet. It's all about balance, and not so much about each morsel of food that goes into your mouth. Your overall diet is what matters most, not that can of Pringles you had for lunch. (You had a can of Pringles for lunch? Shame on you!) A better and easier way to control your fat intake is to count fat grams, not percentages. Based on a 2,000-calorie-a-day diet, your daily fat target would be 67 grams. Inactive women and older adults need slightly less fat, and most men and active teenagers need more. But whatever you do, don't let all the calculations give you palpitations. Healthy eating should be common sense, not percents!

She Sells Stuffed Shells

Spinach- and ricotta-stuffed shells with tomato sauce

Get 'em while they're hot! Full of fat, they're not!

- **18 jumbo pasta shells, uncooked**
- **1 tsp olive oil**
- **1/2 cup minced onions**
- **1/2 cup grated carrots**
- **1 clove garlic, minced**
- **1 pkg (10 oz) frozen spinach, thawed, squeezed dry, and chopped**
- **1 cup part-skim ricotta cheese**
- **1/2 cup low-fat (1%) cottage cheese**
- **1/4 cup grated Parmesan cheese**
- **1 egg white**
- **2 tbsp chopped, fresh basil**
- **2 cups of your favorite, low-fat spaghetti sauce**

Get yer stuffed shells!

- Cook pasta shells according to package directions. Drain. Rinse with cold water and drain again. Set aside.

- Heat olive oil in a small, non-stick saucepan over medium heat. Add onions, carrots, and garlic. Cook and stir for 2 to 3 minutes, until vegetables begin to soften. Remove from heat and let cool.

- In a medium bowl, combine carrot-onion mixture, spinach, cheeses, egg white, and basil. Mix well. Stuff each cooked shell with a heaping tablespoonful of filling.

- Pour 1 cup spaghetti sauce over bottom of a 9 x 13-inch baking pan. Arrange stuffed shells in a single layer over sauce. Spoon remaining sauce over shells. Cover and bake at 350° for 30 minutes. Serve hot.

Makes 6 servings

Per serving: 259 calories, 5.8 g fat, 2.4 g saturated fat, 15.6 g protein, 35.4 g carbohydrate, 3.2 g fiber, 17.4 mg cholesterol, 501.2 mg sodium % calories from fat: 20%

What's in it for me?

Laughter is the shortest distance between two people.

Victor Borge

THE SIDE SHOW

Busy Beans

Super-quick, steamed green beans
tossed in a light vinaigrette

Rushing to make dinner? These beans are a winner! In just a few minutes, you can gussy up plain beans with a tasty, light dressing. Perfect for busy bees!

1 pound fresh green beans, stems removed
1 tbsp each red wine vinegar and apple juice
1 tsp honey mustard
1/2 tsp sugar
1/4 tsp each dried oregano and black pepper

- Steam green beans in a steamer basket for 5 minutes, or until tender. Transfer beans to a serving bowl.

- Combine remaining ingredients in a small bowl. Add to beans and toss to coat. Serve immediately.

Makes 4 servings

What's in it for us?

Per serving: 46 calories, 0.1 g fat, 0 g saturated fat, 1.9 g protein, 9.4 g carbohydrate, 1.4 g fiber, 0 mg cholesterol, 41.2 mg sodium
% calories from fat: 3

The way he eats, no wonder he gets thick to his stomach.

Spilling the Beans

Beans, beans, the musical fruit. The more you eat, the more you...lower your cholesterol, stabilize blood sugar levels, and protect yourself against cancer. No wonder it's the musical fruit! We should sing the praises of these low-fat wonders more often. Super-high in vitamins, minerals, and of course, soluble fiber, beans are an important part of every known cuisine. In fact, they've been eaten for thousands of years. The most famous bean eaters were the pilgrims in Boston, or Beantown, as they say. Because their strict religion forbade them to cook on the Sabbath, they designed a bean pot that baked beans overnight so they'd be ready to eat for Sunday supper. The Pilgrims knew, even back then, that beans were a fantastic food. Darn tootin'!

SAY IT AIN'T SO!

Polly want a cracker? OK, but not too many, or Polly might need a stretcher. Ounce for ounce, some popular crackers contain as much fat and sodium as the cheese you put on them. Though many of their labels scream "no cholesterol," they often contain partially hydrogenated fats, which may raise cholesterol levels as much as saturated fat does. This simple test will help you crack the cracker fat code: If a cracker makes your fingers feel greasy or leaves an oily mark on a paper napkin, it's too fatty for you—and Polly.

I can't believe I ate the whole thing—again!

Use kitchen shears or a sharp knife to chop dried apricots. To prevent the fruit from sticking, spray the scissors or knife with non-stick cooking spray, or dip them in hot water every once in a while. You can soften dried fruit that has hardened by covering it with boiling water and letting it sit for 15 minutes. Blot the fruit dry with paper towels before using.

Since olive oil is "heart healthy," the more you eat, the better.

FAT OR **FICTION?**

A low-fat diet, especially one low in saturated fat, is recommended for heart health. Both olive and canola oils are not only low in saturated fat, but they're also high in monounsaturated fat, the kind of fat that may help lower blood cholesterol levels. That's why experts have deemed them the "heart-healthy" oils. But that doesn't mean you should start pouring olive oil on your breakfast cereal and ladling it onto your salad with reckless abandon. Remember: All oils are 100% fat, whether they're *the good* (olive and canola), *the bad* (palm and coconut), or *the ugly* (hydrogenated vegetable). Likewise, they all have 14 grams of fat and 120 calories per tablespoon. So, overdoing it on the good stuff can still be a bad thing for your waistline. What the experts are suggesting is that, when you do use oil, choose the varieties that are high in monounsaturated fat over the unhealthy types. And that's *oil* she wrote.

The Spice of Rice

Long-grain white rice with dried apricots and lots of spice

There's variety in the spice of rice! Four fragrant spices add jazz and pizazz to this savory, flavory rice dish.

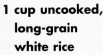

1 tsp olive oil
1/2 cup each diced carrots, diced green bell pepper, and minced onions
1 cup uncooked, long-grain white rice
1 tsp ground coriander
1/2 tsp ground cumin
1/4 tsp each ground ginger and cinnamon
2-1/4 cups low-fat chicken or vegetable broth
1/4 tsp salt
1/2 cup chopped, dried apricots (see Cooking 101)
2 tbsp chopped, fresh cilantro or parsley

- Heat olive oil in a medium, non-stick saucepan over medium heat. Add carrots, green pepper, and onions. Cook and stir until vegetables begin to soften, about 3 minutes.

- Add rice, coriander, cumin, ginger, and cinnamon. Cook and stir for 1 more minute. Add broth, salt, and apricots. Bring to a boil. Reduce heat to low. Cover and simmer for 15 to 20 minutes, until liquid has been absorbed and rice is tender. Stir in cilantro. Remove from heat and let stand for 5 minutes before serving.

Makes 6 servings

Per serving: 157 calories, 1.2 g fat, 0.1 g saturated fat, 4.1 g protein, 32.8 g carbohydrate, 2 g fiber, 0 mg cholesterol, 280.5 mg sodium
% calories from fat: 7

What's in it for me?

TRIVIAL TIDBIT

Why would anyone prefer an apple with a worm in it to one without? The presence of a worm ensures the absence of pesticides.

See Ya Later, Sweet Potater!

Sweet-potato casserole with maple syrup, pecans, and coconut

You'll say "Adios, potatoes!" when this scrumptious side dish lands on your plate. It's a sweet treat for Thanksgiving dinner or special occasions.

1/2 cup evaporated skim milk
1/3 cup pure maple syrup
1 tbsp light butter or margarine, melted
1 tsp vanilla
1/4 tsp pumpkin pie spice
4 large sweet potatoes, peeled and sliced into 1/4-inch-thick rounds
1/4 cup chopped pecans
1/4 cup shredded, sweetened coconut

- In a small bowl, whisk together evaporated milk, maple syrup, melted butter, vanilla, and pumpkin pie spice. Set aside.

- Spray a 9 x 13-inch baking pan with non-stick spray. Arrange sweet-potato slices over bottom in layers. Sprinkle with pecans and coconut. Pour milk mixture evenly over potatoes.

- Bake, uncovered, at 400° for 25 minutes. Remove pan from oven and give potatoes a stir. Return to oven and bake an additional 20 minutes, until potatoes are tender. Stir again, and let cool slightly before serving.

Makes 6 servings

What's in it for me?

Per serving: 284 calories, 6.3 g fat, 1.8 g saturated fat, 4.6 g protein, 53.6 g carbohydrate, 5.1 g fiber, 0.8 mg cholesterol, 77.7 mg sodium
% calories from fat: 20

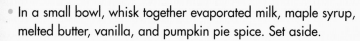

Cultivate the habit of early rising. It is unwise to keep the head long on a level with the feet.

Henry David Thoreau

THE E FILES

"Ninety-eight, ninety-nine, one hundred. Phew! Did it. One hundred sit-ups—that'll flatten my stomach for sure!" If you believe that a daily dose of sit-ups will give you a washboard stomach, you're sadly mistaken. Sit-ups strengthen and tone your abs, but they do not—even if you do 1,000 a day—make stomach fat disappear. Your body can't zap fat just in problem areas. To get a flat stomach, you need to shed overall body fat, and the best way to do that is by cutting down on the fat you eat and by putting your muscles to work. When you burn more calories than you consume, your body draws energy from all of its fat stores, including those nasty, hard-to-reach trouble spots. That's not to say that you shouldn't do sit-ups and other tummy-toning exercises. Any strengthening, calorie-burning activities are a boon to your physique, and having strong abdominal muscles lightens the load on your back, too. So, even though they may not lead to abs of steel, crunches aren't a *waist* of time.

YOU DO THE MATH

If you love pastries, it's time to upset the apple cart. That's because your average apple turnover contains 300 calories and 17 grams of fat! Why not swap that turnover for an apple-flavored, low-fat cereal bar? If you make the trade just once every two weeks, you'll save 8,320 calories and 728 grams of fat a year! That's more than 10 days' worth of fat—a good reason to *turnover* a new leaf.

When peeling and cutting a whole pineapple, be sure to use a very sharp knife. Cut off the top and the base. Stand the pineapple upright and, working from top to bottom, trim off the skin in even strips. Be careful not to cut away too much of the flesh. Don't bother removing the tough core for this recipe. You can cut around it as you eat the grilled slices.

Shaking the Salt Habit

Historically, salt has held strong symbolic value. It was believed to keep evil spirits away, it was a customary gift to newborns in ancient times, and it was one of the first edible items to be taxed. Salt and sodium are not the same thing, but because the two words are used interchangeably, people are often confused about the difference. Sodium is a mineral that combines with chlorine to form salt, and it's a necessary nutrient that helps our bodies maintain water balance, transmit nerve impulses, and contract muscles. For some people, too much sodium may contribute to high blood pressure and other related diseases. We need about 500 mg of sodium a day for normal bodily functions, but it's estimated that the average person consumes 4,000 to 5,000 mg daily. Experts recommend that we limit our sodium intake to no more than 2,400 mg a day. And while most people think that an overactive salt shaker is to blame for a high-sodium diet, salt added at the table accounts for only 25% of our total intake. So, there really isn't a whole lotta shakin' goin' on. Most dietary sodium comes from salt added during food processing. Large amounts of salt are often added to soups, salad dressings, dry dinner mixes, crackers, bouillon, sauces, condiments, canned vegetables, olives, pickles, canned meats, and cold cuts, to name some culprits. Your best bet for shaking the salt habit is to read the label before you buy.

Pine and Dine

Spicy, grilled pineapple slices

Our mouthwatering pineapple sure is a *fineapple*! The spicy basting sauce is what gives it a *brush* with greatness.

1 tbsp each lime juice and brown sugar
2 tsp honey mustard
1/2 tsp each ground cumin and chili powder
1/8 tsp cayenne pepper
1 large sweet pineapple, peeled and cut into 8 round slices (see Cooking 101)

- Preheat grill.
- To prepare basting sauce, combine lime juice, brown sugar, honey mustard, cumin, chili powder, and cayenne in a small bowl.
- Grill pineapple slices over medium-hot coals for 3 to 4 minutes per side, until lightly browned and warmed through. Brush both sides generously with sauce during cooking. Serve warm.

Makes 4 servings

Per serving: 103 calories, 0.9 g fat, 0.1 g saturated fat, 0.9 g protein, 25.5 g carbohydrate, 2.2 g fiber, 0 mg cholesterol, 43.3 mg sodium
% calories from fat: 7

What's in it for me?

'98 was a fine year for tomatoes.

I asked for a bottle of house red. He brought me the ketchup.

Rotini Bopper

Cheesy broccoli and pasta bake

Can't get your kids to eat broccoli? They'll dance with delight when they taste this creamy rotini and broccoli casserole. It takes a bit of slicing and dicing on your part, but it's not like you have to chop 'til you drop, or anything.

**8 oz rotini pasta, uncooked
(about 3 cups dry)
2 tsp butter or margarine
1-1/2 cups chopped mushrooms
1 cup diced carrots
1/2 cup minced onions
1 can (10-3/4 oz) reduced-fat
cream of celery soup, undiluted
1 cup shredded, reduced-fat sharp
cheddar cheese (4 oz)
3/4 cup 1% milk
1/4 cup grated Parmesan
cheese
3/4 tsp dried basil
1/2 tsp dried oregano
1/4 tsp black pepper
2 cups broccoli florets
1/4 cup minced red bell pepper**

• Cook rotini according to package directions. Drain well and place in a large bowl.

• While pasta is cooking, prepare sauce. Melt butter in a medium saucepan over medium-high heat. Add mushrooms, carrots, and onions. Cook and stir until mushrooms are tender, about 4 minutes. Add soup, cheddar cheese, milk, Parmesan cheese, basil, oregano, and pepper. Reduce heat to medium. Cook until cheeses are melted. Stir in broccoli and remove from heat.

• Pour broccoli mixture over pasta in bowl. Mix well. Spray a 9 x 13-inch baking pan with non-stick spray. Pour pasta mixture into pan and spread evenly. Sprinkle with red pepper. Cover with foil and bake at 350° for 30 minutes. Stir before serving.

Makes 8 servings

What's in it for me?

Per serving: 218 calories, 6 g fat, 3 g saturated fat, 11.5 g protein, 30.1 g carbohydrate, 1.1 g fiber, 17.6 mg cholesterol, 349.4 mg sodium
% calories from fat: 24

Crunch and Munch

Forget what your parents told you about snacking between meals. Studies now show that snacking is good for you. It's just too bad that our taste buds prefer banana cream pie over plain bananas. But, with so many healthy alternatives out there, we don't have to clog our arteries with lard-laden foods. When you reach for a snack, it's often a food's characteristic—crunchy, creamy, sweet—that appeals to you, rather than the food itself. Once you've decided what you're looking for, choose a low-fat, heart-healthy food that can satisfy your craving. Here are a few suggestions to get you going:

Crunchy: low-fat microwave popcorn, veggies with low-fat dip, pretzels, baked tortilla chips with salsa, reduced-fat crackers, toast with jam

Creamy: low-fat pudding or yogurt, frozen yogurt, part-skim cheeses, low-fat Fudgsicle, reduced-fat cream soups

Sweet: frozen juice bars, Fig Newtons, fresh fruit, fruit smoothies, angel food cake, low-fat, fruit-filled cereal bars.

YOU DO THE MATH

If "fast food" sounds a lot like "fat food," it's no coincidence. A typical fast-food cheeseburger holds up to 30 grams of fat and 500 calories! Next time you're at the drive-thru, order a grilled chicken sandwich (without mayo) instead. Make the trade once a week and you'll save 9,880 calories and 1,248 grams of fat a year. That's more than 18 days' worth of fat! If you boycott the burger, the savings could be big, Mac.

Where did the pretzel originate?

The pretzel, a great low-fat snack, was invented in the Middle Ages by an Italian monk. He twisted leftover bread dough into the unique pretzel shape, which represented arms being folded in prayer. He and his fellow monks used the baked treats as rewards for children who had learned their prayers. In fact, "pretzel" is from the Latin word *pretiola*, meaning "little award."

Who'da Thunk?

SAY IT AIN'T SO!

If your basic instinct is to lust for movie popcorn, it could be a fatal attraction. Traditionally, movie popcorn has been popped in super-fatty coconut oil. Nowadays, most theaters have switched to canola oil—partially hydrogenated canola oil, that is. Unfortunately, hydrogenation turns a good fat (monounsaturated) into a very bad fat (trans fatty acid), and that's bad news for your heart. Your hips won't like the news, either. All oils, "healthy" or not, have 14 grams of fat per tablespoon. So, how's a poor soul to prevent popping his pants by pigging out on popcorn? Try bringing along healthier snacks—maybe even sneak in some low-fat microwave popcorn. (Shhh! Don't tell!) But if you just can't resist, order a small bag, enjoy every bite, and cut back on your fat intake the next day. That way, it won't be a blockbuster night for your cardiologist.

New Year's Resolution: Something that goes in one year and out the other.

My Yammy Spice

A nutritious twist on regular, oven-baked fries

Police! Put your yams up! You're under arrest for tasting so good! You have the right to remain spicy! Any fries you bake can, and will, be used to lure your kids to the dinner table.

4 medium yams or sweet potatoes
1 tbsp olive oil
1/2 tsp each ground cumin, paprika, and dried oregano
1/4 tsp each salt and black pepper

- Spray a baking sheet with non-stick spray and set aside.

- Wash potatoes and pat dry using paper towels. Leave skins on. Slice potatoes into French-fry-like wedges, about 1/2-inch thick. Toss wedges with olive oil in a large bowl.

- In a small bowl, stir together remaining ingredients. Add to potatoes and toss until they're evenly coated with spice mixture.

- Arrange potatoes in a single layer on baking sheet. Bake at 450° for 25 minutes, turning wedges over halfway through cooking time. Serve hot.

Makes 4 servings

Per serving: 169 calories, 4 g fat, 0.1 g saturated fat, 2.3 g protein, 32 g carbohydrate, 4 g fiber, 0 mg cholesterol, 163 mg sodium % calories from fat: 21

What's in it for me?

THE SIDE SHOW

The Bulgur, the Better

Bulgur pilaf with five-spice powder and cranberries

We know what you're thinkin': Bulgur? You gotta be kidding! Is that something that comes from Bulgaria? Just calm down. There's no need to report us to the Better Bulgur Bureau. We just felt it was time for you to try something new, that's all.

2 tsp olive oil
1 cup diced celery
3/4 cup minced onions
2 cloves garlic, minced
1 cup coarse bulgur
  (see tip below)
1/4 cup dried cranberries (see p. 62)
1 tsp grated orange zest
1/2 tsp Chinese five-spice powder
2 cups low-fat chicken broth
1/4 tsp salt

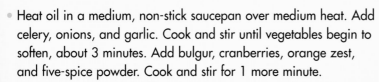

- Heat oil in a medium, non-stick saucepan over medium heat. Add celery, onions, and garlic. Cook and stir until vegetables begin to soften, about 3 minutes. Add bulgur, cranberries, orange zest, and five-spice powder. Cook and stir for 1 more minute.

- Add broth and salt. Bring to a boil. Reduce heat to low. Cover and simmer for 10 to 15 minutes, until liquid has been absorbed and bulgur is tender. Remove from heat and let stand for 5 minutes before serving.

Makes 4 to 6 servings

What's in it for me?

Per serving (based on 6 servings): 128 calories, 2 g fat, 0.1 g saturated fat, 4.3 g protein, 25.2 g carbohydrate, 5.3 g fiber, 0 mg cholesterol, 275.9 mg sodium
% calories from fat: 13

Partying is Such Sweet Sorrow

There's an old rule that says you should never go to the grocery store hungry. Well, the same rule applies to parties. Arriving at a social gathering accompanied by an empty stomach can wreak havoc on your willpower—and your physique—especially when you're surrounded with a smorgasbord of high-fat goodies. What you need is a pre-emptive snack, like a banana, to tame your appetite. And how about stacking the deck in your favor by bringing along some low-fat party food that fits into your healthy eating plan? Baked tortilla chips with salsa or a veggie plate with low-fat dip will do nicely. Once you're at the party, go ahead and sample the treats (note the word "sample"). That third handful of peanuts is tempting, but surely you can find something healthier to snack on. Oh, and whatever you do, don't engage in lengthy conversations while standing right beside the food table. That's when the automatic eating motion sets in. There you are, just gabbin' away, when your hand—unbeknownst to you—reaches down, grabs another potato skin, and moves it directly toward your mouth. *Brain to hand, brain to hand: That potato skin has not been cleared to land! Repeat: Not cleared to land!* You'll have more control if you grab a plate, put a few nibbles on it, and move away. Better yet—use a napkin. You'll be less inclined to pile it high.

What the heck is bulgur and where can I buy it?

Bulgur is a nutritious, quick-cooking form of whole wheat. It's often confused with, but is not exactly the same as, cracked wheat. Bulgur is created when wheat kernels are steamed, dried, and crushed. When cooked, it has a nutty flavor and chewy texture. Look for bulgur in well-stocked supermarkets or natural-food stores.

No disease that can be treated by diet should be treated by any other means.

Maimonides
Jewish father of medicine

COOKING 101

Italian balsamic vinegar is made from white Trebbiano grape juice. It gets its dark color and pungent sweetness from aging in wooden barrels over a period of several years. It's more expensive than other vinegars, but a little balsamic vinegar goes a long way.

Who'da Thunk?

How was cheese discovered?

Legend has it that cheese was accidentally created by a traveling Arab merchant named Kanana. When he started on a long trip across the Sahara, Kanana put his supply of milk in a pouch made of a sheep's stomach, and slung it over his camel. Apparently, there were still traces of the digestive enzyme, rennet, in the stomach lining. The rennet, heated by the sun and stirred by the camel's trot, caused the curds in the milk to separate from the whey. When he sat down to eat his lunch, Kanana discovered his good fortune.

This Spud's For You!

Simple, roasted potatoes with green beans and onions, tossed in balsamic vinegar

For all you do, this spud's for you! Makes a great accompaniment to roasted or barbecued meats.

1-1/2 pounds small red potatoes, unpeeled, quartered (see hint below)
2 medium onions, peeled and quartered
1 tbsp olive oil
8 oz fresh green beans, stems removed
2 tbsp balsamic vinegar (see Cooking 101)
1 tsp dried thyme
1/2 tsp salt
1/4 tsp black pepper

- Spray a medium roasting pan with non-stick spray. Add potatoes, onions, and olive oil. Mix well. Cover with foil and roast at 400° for 30 minutes.

- Add beans, vinegar, thyme, salt, and pepper to potatoes in pan. Stir until vegetables are coated with vinegar and seasonings. Roast, uncovered, for 25 more minutes, until potatoes are tender and crisp around edges.

Makes 6 servings

Hint: If using mini red potatoes, cut them in half instead of quartering them.

Per serving: 173 calories, 2.6 g fat, 0 g saturated fat, 3.7 g protein, 34.7 g carbohydrate, 3.9 g fiber, 0 mg cholesterol, 212 mg sodium % calories from fat: 13

What's in it for me?

Did you hear about the bag of popcorn that was arrested down at the theater? He was charged with a salt and buttery.

The Sweets of San Francisco

You deserve a cake today (and squares and cookies, too!)

Abracadaiquiri Pie

Frozen strawberry daiquiri pie
with a graham crust

Ta daa!

Presto! It's the best-o! Not even
The Amazing Kreskin can figure
out how this magical treat
could also be low in fat.

**1 cup crushed, low-fat
graham crackers**
2 tbsp sugar
**2 tbsp light butter or
margarine, melted**
**1 can (14 oz) low-fat
sweetened condensed milk**
**1/2 cup frozen strawberry
daiquiri mix concentrate, thawed**
1 cup frozen strawberries in light syrup, thawed
2 cups light frozen whipped topping, thawed
Fresh strawberries for garnish (optional)

- To make crust, combine graham crumbs, sugar, and butter in a
  small bowl. Spray an 8-inch springform pan with non-stick spray.
  Press crumb mixture evenly over bottom of pan. Place crust in
  freezer while you prepare filling.

- Beat sweetened condensed milk and daiquiri mix on low speed
  of electric mixer. Add strawberries and beat again until well
  blended. Fold in whipped topping. Pour into prepared crust.
  Cover with plastic wrap and freeze overnight.

- To serve, run a knife around edge of pan and remove sides.
  Garnish individual pieces with fresh strawberries, if desired.

Makes 10 servings

What's
in it
for me?

Per serving: 293 calories, 6 g fat,
3.6 g saturated fat, 5.1 g protein,
54.9 g carbohydrate, 1.2 g fiber,
7 mg cholesterol, 147 mg sodium
% calories from fat: 18

Nondairy coffee whiteners may boast a
"cholesterol-free" banner, but they're
certainly not fat-free. Often they're
made with palm or coconut oil, or
with hydrogenated vegetable oil, all
heavyweight fat offenders that are too
much for your heart to handle. Many
coffee whiteners have more calories per
serving than light cream! They can brag
all they want about being "nondairy," but
when your hips start rustlin' up all that fat,
you'll be in a bad mooood.

Who'da
Thunk?

What are graham
crackers made of?

They're made of graham
flour, silly. But what the
heck is graham flour?
Well, it's a type of flour
that was promoted by a
19th century Presbyterian
minister named Sylvester Graham, who
was active in the temperance movement.
He felt that eating a healthful diet could
cure alcoholism and lead to a more
wholesome lifestyle, so he travelled across
the United States preaching the evils of
eating meats and fats, which he was sure
led to sexual promiscuity. His answer to
man's (and woman's) lack of virtue was a
diet of vegetables, fruits, and whole wheat
bread made with graham flour in place of
white bread—more dietary fiber to
strengthen society's moral fiber!

Why is it that lemonade and lemon pie filling are made with
artificial lemon flavoring, but dish soap and furniture polish are
made with real lemon juice?

FAT OR **FICTION?**

Chocoholics rejoice! Even though this bittersweet treat is high in saturated fat, a recent study showed that men who consumed stearic acid, the saturated fat in chocolate, reduced their risk of developing blood clots. Chocolate is also rich in flavonoids, the natural chemicals credited with making red wine heart-healthy, and it also contains anandamide, a chemical that stimulates the same areas of the brain that marijuana does. But don't worry. There's not enough of the chemical to get you thrown in the slammer. Realistically, you'd have to consume 25 pounds or more at one sitting to get the smallest marijuana-like effect. While chocolate doesn't qualify as a health food, it sure is good for the soul, especially on Valentine's Day when it comes in a heart-shaped box. Looks like what's good for your sweetheart may be good for your heart, too!

Choco Doodle Do's

Super-moist, chocolate-mint brownies

Stomach alarm going off? Then awaken your taste buds with a chocolaty treat so sinfully delicious, you'll think you're dreaming.

1/2 cup all-purpose flour
1 pkg (4 oz) instant chocolate fudge pudding mix
1/2 tsp baking powder
1/4 tsp salt
2/3 cup sugar
3 tbsp butter or margarine, softened
1 egg
1 egg white
1/4 cup baby food prunes (see hint below)
1 tsp vanilla
1/3 cup mint chocolate chips

- Preheat oven to 350°. Spray an 8-inch square baking pan with non-stick spray and set aside.
- In a medium bowl, mix together flour, pudding mix, baking powder, and salt. Set aside.
- In a large bowl, beat together sugar, butter, egg, and egg white on medium speed of electric mixer. Add prunes and vanilla and beat again. Add flour mixture and beat until smooth. Fold in mint chips.
- Spread batter evenly in prepared pan. Bake for 30 to 35 minutes. Brownies should be dry to touch and appear somewhat puffy. Place pan on a wire rack and let brownies cool before cutting. Cut into 12 pieces and store in an airtight container or covered with plastic wrap.

Makes 12 brownies

Hint: Baby food prunes help keep the brownies moist, but you won't taste the prune flavor—honest!

Don't tell jokes in the kitchen. The dishes might crack up.

Per brownie: 155 calories, 4.5 g fat, 2.7 g saturated fat, 2.1 g protein, 27.1 g carbohydrate, 0.3 g fiber, 25.8 mg cholesterol, 117.6 mg sodium
% calories from fat: 26

What's in it for me?

Impeached Rice Pudding

Creamy, rich-tasting, baked rice pudding with a hint of peach

Come on! Look us in the eye and just admit it: Our rice pudding is too good to be truthful. (But that depends on what your definition of the word "is" is.)

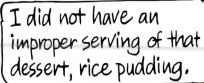

I did not have an improper serving of that dessert, rice pudding.

2 cups 2% milk
1/2 cup honey
2 eggs
2 tsp vanilla
4 cups cooked short- or medium-grain rice (see Cooking 101)
1/3 cup raisins
1 cup low-fat, peach-flavored yogurt
1/2 tsp cinnamon

- Preheat oven to 350°.

- In a large bowl, whisk together milk, honey, eggs, and vanilla. Add cooked rice and raisins and mix well. Pour mixture into a 2-quart casserole dish that has been sprayed with non-stick spray. Cover and bake for 40 minutes, stirring twice during cooking time.

- Remove pudding from oven and let cool. Stir in yogurt and cinnamon. Tastes great warm or cold. Store leftovers in refrigerator.

Makes 8 servings

What's in it for us?

Per serving: 262 calories, 2.5 g fat, 1.2 g saturated fat, 7.1 g protein, 52 g carbohydrate, 0.3 g fiber, 59 mg cholesterol, 61.8 mg sodium
% calories from fat: 9

COOKING 101

Short-grain rice is small, oval-shaped, starchy, and somewhat sticky. When cooked, it makes a creamy, velvety dish, but the centers of the rice kernels remain chewy. Arborio is an Italian short-grain rice used in making risottos, and it works beautifully in this rice pudding, too. Just be aware that our recipe calls for cooked rice. Medium-grain rice has slightly longer grains and is less sticky, but works equally well here.

YOU DO THE MATH

Eggstra! Eggstra! Read all about it! If you enjoy having scrambled eggs once a week, make the following minor change to avoid gaining major poundage: Instead of scrambling two eggs in a tablespoon of butter, cook one egg and one egg white in butter-flavored cooking spray. You'll save 8,100 calories and 825 grams of fat in a year. That's more than 12 days' worth of fat! What a shell-shocker.

Broomhilda running a spell check.

Let's see... One cup eye of newt, two cups chopped tongue of bat

Do the Cocoa Motion Cheesecake

Creamy, dreamy, chocolate and Kahlúa cheesecake

C'mon, baby! Taste the cocoa motion! Your little baby sister could make it with ease. It's easier than learning your ABCs. One bite and you'll be dancing with delight!

1 cup chocolate Oreo baking crumbs
1 tbsp brown sugar
1 tbsp butter or margarine, melted
2 cups low-fat (1%) cottage cheese
2 cups low-fat sour cream
8 oz light cream cheese, softened
1 cup sugar
1/2 cup packed brown sugar
2/3 cup unsweetened cocoa powder
3/4 cup fat-free egg substitute, or 3 whole eggs
2 tbsp cornstarch
1 tsp vanilla
1/4 cup Kahlúa or coffee liqueur
Fresh strawberries for garnish (optional)

- Preheat oven to 350°.

- To make crust, combine crumbs, brown sugar, and melted butter in a small bowl. Mix well. Spray a 9-inch springform pan with non-stick spray. Press crumb mixture evenly over bottom of pan. Bake for 10 minutes. Remove from oven and let cool. Reduce heat to 325°.

- In a blender or food processor, whirl cottage cheese, sour cream, and cream cheese until smooth. Set aside.

- In a large bowl, beat together both sugars, cocoa powder, and egg substitute on medium speed of electric mixer. Add cream cheese mixture and beat until smooth. Add cornstarch and beat again. Add vanilla and Kahlúa and beat until mixture is well blended.

- Pour batter into prepared crust. Bake for 1 hour and 20 minutes. Cheesecake will appear puffy and will jiggle slightly when shaken. Turn off heat. Open oven door halfway and let cake cool in oven for 2 hours. Chill overnight. Before serving, run a knife around edge of pan and remove sides. Garnish with fresh strawberries, if desired.

Makes 12 servings

Per serving: 283 calories, 6.6 g fat, 3.2 g saturated fat, 12.1 g protein, 44.3 g carbohydrate, 1.6 g fiber, 37.6 mg cholesterol, 412.4 mg sodium
% calories from fat: 21

What's in it for me?

Actual announcement on church bulletin: Potluck dinner Saturday night. Prayer and medication to follow.

The Trifle Tower

Berry trifle with angel food cake
and creamy custard

It's a trifle, but it certainly isn't trifling, if you know what we mean. No siree. In fact, this wondrous creation is quite significant. It's the skyscraper of desserts, piled high with heavenly delights.

1-1/2 cups evaporated skim milk
1 cup 1% milk
1/3 cup sugar
3 tbsp custard powder
  (see tip in margin)
1/4 cup seedless raspberry jam
1 tbsp frozen orange juice concentrate,
  thawed
1 prepared angel food cake,
  cut into bite-sized pieces
2 cups sliced, fresh strawberries
1-1/2 cups each fresh blueberries and raspberries
Fresh mint for garnish (optional)

• To prepare custard, combine evaporated milk, 1% milk, sugar, and custard powder in a medium saucepan. Cook and stir over medium heat until mixture begins to bubble and has thickened. Remove from heat. Cover top of custard with a small piece of plastic wrap to prevent a skin from forming. Let cool for 10 minutes.

• Meanwhile, melt raspberry jam in microwave or in a small saucepan over medium heat. Stir in orange juice concentrate.

• To assemble trifle, arrange 1/3 cake pieces over bottom of a trifle bowl or straight-sided glass bowl. Drizzle with 1/3 raspberry jam mixture. Spread 1/3 custard evenly over cake, followed by 1/3 fresh berries. Repeat layering twice, ending with berries. Cover with plastic wrap and refrigerate until cold. Garnish with sprigs of fresh mint before serving, if desired.

Makes 10 servings

What's in it for me? ➤ Per serving: 216 calories, 0.9 g fat, 0.3 g saturated fat, 6.3 g protein, 46.5 g carbohydrate, 3.1 g fiber, 2.4 mg cholesterol, 321.2 mg sodium
% calories from fat: 4

What the heck is custard powder and where can I buy it?

Custard powder is simply a combination of cornstarch, salt, and artificial flavoring. It's a low-fat, egg-free way to create a thick, cooked, pudding-like dessert or a creamy dessert sauce, depending on how much of it you use. You'll find custard powder in tins or boxes near the pudding at your grocery store.

Tea for Tooth

Let's talk tea, the world's other caffeine drink. Tea has the same mood-elevating effects as coffee, thanks to caffeine, and like chocolate, it has the muscle stimulant theobromine. But that's only the beginning of tea's greatness. It seems to lower blood pressure and cholesterol levels, stabilize blood sugar levels, and lower the risk of heart disease and cancer. Most of this good stuff is because of antioxidants that occur naturally in both green and black tea. But did you know that some of the compounds in tea can actually kill the bacteria that get a cavity rolling? It's true! We're telling the tooth, the whole tooth, and nothing but the tooth! The tea chemicals prevent acid-generating bacteria from sticking to your teeth and gnawing at the surface. No sticking. No cavities. No kidding!

They say figures don't lie, but girdles sure condense the truth!

Some popular activities just don't burn as many calories as people would like to think. Take running off at the mouth, for example. Sure sounds strenuous. So does playing the field, jogging your memory, raking in the bucks, building a reputation, sweeping it under a rug, hiking up your hemline, and social climbing. Calories expended during these Olympic-like feats of physical fitness: Zip, zero, zilch! Sorry to burst your bubble (bursting bubbles—zero calories burned). If you're aiming for a leaner, stronger, healthier you, remember that actions speak louder than words. Run, play, jog, rake, build, sweep, hike, and climb. Whatever you do, don't rest on your laurels.

Who'da Thunk?

Why do we like sweets?

It's simply a matter of evolution. Most things found in the wild that taste sweet are good to eat. On the other hand, most bitter things are poisonous or just not good for you. Over the course of human history, those who preferred sweet things tended to survive better than those who ate bitter things. And four out of five dentists surveyed are very happy about this!

Marsha, Marsha, Marshmallow Squares

Our toasted-oat cereal squares are sure to be a hit with children

Why do our chewy cereal squares get all the attention? 'Cause they're packed with a delicious combination of crispy oat flakes, raisins, almonds, marshmallows, and chocolate chips! Makes a big batch for a big bunch.

1 pkg (16 oz) marshmallows
1/3 cup light margarine or butter (see hint below)
1 tsp vanilla
1 box (19-1/4 oz) Oatmeal Crisp Raisin cereal
1/2 cup semisweet chocolate chips

- In a large saucepan, melt marshmallows and margarine over medium heat, stirring constantly. When mixture is smooth, remove from heat and stir in vanilla. Add cereal in small batches, stirring well after each addition. Stir in chocolate chips.

- Spray a 9 x 13-inch baking pan with non-stick spray. Press cereal mixture evenly into pan. Cover with plastic wrap and refrigerate until firm, about 1 hour. For crunchy squares, store in an airtight container in the refrigerator. For chewy squares, store at room temperature.

Makes 24 squares

Hint: You can find reduced-fat varieties of margarine or butter (25% less fat) beside the regular brands in the dairy case.

Per square: 172 calories, 3.2 g fat, 0.9 g saturated fat, 2.4 g protein, 34 g carbohydrate, 1.5 g fiber, 0 mg cholesterol, 122.7 mg sodium
% calories from fat: 17

What's in it for me?

She feeds him like he's a god.
Every meal is a burnt offering.

Bonbon Jovi

Chewy, chocolaty, oatmeal
and coconut clusters

Hunky treats that will make your
heart throb for more! Not technically
"bonbons," but we loved the name and
figured these were pretty close.

2 cups sugar
6 tbsp unsweetened cocoa powder
1/2 cup evaporated 2% milk
1/3 cup margarine
   (see hint below)
1/2 tsp vanilla
3 cups quick-cooking rolled oats
1 cup sweetened, shredded coconut

• In a medium saucepan, combine sugar, cocoa, evaporated milk,
  and margarine. Cook and stir over medium-high heat until
  mixture comes to a boil. Boil for 1 minute, stirring constantly.

• Remove from heat. Stir in vanilla. Add rolled oats and coconut
  and mix well. Drop by tablespoonfuls onto a cookie sheet lined
  with waxed paper. Refrigerate until firm, about 30 minutes to
  1 hour. Store in an airtight container in the refrigerator or at
  room temperature.

Makes 35 bonbons

Hint: For the healthiest type of margarine, look for the word
"non-hydrogenated" on the label.

What's
in it
for me?

Per bonbon: 104 calories, 3.4 g fat,
1.3 g saturated fat, 1.6 g protein,
18.3 g carbohydrate, 1.1 g fiber,
0.3 mg cholesterol, 24 mg sodium
% calories from fat: 28

He used to be quite an athlete in his time—
big chest, washboard stomach. But that's all
behind him now.

It's Good to be Dense

Most people know that 99% of the
calcium in our bodies is found in the
bones and teeth. It's the remaining one
percent that's shrouded in mystery. The
role of calcium found in our cells and in
the fluid that surrounds them is nothing to
shake a bone at. Uh...that's shake a stick
at. Calcium helps regulate blood pressure,
nerve transmission, muscle contractions,
blood clotting, and secretion of hormones
and digestive enzymes. But back to the
bone-building business. Think of your
bones as a bank. If your diet is low in
calcium, your blood *withdraws* it from
your bones. When your diet is rich in
calcium, you make *deposits* in your
calcium bank. Over time, if withdrawals
exceed deposits, your bones begin to
weaken, and when they're less dense,
they're more susceptible to breaking.
Make no bones about it, there's no
overdraft protection in this bank account!
Good sources of calcium are skim milk,
low-fat yogurt, part-skim cheeses, tofu,
soy milk, and dark, leafy green
vegetables.

TRIVIAL
TIDBIT

The average person eats
about 2,000 pounds
of food each year,
equivalent to a pickup
truckload.

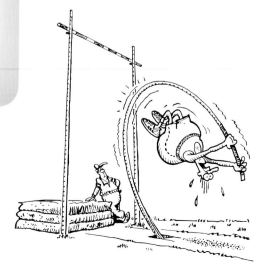

A 20-ounce can of crushed pineapple will yield about 1-1/2 cups after you drain it well. Empty the can into a wire strainer, and press down on the pineapple to remove the juice. Incidentally, pineapple was named for its resemblance to the pine cone, and has been used for centuries as a symbol of hospitality.

SAY IT AIN'T SO!

Don't be lulled into a false sense of security by food products with healthy-sounding names. Take carrot cake, for example. Nearly all store-bought varieties contain refined flour, eggs, and shortening, plus high-fat cream cheese and loads of sugar in the frosting. And that's not even the icing on the cake... well, actually...it is. Anyway, this popular dessert may contain more than one cup of oil, which has nearly 2,000 hip-hugging calories! Now that takes the cake! (Avoid the oil spill by making our recipe over yonder—it's 24-*carrot*-gold delicious.)

If you think you have someone eating out of your hands, it's a good idea to count your fingers.

Must Bake Carrot Cake

Our test-kitchen dummies said this was the best carrot cake they've ever tasted

It's simply the best. Better than all the rest. But don't take our word for it. Just bake it!

2-1/2 cups all-purpose flour
2 tsp cinnamon
1-1/2 tsp each baking powder and baking soda
1/2 tsp salt
1-1/2 cups packed brown sugar
1 cup drained, crushed pineapple (see Cooking 101)
3/4 cup fat-free egg substitute, or 3 whole eggs
3/4 cup buttermilk
1/2 cup unsweetened applesauce
1/3 cup vegetable oil
2 tsp vanilla
3 cups grated carrots
1/2 cup chopped walnuts
Cheater's Icing
1 tub (16 oz) Betty Crocker low-fat vanilla icing
1 tbsp frozen orange juice concentrate, thawed
1 tsp grated orange zest

- Preheat oven to 350°. Spray a 9 x 13-inch baking pan with non-stick spray and set aside.

- Combine first 5 ingredients in a medium bowl. Set aside.

- In a large bowl, whisk together brown sugar, pineapple, egg substitute, buttermilk, applesauce, oil, and vanilla. Stir in grated carrots. Add flour mixture to carrot mixture and stir until well blended. Stir in walnuts.

- Pour batter into prepared pan. Bake for 35 to 40 minutes, or until a toothpick inserted in center of cake comes out clean. Set pan on a wire rack and cool cake completely.

- While cake is cooling, prepare icing. Transfer icing from tub to a medium bowl. Add orange juice concentrate and orange zest. Mix well. Refrigerate until ready to use. When cake is cool, spread icing evenly over top. Cover with plastic wrap and store in refrigerator.

Makes 24 servings

Per serving: 235 calories, 5.8 g fat, 0.6 g saturated fat, 3.1 g protein, 43.3 g carbohydrate, 1.1 g fiber, 0.3 mg cholesterol, 182.3 mg sodium
% calories from fat: 22

What's in it for me?

Copabanana Cake

Banana snack cake with chocolate chips

Her name was Lola. She was a showgirl. But that was 30 years ago, when she used to have a show. Today she prefers to stay home and bake scrumptious cakes like this one.

2 cups all-purpose flour
1 tsp each baking powder and
   baking soda
1/2 tsp salt
1 cup sugar
1/2 cup fat-free egg substitute,
   or 2 whole eggs
1/4 cup butter or margarine,
   softened
1 cup mashed, ripe bananas
1/2 cup low-fat sour cream
1 tsp vanilla
1/2 cup mini chocolate chips

- Preheat oven to 350°. Spray a 9 x 13-inch baking pan with non-stick spray and set aside.

- In a medium bowl, combine flour, baking powder, baking soda, and salt. Set aside.

- In a large bowl, beat together sugar, egg substitute, and butter on medium speed of electric mixer. Add bananas, sour cream, and vanilla. Beat again until smooth.

- Gradually add flour mixture to banana mixture, beating after each addition. Batter will be thick. Fold in chocolate chips.

- Spoon batter into prepared pan and spread evenly using a spatula. Bake for 25 to 28 minutes, or until a toothpick inserted in center of cake comes out clean. Cool completely on a wire rack. Cut into 16 pieces and store in an airtight container.

Makes 16 servings

When it comes to cream cheese, a little dab'll do ya. That's because regular cream cheese has 100 calories and 10 grams of fat per ouch. (Oops. That's ounce.) If you spread light cream cheese on your bagel twice a week instead of the full-fat kind, you'll save over 4,160 calories and 520 grams of fat in a year. That's almost eight days' worth of fat! No need to get cheesed off—just lighten up!

Banana Banter

A recent California study showed how one banana a day can reduce the risk of stroke by as much as 40%. Ai Chiquita! Patients in the study were on medication to control high blood pressure. Unfortunately, the medication was depleting their bodies' stores of potassium. Low potassium can lead to an increased risk of stroke. By eating one banana each day, they restored the correct level. Need another reason to reach for bananas? They're packed in their own biodegradable container. No wonder environmentalists think bananas have *appeel*!

What's in it for me?

Per serving: 185 calories, 5.1 g fat, 2.1 g saturated fat, 3.2 g protein, 32.2 g carbohydrate, 0.8 g fiber, 9 mg cholesterol, 183 mg sodium
% calories from fat: 25

He takes vitamins A, B, C, D, E, F, G, and still looks like H.

If you want to melt fat effortlessly, try the grapefruit diet.

FAT OR FICTION?

Remember this one? A grapefruit for breakfast, lunch, dinner, and presto—kiss cellulite good-bye. (Yuk! Not a very pleasant thought.) Supposedly, this diet could melt the pounds away. The truth is, no food can miraculously burn fat. People following grapefruit diets lose weight because they eat little else. That can be dangerous because your body isn't getting all the nutrients it needs to function properly. However, it's still very smart to eat grapefruit. Besides containing vitamin C, potassium, iron, and calcium, grapefruits are also high in pectin, a soluble fiber that lowers blood cholesterol. In addition, they contain flavonoids and other plant chemicals that protect against cancer and heart disease. Lots of juicy reasons to eat more grapefruit...more than meets the eye, in fact.

THE E FILES

Got a bad case of the TV-jeebies? Congratulations! Voluntarily boycotting the tube puts you squarely on the road to a healthier lifestyle! Almost any activity burns more calories than watching TV. A study of 6,000 men found that those who watched more than three hours daily were twice as likely to be overweight as those who watched less than an hour a day. Another study says that we watch television 40% of the time that we don't spend eating, sleeping, working, or doing chores. Shouldn't we live, rather than watch, the *Days of Our Lives*?

The City of Happiness is found in the State of Mind.

Cookies for Rookies

Peanut-butter, oatmeal, and chocolate-chip cookies

If you're kookie over cookies, these easy-to-make treats are no sweat and no threat, even for the confirmed kitchen klutz.

1-1/4 cups all-purpose flour
1 cup quick-cooking rolled oats
1/2 tsp each baking soda and salt
3/4 cup packed brown sugar
1/3 cup light margarine or butter (see hint below)
1/3 cup light peanut butter
1/4 cup buttermilk
1/3 cup mini chocolate chips

- Preheat oven to 350°. Spray a large cookie sheet with non-stick spray and set aside.

- In a medium bowl, combine flour, oats, baking soda, and salt. Set aside.

- In another medium bowl, cream together brown sugar, margarine, peanut butter, and buttermilk. Add dry ingredients and stir to form a smooth dough. Stir in chocolate chips.

- Roll dough into 1-1/2-inch balls, and place 2 inches apart on prepared cookie sheet. Using a fork dipped in flour, flatten cookies to 1/4-inch thickness. Bake for 10 minutes. Be careful not to overbake, as cookies will dry out.

- Remove cookies from tray immediately and cool on a wire rack. Store covered with plastic wrap or in an airtight container.

Makes 30 cookies

Hint: You can find reduced-fat varieties of margarine or butter (25% less fat) beside the regular brands in the dairy case.

Per cookie: 80 calories, 2.7 g fat, 0.7 g saturated fat, 1.6 g protein, 13 g carbohydrate, 0.4 g fiber, 0 mg cholesterol, 94.6 mg sodium
% calories from fat: 30

What's in it for me?

Girls Just Wanna Have Fudge

Chocolate and peanut-butter fudge, that is

It's my party, and I'll eat fudge if I want to...fudge if I want to. You'd eat fudge, too, if it happened to you.

1-1/2 cups sugar
3/4 cup brown sugar
1/3 cup unsweetened cocoa powder
2/3 cup evaporated 2% milk
1 cup miniature marshmallows
1/4 cup light peanut butter
2 tbsp butter

- In a medium, non-stick saucepan, combine sugar, brown sugar, cocoa, and milk. Bring to a boil slowly over medium-low heat, stirring frequently. Boil until a few drops of hot syrup form a soft ball when dropped in a cup of ice water. (This stage of fudge-making is usually reached when a candy thermometer registers between 234° and 240°.)

- Remove from heat and stir in marshmallows, peanut butter, and butter. Stir until marshmallows are completely melted. Let fudge stand for 15 minutes without stirring.

- Meanwhile, line bottom of a 9 x 5-inch loaf pan with a piece of waxed paper that sticks up 2 inches at both ends of pan (so you can lift out the fudge when it's ready). Spread fudge in pan. Refrigerate until firm, about 1 to 1-1/2 hours. Cut into 24 pieces and store covered in refrigerator.

Makes 24 pieces

What's in it for me?

Per piece: 112 calories, 2.2 g fat, 1 g saturated fat, 1.2 g protein, 23 g carbohydrate, 0.4 g fiber, 3.1 mg cholesterol, 23.4 mg sodium
% calories from fat: 17

She's in such bad shape, she breathes hard when her stockings run.

Cholesterol's Split Personality

Your LDL level is too high. Your HDL level is too low. Wondering what the H_LL your doctor is talking about? Here's the lowdown on Low-Density Lipoprotein (LDL) and High-Density Lipoprotein (HDL), the fat and protein particles that carry cholesterol throughout your body. In simple terms, LDL is like a raft on which cholesterol sails into your system. If the cholesterol isn't used for cell metabolism and if it's not cleared, it accumulates in the arteries and can lead to a heart attack or stroke. That's why LDL is called "bad" cholesterol. The "L" stands for lousy, as far as your arteries are concerned. HDL is the kinder, gentler alter ego. It seems to have the beneficial capacity to pick up cholesterol and bring it back to the liver for reprocessing or excretion. So the "H" stands for healthy in your books. Now, rather than obsess over the ABCs of HDLs, just remember this: If your doctor tells you that your cholesterol levels are too high, you need to limit your intake of animal-based foods like eggs, meat, poultry, cheese, and high-fat milk products, which are cholesterol culprits. But overall, it's the total amount of fat (and saturated fat, in particular) in your diet that has the greatest impact on blood cholesterol. So, if you mind the fats, you'll score an A+ on your cholesterol report card.

SAY IT AIN'T SO!

Beware of high-fat snacks masquerading as healthy choices. Take banana chips, for example. They must be good for you—they're fruit, right? Actually, they're fried fruit. *Dole* out a three-ounce serving (a small bag) and you're looking at 441 calories and 28 grams of fat. That's enough to knock your lipid levels a few notches closer to a maybe-we-should-consider-medication chat with your doctor. If you don't want your health to slip, eat the real thing, not the chip.

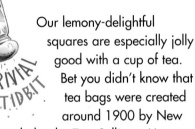

TRIVIAL TIDBIT

Our lemony-delightful squares are especially jolly good with a cup of tea. Bet you didn't know that tea bags were created around 1900 by New York tea wholesaler Tom Sullivan. He wrapped his samples in little silk bags, never thinking his customers would brew the tea, bag and all. Needless to say, his invention created quite a brew-haha!

I'm afraid your condition is hereditary.

In that case, send the bill to my parents!

Jollygood Squares

Light and lemony, no-bake cheesecake squares

Our prayers have been answered! God save our gracious Queen's leftovers. Send us victorious, happy, and glorious lemon squares.

1 pkg (3 oz) lemon-flavored jelly powder
1 cup boiling water
1-1/2 cups crushed, low-fat graham crackers
3 tbsp light butter or margarine, melted
1 tbsp packed brown sugar
8 oz light cream cheese
1 cup sugar
2 tbsp lemon juice
2 tsp grated lemon zest
1 tsp vanilla
4 cups light frozen whipped topping, thawed

They're jolly good!

- In a small bowl, dissolve jelly powder in boiling water. Refrigerate until slightly thickened, but not set (about 45 minutes).

- Meanwhile, prepare crust. In a small bowl, combine graham crumbs, melted butter, and brown sugar. Stir well using a fork. Spray a 9 x 13-inch baking pan with non-stick spray. Press crumb mixture evenly over bottom of pan. Refrigerate while you make filling.

- To prepare filling, beat together cream cheese, sugar, lemon juice, lemon zest, and vanilla on high speed of electric mixer. Beat until smooth. Add thickened jelly and beat on medium speed until well blended. Fold in whipped topping.

- Pour lemon mixture over prepared crust and spread evenly to edges of pan. Refrigerate for 4 hours, until set. Cut into squares and serve.

Makes 24 squares

Hint: This dessert looks and tastes great when served with fresh berries or a spoonful of blueberry or cherry pie filling on top of each square.

Per square: 133 calories, 4.5 g fat, 2.8 g saturated fat, 1.9 g protein, 21.8 g carbohydrate, 0.5 g fiber, 3.3 mg cholesterol, 122.6 mg sodium % calories from fat: 30

What's in it for me?

THE E FILES

If you take in just 100 extra calories a day—the amount in a single tablespoon of mayonnaise—you could gain 11 pounds in one year. On the other hand, if you went for a brisk 30- to 40-minute walk each day, you could burn about 100 calories and lose 11 pounds in one year. Although this formula is a bit simplistic (not everyone acquires or expends pounds at that rate), it shows how small changes can make a big difference in your weight over time. Now, we wouldn't want you to become obsessed with the math of calorie-counting, so we'll sum it up like this: Calories count. They add up. And they multiply, too—all over your body, until your figure spans the great divide. Fortunately, you can subtract from that figure with the addition of any kind of physical activity, however big or small, to your everyday life. All that's required is a calculated effort.

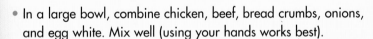

It's no wonder television became known as the "boob tube." Researchers at Kansas State University found that people who had just watched television for a mere 15 minutes had diminished brain-wave activity. Switch off the telly or your brain turns to jelly!

Those who think they have no time for bodily exercise will sooner or later have to find time for illness.

Edward Stanley

Burger, She Wrote

Teriyaki-seasoned beef and chicken burgers for the barbecue

It's an unsolved mystery: How could burgers that taste this great also be low in fat? All clues point to the same suspect: Teri Yaki. Throw the cookbook at her!

3/4 pound skinless ground chicken or turkey
3/4 pound extra-lean ground beef
1/3 cup unseasoned, dry bread crumbs
1/3 cup minced green onions
1 egg white
1/4 cup ketchup
2 tbsp reduced-sodium soy sauce
1 tbsp brown sugar
1-1/2 tsp grated gingerroot
1 clove garlic, minced
1/2 tsp sesame oil
6 hamburger rolls
Lettuce, sliced tomatoes, and your favorite burger toppings (optional)

- In a large bowl, combine chicken, beef, bread crumbs, onions, and egg white. Mix well (using your hands works best).

- In a small bowl, combine ketchup, soy sauce, brown sugar, gingerroot, garlic, and sesame oil. Add 3 tablespoons of this mixture to ground meat, and mix well. Reserve remaining sauce to brush on burgers while grilling.

- Shape meat mixture into 6 patties. Cook burgers over medium-hot coals for about 5 minutes per side, or until desired "doneness" is reached. Baste with reserved sauce.

- Serve on hamburger rolls with your favorite toppings.

Makes 6 burgers

Per burger: 318 calories, 7.3 g fat, 1.9 g saturated fat, 31.3 g protein, 31.3 g carbohydrate, 1.5 g fiber, 57.1 mg cholesterol, 664.2 mg sodium % calories from fat: 21

What's in it for me?

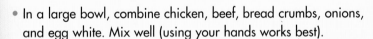

MISCELLOONEYOUS

163

It's a Wonderful Loaf

Ground chicken and beef are paired
in this twist on traditional meat loaf

Nominated for Best Meat Loaf in a Starring Role,
our recipe is sure to become a classic!

1/4 cup ketchup
1 tbsp brown sugar
1/2 tsp dry mustard
   powder
3/4 pound skinless ground
   chicken or turkey
3/4 pound extra-lean
   ground beef
1 cup Italian-style dry
   bread crumbs
1/2 cup peeled, grated sweet potato or carrots
1/2 cup unpeeled, grated zucchini
1/2 cup minced onions
1/4 cup chopped, fresh parsley
1/4 cup milk (1% or 2%)
2 egg whites
1 tsp dried thyme
1/2 tsp each dried sage and salt
1/4 tsp black pepper

- Combine first 3 ingredients in a small bowl. Set aside.

- Using your hands, combine all remaining ingredients in a large
  bowl. Mix well. Pat mixture into a 9 x 5-inch loaf pan. Spread
  ketchup mixture evenly over loaf.

- Bake, uncovered, at 350° for 1 hour and 10 minutes, until meat
  is browned and juices run clear.

- Pour off liquid in bottom of pan and remove loaf. Slice into
  8 pieces and serve immediately.

Makes 8 servings

What's
in it
for me?

Per serving: 200 calories, 4.3 g fat,
1.4 g saturated fat, 22.6 g protein,
17.5 g carbohydrate, 1.3 g fiber,
44.4 mg cholesterol, 514.1 mg sodium
% calories from fat: 19

COOKING 101

If you don't want your
meat loaf soaking in
drippings of fat and
water while it cooks,
invest in one of those
new meat loaf pans with
a built-in rack. The
holes in the bottom of the rack allow the
juices to drain away from the meat. This
helps cut back on fat, especially when
using regular ground beef or pork.

FAT OR FICTION?

**The most
unhealthy thing
about being
overweight is the
stress it puts on
your heart.**

True. But that's only one of your troubles.
Excess weight raises insulin levels, which
can lead to diabetes and high blood
pressure. What's more, if you're obese,
your body's hormonal balance could be
thrown out of whack. If you're a woman,
that increases your risk of breast and
endometrial cancer. And both genders run
a greater risk of developing gallstones,
arthritis, and even sleep disorders. Yet
another unhealthy thing about being
overweight is that you don't feel like
exercising. And that's a real killer.

I know a place
where we can
eat dirt cheap.

I don't want to
eat dirt at
any price!

MISCELLOONEYOUS

Peter Pancakes

We *tinkered* with this recipe to create pancakes so fluffy and light, they'll fly off your plate. They're fairy, fairy tasty, especially when topped with fruit sauce or maple syrup.

1-1/2 cups all-purpose flour
1/2 cup whole wheat flour
1-1/2 tsp baking powder
1/2 tsp each baking soda and salt
1-3/4 cups buttermilk
2 tbsp reduced-fat butter or margarine, melted (not fat-free)
1 egg
1 tbsp honey
1/2 tsp vanilla
1/2 cup mashed, ripe banana
Strawberry sauce (recipe follows)

- Combine both flours, baking powder, baking soda, and salt in a large bowl. Set aside.

- In a medium bowl, whisk together buttermilk, butter, egg, honey, and vanilla. Add wet ingredients to dry ingredients and stir just until dry ingredients are moistened. Fold in mashed banana.

- Spray a large, wide skillet or electric griddle with non-stick spray. Heat over medium-high heat.

- For each pancake, spoon about 1/2 cup batter onto skillet. Spread batter out to make 4-inch circles. Cook until undersides are lightly browned. Flip and cook other sides until lightly browned, 2 to 3 more minutes. Serve immediately with strawberry sauce.

Makes 10 pancakes

Strawberry Sauce
2 cups diced strawberries
1/3 cup orange juice mixed with 1 tbsp cornstarch
1/4 cup sugar

- Combine all ingredients in a medium saucepan. Cook and stir over medium heat until liquid has thickened and strawberries have softened, about 6 to 7 minutes.

- Let cool slightly before serving. Sauce may be refrigerated for up to 1 week.

Per pancake (with sauce): 176 calories,
2.6 g fat, 0.7 g saturated fat, 5.2 g protein,
34.2 g carbohydrate, 2.3 g fiber,
23 mg cholesterol, 315.7 mg sodium
% calories from fat: 13

What's in it for me?

MISCELLOONEYOUS

Always remember the distinction between contribution and commitment. Take the matter of bacon and eggs. The chicken makes a contribution. The pig makes a commitment.

John Mack Carter

The Sound of Muesli

A high-fiber breakfast blend of oats, yogurt, and fresh fruit

The thrills are alive with the sound of muesli! And our healthy, satisfying breakfast just might *Alp* you lose weight, too.

3 cups quick-cooking rolled oats (not instant)
1-1/2 cups low-fat, strawberry-flavored yogurt
1 cup orange juice
1/3 cup light cream
2 tbsp honey
1-1/2 cups each fresh raspberries and diced strawberries
1 cup fresh blueberries
1 medium apple, peeled, cored, and coarsely grated

- In a large bowl, combine oats, yogurt, orange juice, cream, and honey. Let stand 5 minutes.
- Gently fold in fresh fruit. Cover and refrigerate overnight.

Makes 6 servings

Hint: Refrigerating the muesli overnight makes it creamier. Sprinkle individual servings with a tablespoon of low-fat granola if you want to add some crunch.

What's in it for me?

Per serving: 270 calories, 4.6 g fat, 1.1 g saturated fat, 10.1 g protein, 53.4 g carbohydrate, 8.2 g fiber, 4.6 mg cholesterol, 33.4 mg sodium
% calories from fat: 14

We can make beautiful muesli together!

Oats

Yogurt

He's college-bred. He made a four-year loaf with his father's dough.

Fat Be Nimble, Fat Be Quick

Gaining body fat from large doses of dietary fat can be amazingly easy. That's because fat contains nine calories per gram, more than twice as many calories as the same amount of carbohydrates or protein. A cup of oil has a mammoth 2,000 calories. A cup of flour has just 455. So, if you cut back on fat, you'll be cutting back on calories, too. Now, dietary fat isn't a culprit just because it's calorically dense. Fat in food is more easily turned into body fat. Your body has to burn 25% of the calories contained in carbohydrates and protein in order to turn them into body fat. But 97% of calories from dietary fat are available for immediate storage. In plain English, your body is very efficient at storing fat. That oil-packed salad dressing is like a high-speed Porsche zooming down the highway without a cop in sight. It'll race straight to your gut or butt in no time with no detours!

A popular breakfast cereal, muesli (pronounced MYOOZ-lee) was developed about 100 years ago by Dr. Bircher-Benner, a Swiss nutritionist. The German word muesli means "mixture." Commercially made muesli can be loaded with fat, as it's often laced with heavy cream. Our rendition uses low-fat yogurt and just a touch of light cream to keep the smooth texture while cutting back on fat.

MISCELLOONEYOUS

166

Who'da Thunk?

Help! I'm burnin' up! I just ate a chili pepper and my mouth's on fire!

If you're an unfortunate soul who's chewing a chili pepper that's too hot to handle, forget about dousing the flames with water or beer. It won't work. That's because capsaicin, the potent compound that's the source of the chili pepper's fiery flavor, isn't water soluble—it's an oil. Also, alcohol speeds the absorption of capsaicin, so washing the chili pepper down with a margarita is a blazing no-no. Milk and yogurt, which contain the natural ingredient caesin are more effective at decreasing the mouth-blistering heat. Starchy foods like bread and potatoes may also offer some relief—as will adding 911 to your phone's speed-dial list.

You Do The Math

So, you've made the switch to baked tortilla chips from the fried variety. Olé! But what's that you're dunking them in? If it's high-fat guacamole, don't be surprised if you develop a paunch underneath that poncho! Try substituting a half-cup of low-fat salsa for the same amount of guacamole once every two weeks. You'll save 4,254 calories and 408 grams of fat a year—that's more than 6 days' worth of fat! Adios, adipose!

I told my doctor that I get very tired when I go on a diet, so he gave me pep pills. Now I eat faster.

Bohemian Wrapsody

Stir-fried chicken and vegetables with brown rice, wrapped in warm, flour tortillas

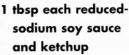

I see a little silhouette-o of a wrap. Add the rice! Add the sauce! Can you fill the tortilla?

1 tbsp each reduced-sodium soy sauce and ketchup
2 tsp each honey and lime juice
1-1/2 tsp grated gingerroot
1 tsp each sesame oil and cornstarch
1/4 tsp ground coriander
4 7-inch flour tortillas
1 tsp olive oil
2 boneless, skinless chicken breast halves, cut into thin strips
1 cup each bean sprouts, halved snow peas, and sliced red bell pepper
1 cup hot, cooked brown rice
1/2 cup grated carrots

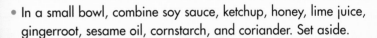

- In a small bowl, combine soy sauce, ketchup, honey, lime juice, gingerroot, sesame oil, cornstarch, and coriander. Set aside.

- Wrap tortillas in a damp kitchen towel and place in a 250° oven for 10 minutes to warm.

- Meanwhile, heat olive oil in a large, non-stick wok or skillet over medium-high heat. Add chicken. Cook and stir until chicken is no longer pink. Continue to cook until chicken is lightly browned. Add bean sprouts, snow peas, and red pepper. Cook for 2 more minutes. Add sauce. Cook until sauce is bubbly and has thickened. Remove from heat.

- To assemble wraps, place a warm tortilla on a serving plate. Spoon 1/4 rice in center, followed by 1/4 grated carrots. Spoon 1/4 hot chicken-vegetable mixture over top. Fold bottom of tortilla up to cover part of filling, then fold in sides. Serve immediately.

Makes 4 wraps

Per wrap: 273 calories, 5.7 g fat, 0.5 g saturated fat, 19.9 g protein, 37.4 g carbohydrate, 3.1 g fiber, 37 mg cholesterol, 354.3 mg sodium % calories from fat: 18

What's in it for me?

Loafing Around

Round, Italian bread loaf stuffed with turkey, Canadian bacon, cheese, and veggies

Relax! Take it easy! This humungous sandwich is a breeze to make. You barely have to lift a finger—except to eat it, of course.

1 tbsp each honey mustard and low-fat mayonnaise
1/2 tsp grated lemon zest
6 oz Canadian bacon
1 10-inch round Italian, sourdough, or pumpernickel loaf
1 cup baby spinach leaves or watercress
8 oz thinly sliced, roasted turkey breast
4 slices reduced-fat Swiss cheese
1 cup alfalfa sprouts
1 large tomato, thinly sliced
1 small cucumber, unpeeled, thinly sliced

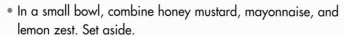

- In a small bowl, combine honey mustard, mayonnaise, and lemon zest. Set aside.

- Heat bacon according to package directions. Set aside.

- Slice loaf in half horizontally. Pick out some of bread from inside of top and bottom pieces (save for bread crumbs), leaving a 1/2-inch border. Line bottom half with spinach leaves or watercress. Arrange cooked bacon slices over spinach, followed by turkey breast, cheese, sprouts, tomato, and cucumber.

- Spread honey mustard mixture inside top half of loaf and place over filling. Press down slightly as you slice loaf into 6 wedges. Serve immediately.

Makes 6 servings

Hint: If you aren't serving the sandwiches right away, wrap the whole, unsliced loaf in plastic wrap and refrigerate for up to 4 hours. Spread the honey mustard mixture inside the top half of the loaf just before serving, to avoid making the bread soggy.

Care for some mixed nuts with your drink? Grab a handful. It's OK—they're roasted, right? Brazil nuts, pecans, almonds, *cashews*...Gesundheit! One cup of these nuts can have close to 1,000 calories and 90 grams of fat, and that ain't *nuttin'* to sneeze at! In fact, roasted nuts are sometimes fried in highly saturated coconut oil. So, how can you eat nuts without going over the edge? Instead of munching on them as a snack, when you'll be tempted to squirrel away huge amounts, use them as a condiment or garnish. Chopped nuts make tasty additions to salads, yogurt, home-baked breads, muffins, pancakes, and casseroles.

TRIVIAL TIDBIT

Licking a lemon or sipping unsweetened, diluted lemon juice can stimulate saliva flow in someone who has a dry mouth. This remedy should be used in moderation, however, since it's been said that highly acidic lemon juice can actually dissolve a pearl. If that's the case, imagine what it might do to your pearly whites!

This is the best bacon we've had for years.

Then show me some you've had more recently!

What's in it for me?

Per serving: 343 calories, 7 g fat, 2.5 g saturated fat, 25.5 g protein, 42.3 g carbohydrate, 2.7 g fiber, 34.3 mg cholesterol, 1171.9 mg sodium
% calories from fat: 19

Jambalaya (pronounced juhm-buh-LI-yah) is a hallmark of Creole cooking. The name comes from the French word *jambon,* meaning "ham," the star ingredient in many of the first jambalayas. This spicy dish is typically a concoction of rice, tomatoes, onions, green peppers, and just about any kind of shellfish, poultry, or meat. You can substitute shrimp for the scallops in this recipe, and use cubed chicken breasts instead of the kielbasa.

Women may have more to gain *and* lose from resistance-training (working out with weights) than men. Of all the calories burned in the body, 50 to 90% are burned by your muscles. This gives men an advantage. Since they naturally have more muscle than women, they burn more calories—even while sleeping! But strength-training puts women on a level playing field as far as metabolism goes. The more muscle mass a woman has, the more calories she can burn, and the better she can effectively wage war against fat. Resistance-training also keeps bones dense and strong, so it's a good weapon against osteoporosis. See what happens when you pick up a dumbbell? (No offense, guys. Really!)

As a child, my family's menu consisted of two choices: take it or leave it.

Buddy Hackett

Pump up the Jambalaya

Spicy jambalaya with turkey sausage and scallops

With traditional jambalaya, you'd be hammin', but with our low-fat version, you'll be jammin'—all kinds of tasty ingredients in one big pot. Get ready for ragin' Cajun flavor!

1 tsp canola oil
1 cup each chopped onions, chopped green bell pepper, and chopped celery
1 clove garlic, minced
8 oz turkey kielbasa, casing removed, cut into bite-sized pieces
2-1/2 cups low-sodium, low-fat chicken broth
1-1/3 cups mild salsa (see hint below)
1-1/4 cups uncooked, long-grain white rice
1 bay leaf
1 tsp Cajun seasoning
1/2 tsp each dried thyme and dried oregano
12 oz uncooked bay scallops
1/4 cup chopped, fresh parsley

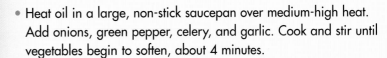

- Heat oil in a large, non-stick saucepan over medium-high heat. Add onions, green pepper, celery, and garlic. Cook and stir until vegetables begin to soften, about 4 minutes.

- Add kielbasa and cook for 2 more minutes. Add all remaining ingredients, except scallops and parsley. Bring to a boil. Reduce heat and simmer, covered, for 15 minutes. Stir occasionally to prevent rice from sticking to bottom of pan.

- Stir in scallops and parsley. Cook for 5 more minutes, until scallops are cooked through and rice is tender.

Makes 6 servings

Hint: Use medium salsa if you like your food very spicy.

Per serving: 292 calories, 6.4 g fat, 1.2 g saturated fat, 22.6 g protein, 41.4 g carbohydrate, 2 g fiber, 45.4 mg cholesterol, 691 mg sodium % calories from fat: 18

What's in it for me?

Sauced in Space

Zesty pizza sauce

All the stars and planets must have been aligned when this flavorful pizza sauce was created. Use a big dipper to pour it on your crust and enjoy!

1 tsp olive oil
1/2 cup minced onions
1 clove garlic, minced
2 cups tomato sauce
1 can (6 oz) tomato paste
1 tbsp dried oregano
1 tbsp red wine vinegar
1 tsp sugar

- Heat olive oil in a small, non-stick saucepan over medium heat. Add onions and garlic. Cook and stir for 2 to 3 minutes, until onions have softened.

- Add all remaining ingredients. Bring to a boil. Reduce heat to low. Cover and simmer for 10 minutes, stirring occasionally.

- Cool before using. Store in an airtight container in refrigerator for up to 1 week.

Makes about 2-1/4 cups

Hint: You can make a double batch and freeze it if you like.

What's in it for me?

Per serving (1/4 cup): 40 calories, 0.9 g fat, 0 g saturated fat, 1.7 g protein, 7.7 g carbohydrate, 0.6 g fiber, 0 mg cholesterol, 343.5 mg sodium
% calories from fat: 18

A bad habit never disappears miraculously. It's an undo-it-yourself project.

Abigail Van Buren

Where did the expression "sell like hotcakes" originate?

Who'da Thunk?

In the early 1800s, hotcakes cooked in bear grease or pork lard were the most popular fast-food item at carnivals and country fairs. Anyone who kept a hotcake stand was sure to make a killing. In fact, they were so popular that by the beginning of the 19th century, the expression came to mean anything that sold quickly and effortlessly in huge quantities. But bear grease and pork lard? A more accurate expression would be "selling like fatcakes!"

YOU DO THE MATH

The fat in candy bars may cause a few Snickers. So, if you're craving chocolate, but don't want to Eatmore, just swap that weekly treat for a low-fat, chocolate-fudge pudding cup. You'll satisfy your sweet tooth and save 7,800 calories and 572 grams of fat a year. That's more than eight days' worth of fat! It's a smart move if you don't want your scale to play Twix on you.

I wish you could bake pies like Ma used to bake.

And I wish you could make the dough that Pa used to make!

Mind Your Peas and Cucumbers

Studies show that people who get plenty of fruits and vegetables in their diets have the lowest risk of illness, including heart disease and cancer. To help your family get their five servings a day—the amount recommended by experts—follow a few simple tips. *Make fruits and veggies the stars of your fridge:* If they're outta sight, they're outta mind. Give fruits and vegetables center stage (eye level) in the fridge. With some decent exposure, your family might reach for cantaloupe instead of candy bars. *Be sneaky:* Fool those finicky kids by hiding grated carrots in pasta sauce or grated zucchini in muffin batter. *Jazz up the presentation:* Stark-naked string beans staring up from your plate aren't exactly a thrill for your taste buds. But some steamed broccoli topped with a bit of melted cheese, a colorful, cozy bowl of homemade vegetable soup, or a cool strawberry and banana smoothie are anything but boring. *Try dried:* Just a quarter cup of either raisins or dried apricots counts as a whole serving, and they're convenient to keep at your desk or to pack in your kid's knapsack.

TRIVIAL TIDBIT Some dairy farmers believe that creating a relaxed, tranquil environment helps cows produce more milk, so farmers sometimes play light country tunes or classical music in the barn. Apparently, rock music makes the cows produce less milk. Looks like The Rolling Stones gather no milk, but when it comes to bigger yields, Beethoven is nothing to Bach at.

Hangover: The wrath of grapes.

Taco of the Town

Spicy ground chicken, peppers, and onions wrapped in a soft flour tortilla

We heard it through the grapevine: These tacos are *di*-vine. Rumor has it they're a real family-pleasing treat.

1-1/2 pounds skinless ground chicken
1 cup diced onions
3/4 cup diced green bell pepper
2 cups seeded and diced tomatoes
1/2 cup grated carrots
1/4 cup ketchup
1 tbsp each chili powder and red wine vinegar
2 tsp brown sugar
1 tsp ground cumin
8 7-inch flour tortillas
8 lettuce leaves
1 cup shredded, reduced-fat sharp cheddar cheese (4 oz)
1/2 cup low-fat sour cream

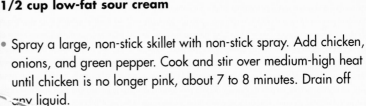

There's that low-fat taco everyone's raving about.

- Spray a large, non-stick skillet with non-stick spray. Add chicken, onions, and green pepper. Cook and stir over medium-high heat until chicken is no longer pink, about 7 to 8 minutes. Drain off any liquid.

- Add 1 cup tomatoes, carrots, ketchup, chili powder, vinegar, brown sugar, and cumin to chicken. Reduce heat to medium-low. Cover and simmer for 10 minutes, stirring occasionally. If mixture is too saucy, simmer uncovered for a few more minutes, until most of liquid has evaporated. Remove from heat.

- To assemble tacos, place one lettuce leaf in center of a tortilla. Spoon 1/8 chicken mixture over top. Sprinkle some of cheese and remaining tomatoes over chicken, followed by a dollop of sour cream. Roll up bottom of tortilla to cover filling, then fold in sides. Serve immediately. A little messy, but worth it!

Makes 8 tacos

Per taco: 288 calories, 6.3 g fat, 2.3 g saturated fat, 29.8 g protein, 28.9 g carbohydrate, 2.8 g fiber, 52.3 mg cholesterol, 389.8 mg sodium % calories from fat: 19

What's in it for me?

Benaddicted to Eggs

Traditionally high-fat eggs Benedict gets a makeover

You might want to *eggsercise* caution when deciding who to make this scrumptious recipe for. Some traitor may give away your secrets.

For heaven's sake—don't tell the British about these.

8 slices Canadian bacon
4 large eggs
1/4 cup each low-fat mayonnaise and low-fat sour cream
1 tbsp each honey mustard and lemon juice
Pinch of salt and cayenne pepper
2 English muffins, split and toasted
Fresh dill or parsley for garnish (optional)

- In a large skillet over medium heat, lightly brown bacon (about 3 minutes per side). Remove from skillet and keep warm.

- Fill a medium skillet half full of water. Bring to a boil, then reduce heat to simmering. Break 1 egg into a small dish, then slide egg into simmering water. Repeat with remaining eggs. Simmer eggs, uncovered, for 4 to 5 minutes, until yolks are set, but not hard.

- Meanwhile, in a small saucepan, whisk together mayonnaise, sour cream, honey mustard, lemon juice, salt, and cayenne. Cook over medium heat just until mixture is heated through. Do not boil. Remove sauce from heat.

- For each serving, place 1 toasted muffin-half on a plate. Top with 2 slices bacon. Remove 1 egg from water using a slotted spoon. Place egg over bacon. Pour 2 tablespoons sauce over egg. Garnish with fresh dill or parsley, if desired. Serve immediately.

Makes 4 servings

What's in it for us?

Per serving: 188 calories, 6.2 g fat, 1.9 g saturated fat, 13.5 g protein, 19.7 g carbohydrate, 0.6 g fiber, 226.3 mg cholesterol, 784 mg sodium
% calories from fat: 30

FAT OR FICTION?

Skipping meals means you'll "save" fat calories and lose weight quickly.

If eating less helps you lose weight, why not speed up the process and skip lunch altogether? Though it seems like the most obvious tactic in the world, this strategy could result in metabolic mutiny. You may find yourself fighting a never-ending battle of the bulge when you give your body a big zero at meal time. When you go half a day without food, your body reacts the only way it can: It hoards the fuel you've already given it, with fat being the primary hostage since it lasts the longest in times of famine. This instinct for survival causes the body to efficiently adapt when its fuel supply is threatened. Soon you can get by on fewer calories, meaning you'll have to eat less just to maintain your weight. And that's nothing to skip about.

TRIVIAL TIDBIT

If you think that brown eggs are more nutritious than white eggs, the yolk's on you! Shell color depends on the breed of hen, and no one breed is known to lay better eggs than another, though a few biased farmers may consider their product *eggstraordinary*.

There are no shortcuts to any place worth going.

Beverly Sills

Back Matter

Appendix, index, bibliography

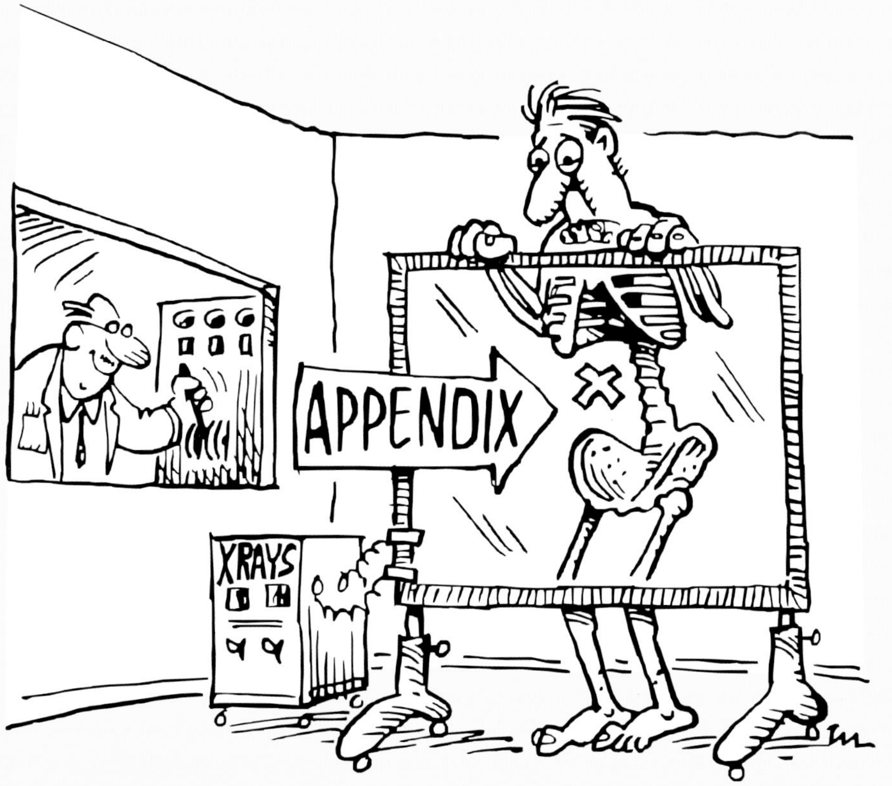

The CRAZY PLATES 12-Step Program for a Healthier Lifestyle

Small, gradual changes in your lifestyle and diet can pay huge health dividends over the long run. For improved overall health, including lower cholesterol, higher energy levels, and weight loss, try incorporating one new, healthy habit into your life each month for the next year. Unlike restricted eating plans and fad diets, this is a plan you can stick to forever!

Step 1
Avoid the Fat-free Free-for-all
Yes, you can save fat grams by eating low-fat or fat-free cookies, cakes, ice cream, and other sweets, but you're not helping the healthy-eating cause when you polish off the whole box. Remember, those foods still have calories, and if you consume more calories than you burn, the excess is stored as fat. When you shop for treats, even the fat-free kind, buy smaller, single servings—just enough to satisfy your cravings. Sometimes a chocolate urge can be suppressed by one, bite-sized chocolate bar, for instance. Let's face it, there are times when you've just got to have some candy, cookies, or cake. But to keep your weight down—and stay healthy—make fresh fruits and vegetables your snacks of choice. Not only will they fill you up, but also the phytochemicals, fiber, folic acid, and potassium in them may help reduce your risk of cancer and heart disease.

Step 2
Remember: Less Is More
Thanks to ballooning, industrial-sized portions, even some lower-fat restaurant meals, such as linguini with clam sauce, and chicken fajitas, can have close to 1,000 calories. (By the way, some of the fattier meals can run close to 2,000 calories!) Your best bet: Think kid size not mammoth size. Although large servings may seem like a bargain, is an extra 250 calories for 39 cents more really such a wise expenditure? Those are the differences, in calories and cost, between a small order of fries and a large one. A child-size soda (8 ounces) has about 95 calories, whereas a super-size, 36-ounce soda contains at least 400. And all-you-can-eat buffets? Let's not go there...literally and *figuratively*.

Step 3
Think "Fitness," Not "Thinness"
Throw unrealistic notions of becoming pencil thin or perfectly chiseled out the window. If you want to work on changing your body shape, don't model yourself after supermodels. Do it for the right reasons: to develop a sense of well-being and to have the optimal energy, vitality, and fitness level to enjoy life. Anyone, of any body type, of any age, of any height, can become fit through regular exercise and a healthy diet. It's smarter to make health and fitness—not appearance—your number-one priority. Remember, if you're dreaming of a body that's pencil thin, you're not being very sharp!

Step 4
Kill Two Birds with One Stone
Doing two things at once may be just the way to fit exercise into a hectic schedule. Wear your running shoes when you take your kids to soccer practice, so you can walk around the field instead of just sitting for an hour. Do stretching exercises or lift weights while watching television. Grab a friend and go for a walkie-talkie session instead of gabbing on the phone.

Since exercise doesn't have to be intense to be beneficial, brisk walking is an ideal choice for beginners. You can also gab and burn flab while hiking, biking, or golfing.

Step 5
Follow the 80/20 Rule
Food is one of life's simple pleasures. That's why it's important to give yourself an occasional treat. If you just can't face the day without your favorite high-fat food, eat a small portion, enjoy every bite of it, and then get back on the healthy-eating track. Choose foods that are nutritious, low in fat, and high in fiber, 80% of the time. Twenty percent of the time, allow yourself to have an indulgence. This way, you'll never feel deprived, and no foods will be "off limits" or "taboo." It's not every morsel of food you eat that's important, it's what you do consistently, over the long haul, that matters most.

Step 6
Think Before You Drink
Start cutting back on your alcohol consumption. If you drink regularly, say, two beers or two glasses of wine a day, that's about 1,400 calories a week, or 73,000 calories a year—enough to create 20 pounds of excess flab. You booze, you lose...well, actually, you gain! And don't forget that soft drinks, fruit drinks, Frappaccinos, and other fancy coffee drinks can have anywhere between 100 and 300 calories per serving. (Water, seltzer, coffee, and tea are calorie-free, as long as you're not adding sugar.)

Step 7
Beef Up On Your Fast Food IQ
Most people know that a Quarter Pounder isn't diet food. But few realize that a serving of fries has the same amount of calories. Order one or the other, not both. The best fast-food options: A grilled chicken sandwich (hold the mayo), a grilled chicken salad (with fat-free or low-fat dressing), a stuffed veggie or chicken pita without the fatty dressing, or a turkey or chicken sub (without mayo and easy on the cheese).

If at all possible, don't eat cheese-drenched foods more than twice a month. Much of the cheese we eat comes from prepared foods like lasagna, cheeseburgers, and pizza. And just two slices of pepperoni pizza contain more than 40% of your saturated fat budget for the day. Eat pizza less often, or buy it at places that offer veggie toppings and flavorful tomato sauces that allow you to go easy on the cheese.

Step 8
Don't Overload on Sweet Nothings
The average North American consumes more than 50 gallons of soda a year. Hey, we like a cold pop as much as anyone, but 50 gallons...wow! That's nearly double our intake of beer, more than double our consumption of milk and coffee, and, amazingly, six times the amount of fruit juice and tea we drink. What's more, over 75% of the soda chugged is the high-calorie, non-diet variety. Each 12-ounce can contains 10 teaspoons of sugar, 150 calories, and no vitamins, minerals, or fiber. Other sweets such as brownies, cookies, and cakes can saddle us with an entire meal's worth of calories and fat. Even worse, they often take the place of fruit, vegetables, whole grains, and other nutrient-packed foods.

Step 9
Plan Menus in Advance
When you know what you're going to eat ahead of time, you avoid impulsive, high-fat, high-calorie food selections. Try to plan weekly menus on the weekend when you're less busy, then shop for the ingredients you'll need. Make a casserole on Sunday that can be frozen and served later in the week. Planning ahead makes weekday mealtimes a lot less hectic...and, probably, a lot healthier.

Step 10
Put the Skids on Grease
All cooking oils, whether monounsaturated (healthy) or saturated (unhealthy), have 14 grams of fat and 120 calories per tablespoon. They're one of the

biggest sources of hidden fat in our diets, yet one of the easiest to cut back on. Here are a few ways to get the grease out of meals: (1) *Wipe it thin.* Food doesn't have to float in order for oil to do its work. Rather than dumping it into a pan, apply a light coating with a brush or a paper towel; (2) *Measure precisely.* If you must use oil in a recipe, dole it out with a measuring spoon. When pouring straight from the bottle, for example, people often overestimate the amount of oil that equals a tablespoon; (3) *Ready... aim...fire* a short burst of non-stick cooking spray (like Pam) into your pan. You'll be adding next to no fat and negligible calories because you apply so little; (4) *Invest in good-quality, non-stick cookware.* Instead of cooking in a cast-iron or stainless steel skillet, try using a non-stick pan. With this type of surface, you'll need only a smidgen of oil to keep food from sticking; (5) *Don't be a frequent fryer.* Choose cooking methods that don't add fat to your foods: baking, broiling, boiling, grilling, roasting, poaching, and steaming.

Step 11
Kick the Habit
Nothing to fear, Sister Mary Theresa—we're talking *fat* habit! It's second nature to add butter to toast, mayonnaise to sandwiches, and fat-laden dressings to salads. Try replacing these high-fat habits with new low-fat ones, like putting jam on your toast instead of butter, spreading low-fat mayonnaise or honey mustard on your sandwiches, or trying one of the many new, low-fat salad dressings on the market. If you must have cream cheese on your bagel, order fat-free or light cream cheese on the side and use it sparingly. When eating baked potatoes, top them with low-fat sour cream or other healthy choices such as salsa, tzatziki, or cottage cheese.

Step 12
Serve in the Kitchen/Eat in the Dining Room
When you eat in the dining room and leave the serving bowls in the kitchen, you won't be as tempted to pick at the leftovers. You're also forced to go out of your way for seconds. And as silly as this sounds, make sure you eat off plates or out of bowls. Nibbling from packages of crackers, taking forkfuls of cake from a platter, or eating ice cream straight from the container can add up to plenty of calories—a lot more than you think you've eaten. Put the packages away. Out of sight, out of mouth.

Let's Make a Meal

You Go, Grill!
For a backyard barbecue party, grill up Burger, She Wrote (p. 163), juicy, teriyaki beef and chicken burgers, and some Low-Fatty Patties (p. 113) for the fish lovers in the crowd. A fruit platter with a bowlful of Dippity-do-da Fruit Dip (p. 13) in the center, Nat's King Coleslaw (p. 32), and some Crabsolutely Fabulous Pasta Salad (p. 28) make nice accompaniments to the burgers. Serve Copabanana Cake (p. 156) and Choco Doodle Do's (p. 149) for dessert.

Hit the Stove, Jack
And she'll be comin' back for more, for more, for more, for more! Impress her with your culinary expertise, even if you don't have any. Our delicious chicken stir-fry, To Stir, With Love (p. 95) tastes great served over Twice As Nice Coconut Rice (p. 136), and it's easy enough for the cooking-challenged.

When Ya Hasta Have Pasta

If you're a big fan of pasta, but you're tired of the same ol', boring tomato sauce on top, have we got a meal for you! Mr. Bowjangles (p. 80) pairs bow-tie pasta with chicken, broccoli, and sun-dried tomatoes, then the whole mix gets tossed with an amazing broth made of soy sauce, honey, lime, and balsamic vinegar. Add a tossed salad and some fresh Italian bread and it's *mangia* time!

Sea of Love

For the seafood lover in you, we tempt your taste buds with the exquisitely flavored Tuna Turner (p. 111) topped with a serving of Sammy Salsa (p. 134), and accompanied by The Rice Squad (p. 24). Those who prefer shellfish may opt for the divine Penne from Heaven (p. 89) served with caesar salad and fresh bread sticks.

Bowled Over

Come in from the cold and turn up the heat with a brimmin' bowlful of Looking for Mr. Goodbarley (p. 38) with chunks of beef and vegetables, served with warm Corn in the U.S.A. (p. 54) muffins for dunking. If you're in a *fowl* mood, go for highly seasoned Mulligatawnski (p. 50) and bake up a batch of Takin' Care of Biscuits (p. 53).

Another Steakout

If you're longing for barbecued beef, then For Goodness Steak (p. 122), go ahead and have some! Throw on a few De-lish Kebabs (p. 135) while you're at it, to make the meal nutritious and complete.

You've Got Male

And if he's a hungry, pork chop lovin', meat and potatoes kinda male, you might want to whip up Barbiechop Quartet (p. 127) with a side of This Spud's For You! (p. 145). There's no way he'll mark his plate "return to sender."

Don't Have a Cow, Man!

You won't miss the meat when you sink your teeth into this vegetarian dinner. Start off with a bowl of either We're Yammin' (p. 44) roasted sweet-potato soup or creamy, minty Give Peas a Chance (p. 43), followed by a generous serving of Piled-High Veggie Potpie (p. 76). If you still have room, you might want to end the meal with a small piece of Must Bake Carrot Cake (p. 155).

One Night in Bangkok

When you're in the mood for Thai food, try Satayday Night Fever (p. 22), our grilled chicken skewers with spicy peanut sauce, followed by Thai for Two (p. 88), linguini with shrimp in a spicy plum sauce. Vegetarians will love our Jerry Springrolls (p. 16), followed by Pod's Pad Thai (p. 67).

Holidays are Here Again

Concerned about putting on weight over the holidays? With The Roast of Christmas Past (p. 120), thoughts of packing on the pounds won't haunt you. This hearty meal-in-a-pot can be followed by a light dessert, such as our Jollygood Squares (p. 159). It's perfect for a Sunday dinner, too.

He's such a bad cook, last week Gourmet magazine tried to buy back his subscription.

Metric Conversion

If you are converting the recipes in this book to metric measurements,
use the following charts as a guide.

VOLUME

Conventional Measure	Exact Metric Conversion (mL)	Standard Metric Conversion (mL)
1/4 teaspoon	1.2 mL	1 mL
1/2 teaspoon	2.4 mL	2 mL
1 teaspoon	4.7 mL	5 mL
2 teaspoons	9.4 mL	10 mL
1 tablespoon	14.2 mL	15 mL
2 tablespoons	28.4 mL	30 mL
3 tablespoons	42.6 mL	45 mL
1/4 cup (4 tablespoons)	56.8 mL	50 mL
1/3 cup (5-1/3 tablespoons)	75.6 mL	75 mL
1/2 cup (8 tablespoons)	113.7 mL	125 mL
2/3 cup (10-2/3 tablespoons)	151.2 mL	150 mL
3/4 cup (12 tablespoons)	170.5 mL	175 mL
1 cup (16 tablespoons)	227.3 mL	250 mL
4-1/2 cups	1022.9 mL	1000 mL (1 L)

WEIGHT

Ounces (oz)	Exact Metric Conversion (g)	Standard Metric Conversion (g)
1 oz	28.3 g	30 g
2 oz	56.7 g	55 g
3 oz	85.0 g	85 g
4 oz	113.4 g	125 g
5 oz	141.7 g	140 g
6 oz	170.1 g	170 g
7 oz	198.4 g	200 g
8 oz	226.8 g	250 g
16 oz	453.6 g	500 g
32 oz	907.2 g	1000 g (1 kg)

OVEN TEMPERATURES

Fahrenheit (°F)	Celsius (°C)
175°	80°
200°	95°
225°	110°
250°	120°
275°	140°
300°	150°
325°	160°
350°	175°
375°	190°
400°	205°
425°	220°
450°	230°
475°	240°
500°	260°

Index

Where We Learned the Stuff We Didn't Know

Balch, Phyllis A., C.N.C., and Balch, James F., M.D. **Prescription for Nutritional Healing, Second Edition.** Avery Publishing Group, 1997.

Bauer, Joy, M.S., R.D. **The Complete Idiot's Guide to Eating Smart.** Alpha Books, 1996.

Brody, Jane E. **The New York Times Book of Health: How to Feel Fitter, Eat Better, and Live Longer.** The New York Times Company, 1997.

Chalmers, Irena. **The Great Food Almanac.** Collins Publishers, 1994.

Claflin, Edward. **Age Protectors: Your Guide to Perpetual Youth.** Rodale Press, 1998.

Colton, Katherine. **Smart Guide to Getting Thin and Healthy.** Cader Company, 1998.

Cooper, Robert K., Ph.D. and Cooper, Leslie. **Low-Fat Living.** Rodale Press, 1996.

Dincin Buchman, Dian and Groves, Seli. **What If? Fifty Discoveries that Changed the World.** Scholastic Inc., 1998.

Foods That Harm Foods That Heal: An A-Z Guide to Safe and Healthy Eating. The Reader's Digest Association, Inc., 1997.

France, Christine. **Cooking Hints and Tips.** Macmillan Canada, 1997.

Gardiner, Anne and Wilson, Sue. **The Inquisitive Cook.** Owl Books, 1998.

Hendrickson, Robert. **Encyclopedia of Word and Phrase Origins: Revised and Expanded Edition.** Facts On File, Inc., 1997.

Herbst, Sharon Tyler. **Food Lover's Companion.** Barron's Educational Series, Inc., 1995.

Herbst, Sharon Tyler. **The Food Lover's Tiptionary.** Hearst Books, 1994.

Josephson, Ramona, R.D.N. **The HeartSmart Shopper: Nutrition on the Run.** Douglas & McIntyre, 1997.

Larson Duyff, Roberta, M.S., R.D. **The American Dietetic Association's Complete Food and Nutrition Guide.** Chronimed Publishing, 1998.

Nutribase Professional Nutrition Manager (software). Cybersoft Inc., 1998.

Nutrition Action Healthletter. The Center For Science in the Public Interest.

Quotable Quotes. Reader's Digest Association Ltd., 1998.

Ronzio, Robert A., Ph.D., C.N.S. **The Encyclopedia of Nutrition and Good Health.** Facts on File, Inc., 1997.

Somer, Elizabeth, M.A., R.D. **Food and Mood: The Complete Guide to Eating Well and Feeling Your Best.** Henry Holt and Company, Inc., 1995.

Ulene, Dr. Art. **Nutrition Facts Desk Reference.** Avery Publishing Group, 1995.

University of California, Berkely Wellness Letter, Editors. **The Wellness Encyclopedia.** Houghton Mifflin Company, 1995.

Voorhees, Don. **Why Does Popcorn Pop?** Citadel Press, 1995.

Couldn't Have Done It Without Ya

Many people consider **Dave Chilton** a smart man when it comes to book publishing, but not us. We consider him a genius. He's our friend, our business partner, our mentor, and our biggest fan. Though he was forced to give up many rounds of golf to help perfect this book, he should really thank *us*. After all, we saved him a ton of money. (Have you seen his swing?)

When **Ted Martin**, the brilliant creator of the syndicated cartoon strip, *Pavlov*, offered his services for *Crazy Plates* (and previously *Looneyspoons*), little did he know it would entail risking social life and sore limb (drawing hand, that is). He was a perfect extension of our imaginations and a pleasure to work with. Besides, who else could draw a bionic manicotti noodle?

We've named **John Duff**, our editor, the official captain of the *Crazy Plates* cheerleading team. He believed in our project from the beginning and always laughed at our corny jokes. (He later informed us that he was just being polite.) We'd also like to extend a big thank-you to the enthusiastic staff at Perigee Books.

Our guardian agent, **Larry Chilnick**, is a man of many connections. He opened a lot of publishing doors for us and was a great "wheeler and dealer" in between his wild nights at the disco.

Although she's accidentally killed every plant and fish in our office, **Jennifer Creed**—our desktop publisher extraordinaire—brought *Crazy Plates* to life. Jen worked long hours with little pay and no breaks, under harsh conditions (dead plants everywhere) and was often isolated from any human contact other than the occasional tryst with the FedEx deliveryman. We owe her a lot...at the very least, a day off.

Peter McMenemy, a.k.a. "Wall Street Pete," is our operations manager, and remarkably, is still Janet's husband. He's always supportive, always good-natured, always willing to help, and always an eager recipe taste tester (when he's not golfing, that is).

John Randall, a Registered Massage Therapist and our neighbor at work, slipped over between clients to offer us encouragement, bad jokes, and Tim Hortons' coffee. Some of *Crazy Plates*' corniest recipe titles came from his twisted mind. This guy really rubs us the right way!

Tania Craan did such a phenomenal job on the interior design of our book, we can hardly wait to see what she does with our office! We thank Tania immensely for her patience and her outstanding eye for detail.

Kevin Strang, our computer coach and 24-hour technical support hot line, made our transition from the PC World to Mac Land a smooth one. He always responded quickly and professionally to our endless "urgent requests."

This is the second book for which **Chuck Temple** has offered us his valuable insight, at no cost. His amazing design skills are only surpassed by his generosity. We love this guy!

Our sincere thanks to the following people who lent us their ears, imaginations, support, time, expert opinions, and not-so-expert opinions:

Alfreda Podleski	Margaret & Gary Robb	Dr. Chris Kuntz	Ken Heinrich
Patti Maxim	Kathy & Eric Johnson	Steve Boynton	Jennifer Berard
Bob & Marge Chilton	Jill Doan	Jim Phillips	Jeff Doan
Scott & Courtney Chilton	Donna Paris	Arlene Lebovic	Janet Tottle
Wayne Mosley	Denis Trottier	Stephen Quick	Mark Ewald
Barry Nicholds	George McMenemy	Lorri Donaldson	Darren Semple
Grethe D. Eifert	Sadie Colson	Steve Rehbein	Dawn & Leo Martin
Helen & Don Clark	Carole Filion	Diane Latraverse	Cheryl Embrett
Donna & George Grabowski	Rhonda Schnurr	Tobi Boisvert	Fina Scroppo
Theresa & Barry Eveleigh	Dave Barker & Lee Eckley*	Paul Moore	

* Didn't actually contribute anything

ACKNOWLEDGEMENTS

We'd Love to Hear from You

Please feel free to contact us by phone or E-mail with
your questions, comments, or recipe suggestions.
(Direct any criticism toward Janet,
as Greta is very sensitive.)

(800) 470-0738
spoons@magi.com